Redeeming Politics

STUDIES IN CHURCH AND STATE

JOHN F. WILSON, EDITOR

---

*The Restructuring of American Religion:
Society and Faith Since World War II*
by Robert Wuthnow

Shintō and the State, 1868–1988
by Helen Hardacre

Redeeming Politics
by Peter Iver Kaufman

Redeeming Politics

Peter Iver Kaufman

PRINCETON UNIVERSITY PRESS

PRINCETON, NEW JERSEY

Library of Congress Cataloging-in-Publication Data

Kaufman, Peter Iver.
Redeeming politics / Peter Iver Kaufman.
p. cm. — (Studies in church and state)
Includes bibliographical references.
1. Christianity and politics—History of doctrines.
2. Church and state—History. 3. Christianity
and politics. 4. Church and state.
I. Title. II. Series.
BR115.P7K28 1990 261.7'09—dc20 90-32871

ISBN 0-691-07372-4 (alk. paper)

This book has been composed in Linotron Sabon

Princeton University Press books are printed on acid-free paper,
and meet the guidelines for permanence and durability of the
Committee on Production Guidelines for Book Longevity of the
Council on Library Resources

Printed in the United States of America by Princeton University Press,
Princeton, New Jersey

1   3   5   7   9   10   8   6   4   2

For Jerald Carl Brauer

———————————

It may be a truism, but it is nonetheless often true,
that we rarely know what we are actually doing until
someone else tells us.
—Martin Jay, *Fin de Siècle Socialism*

CONTENTS

FOREWORD

REDEEMING POLITICS is the third of the "Studies in Church and State" sponsored by the Project on Church and State at Princeton University. *The Restructuring of American Religion: Society and Faith Since World War II*, by Robert Wuthnow, and *Shintō and the State, 1868–1988*, by Helen Hardacre, both published by Princeton University Press, preceded it in 1988 and 1989 respectively. Wuthnow's volume analyzes the general forces that have been redefining the role of religion in the United States over the past four decades. Hardacre's investigates a modernizing nation-state's relationship with religious traditions. The present volume, by a historian of Western religion teaching at the University of North Carolina at Chapel Hill, is a study of how versions of Christianity and political cultures made claims upon each other at a number of junctures in Western history, roughly between the conversion to Christianity of the Emperor Constantine and the end of the Civil War in England.

The Project on Church and State, funded by the Lilly Endowment, has two main goals: one is to sponsor scholarly publications on the interaction of religion and its political environment, primarily but not exclusively in the United States, and the other is to draw on disciplines beyond those traditionally concerned with church-state issues to investigate that interaction. These goals flow from the conviction that religion and politics come together in many settings other than the institutional and the conventional. As earlier scholarly emphasis on the organized life of religious bodies has been superseded by inquiry into the broader role of religion in culture, particularly culture in its political and social dimensions, insights of sociologists and anthropologists have necessarily been added to those of historians of religion, law, and society.

Apart from the series of which this volume is a part, the Project has sponsored a two-volume bibliographical guide to literature on the church-state question in U.S. history and a casebook on church-state law compiled by John T. Noonan, Jr.* The series will eventually comprise some ten studies, including volumes on the interrelationship of church and state in the United States, India, Latin America, and Europe. The authors, all well known in their fields, share the view that the role of religion in society today is necessarily understood by means of many dis-

* John F. Wilson, ed., *Church and State in America: A Bibliographical Guide*, vol. 1, *The Colonial and Early National Periods*; vol. 2, *The Civil War to the Present Day* (Westport, Conn., 1986, 1987). John T. Noonan, Jr., *The Believer and the Powers That Are* (New York, 1987).

ciplines and comparative perspectives. The Project will not publish studies on all the topics that deserve scholarly treatment in its area of interest,
but by demonstrating, as this volume does, the potential for new work on
issues traditionally given the label church-state, we hope to stimulate further scholarship. We trust that the volumes in the series will point up the
complexity of the relationship between religion and politics and prove to
be resources for the rethinking of this vexing topic.

Robert Wood Lynn, now retired from the Lilly Endowment, guided
and supported the Project with great skill. We have greatly appreciated
his most constructive interest. With the closing of the Project office in
1990, Yoma Ullman will no longer be with us, but she leaves a strong and
lasting imprint on our work. We are grateful to Walter H. Lippincott,
director of the Princeton University Press, and Gail Ullman, history editor, for their welcome encouragement.

John F. Wilson
Robert T. Handy
Stanley N. Katz
Albert J. Raboteau

ACKNOWLEDGMENTS

EVERY THIRTY PAGES or so, Captain Cuddle advises anyone listening in Dickens's *Dombey, and Son,* "when found, make a note of." Somehow it happened, however, that after more than a dozen years of teaching and writing about the history of the Christian traditions, I had mountains of notes and few findings. I needed time to reflect on the politics and theology of Latin Christendom, time that the Lilly Foundation furnished with a grant to the Princeton Project on Church and State. To time, add patient friends, five of whom deserve very special thanks. John Wilson was an unfailing source of wise counsel, telling criticism, and encouragement. Marcia Colish put an early and errant draft back on course. Conversations with John Headley and Grant Wacker in situ supplied insight as well as inspiration, increasing my debts to both for a decade of goodwill and good sense. My dedication acknowledges a debt of longer standing, for Jerald Carl Brauer of the University of Chicago wholly convinced one of his struggling graduate students that this kind of work was great fun. The rest (and perhaps the result) is history.

It is difficult to remember all the help I have had from other colleagues and friends. Yet the suggestions and criticisms of some stand out, and I am profoundly grateful to William Bouwsma, Gary Dickson, David Ganz, Frances Hickson, Salim Kemal, Ken Langston, Frederick Russell, Robert Spencer, George Huntston Williams, and Carolyn Wood. David Gardiner and Yoma Ullman kindly and competently groomed the manuscript and made it so much more readable. Nadine Kinsey, Robbie Knowles, Mary Jo Leddy, and Ellen Smith Summers tolerantly indulged an author whose incessant revisions and untimely interventions complicated the manuscript's life in the computer and their life in the front office. I blame only my squash partners for errors that remain. Had they won less frequently, I would have concentrated more completely on *Redeeming Politics.*

ACKNOWLEDGMENTS

EVERY THIRTY PAGES or so, Captain Cuddle advises anyone listening in Dickens's *Dombey, and Son*, "when found, make a note of." Somehow it happened, however, that after more than a dozen years of teaching and writing about the history of the Christian traditions, I had mountains of notes and few findings. I needed time to reflect on the politics and theology of Latin Christendom, time that the Lilly Foundation furnished with a grant to the Princeton Project on Church and State. To time, add patient friends, five of whom deserve very special thanks. John Wilson was an unfailing source of wise counsel, telling criticism, and encouragement. Marcia Colish put an early and errant draft back on course. Conversations with John Headley and Grant Wacker in situ supplied insight as well as inspiration, increasing my debts to both for a decade of goodwill and good sense. My dedication acknowledges a debt of longer standing, for Jerald Carl Brauer of the University of Chicago wholly convinced one of his struggling graduate students that this kind of work was great fun. The rest (and perhaps the result) is history.

It is difficult to remember all the help I have had from other colleagues and friends. Yet the suggestions and criticisms of some stand out, and I am profoundly grateful to William Bouwsma, Gary Dickson, David Ganz, Frances Hickson, Salim Kemal, Ken Langston, Frederick Russell, Robert Spencer, George Huntston Williams, and Carolyn Wood. David Gardiner and Yoma Ullman kindly and competently groomed the manuscript and made it so much more readable. Nadine Kinsey, Robbie Knowles, Mary Jo Leddy, and Ellen Smith Summers tolerantly indulged an author whose incessant revisions and untimely interventions complicated the manuscript's life in the computer and their life in the front office. I blame only my squash partners for errors that remain. Had they won less frequently, I would have concentrated more completely on *Redeeming Politics*.

ABBREVIATIONS

CCSL	*Corpus Christianorum series Latina*
CR	*Corpus Reformatorum*
CSEL	*Corpus scriptorum ecclesiasticorum Latinorum*
DADC	Dante Alighieri, *La Divina Commedia*, ed. Carlo Steiner, 3 vols. (Turin, 1960)
DAOM	Dante Alighieri, *Opera Minore*, ed. Pier Vincenzo Mengaldo, Bruno Nardi, et al., vol. 2 (Milan, 1979)
DCD	Augustine, *De civitate Dei*, in CCSL
ICR	John Calvin, *Institutio Christianae religionis*, in JCOS, vols. 3–5
JCOS	*Joannis Calvini opera selecta*, ed. Peter Barth and Wilhelm Niesel, vols. 2–5 (Munich, 1928–52)
KKP	Percy Ernst Schramm, *Kaiser, Könige und Päpste: Beiträge zur algemeinen Geschichte*, 4 vols. (Stuttgart, 1968–71)
LKK	Eusebius, *Über das Leben des Kaisers Konstantin*, ed. Friedhelm Winkelmann (Berlin, 1975)
MGH	*Monumenta Germaniae Historica*
PL	*Patrologiae Cursus Completus, series Latina*
QGTE	*Quellen zur Geschichte der Täufer, Elsass*, ed. Manfred Krebs and Hans Georg Rott, in *Quellen und Forschungen zur Reformationsgeschichte*, vols. 26–27 (Gütersloh, 1959–60)
QGTS	*Quellen zur Geschichte der Täufer in der Schweiz*, ed. Leonard von Muralt and Walter Schmid, 4 vols. (Zurich, 1952–74)
RG	*Das Register Gregors VII*, ed. Erich Caspar, 2 vols. (Berlin, 1920–23). Citations refer to book and document number.

Redeeming Politics

INTRODUCTION

How SHOULD we think of redeeming politics? In the history of the Christian traditions, from the time of Constantine's conversion to that of Oliver Cromwell's civil war, Christianity and politics were often so closely joined that it is difficult now to tell whether we are looking back at religious or political convictions. That made me curious about apologetic strategies that inspired such convictions and Christian political cultures they created. To ward off imprecision on the route from curiosity to the conclusion of this presentation, I formulated and offer here some preliminary redefinitions.

Political culture is said to refer to activities "in principle open to intervention or control on the part of the state."[1] Although this reference seems eminently adaptable, two difficulties arise if we accept that meaning of political culture in the inquiries that follow. (1) In principle, no activity is beyond government intervention in absolutist regimes. *Redeeming Politics* investigates ideas about rule and redemption that animated an assortment of absolutist regimes, so we would have to call all culture political culture. (2) Moreover, as it now stands, the definition obliges users to contemplate the extent of government control and intervention. To be sure, the study of church-state relations has been well served by exercises of this kind, yet it is not my purpose to add to their growing number. My case studies were composed and assembled primarily to examine unifying ideologies and discover how ideologues staged the courtships between their gods and governments. Having set that course for *Redeeming Politics*, I need a different definition of political culture. In this volume, then, the term refers to any set of doctrines, images, and institutions used by apologists and administrators to distribute or redistribute their governments' powers to intervene and control. Hence, the definition encourages concern with conspicuous and spirited claims to divine sanction, with the realm once identified as *Staatssymbolik*, where ideologies idealize political power, institutionalize charisma, and rewrite history.[2]

I want to define *ideology* in terms of those three functions, but first in terms of the function that seems most problematic because charisma and institution are generally classified as incompatibles. Despite Max Weber's

[1] Anthony Giddens, *The Nation-State and Violence* (Cambridge, 1985), p. 211.
[2] See Abner Cohen, *Two-Dimensional Man* (London, 1974), particularly pp. 21–22, 102–6, and John B. Thompson, *Studies in the Theory of Ideology* (Berkeley, 1984), pp. 133–39, 158–60.

editorials on the process of socialization, theorists usually associate charisma with socially disruptive behavior. Lately, however, Edward Shils
has explained how charisma also "maintains and conserves" social orders, how institutionalized charisma enables officials to perform their vicarial and custodial duties with an authority closely connected (at least in
citizens' imaginations) with some sanctified ideal. Delegates, documents,
and commissions thus acquire the same authority as the theophanic monarch, the inspired council, or the general and glorious will of the people
they are thought to represent. Shils gives a memorable illustration. He
observes that most citizens today, although more sinned against than sin-
ning, still recoil from uniformed police officers. Approaching officers
prompt awe, anxiety, and perhaps resentment traditionally reserved for
the tremendous power at the center or summit of government. The uni-
forms bring that power over the people closer to the people, and when
resentment becomes so strident that respect turns into disrespect, and disrespect into defiance, we may infer that ideology no longer possesses the
voltage necessary to illumine the charismatic qualities of government.[3]

Ideology makes a critical contribution to the maintenance of order. It
discourages disaffection to the extent it can establish its canonicity and
reshape the history of a given government so that present and anticipated
conditions appear as natural developments from a venerable past. To that
end, ideology may suggest history is the playbook for God's providential
work that rewards the righteous and punishes the wicked. Ideology occasionally celebrates a purpose fully realized. Sometimes it refers to a purpose, reward, or punishment only partially revealed to (and by) ideologues and their patrons; the promise of greater things to come then
sanctifies the way things are. The range of variations is too great for a
single definition to compass, yet ideologies' histories have a common
theme or orientation. Their narratives invariably give the governments
they eulogize the appearance of necessity.[4]

Such talk of appearances, however, raises an important question: Do
ideologies always promote false consciousness? Undeniably, specious rationalizations and outrageous self-deceptions often pass as history and
political theory, only to be savaged once scholars have appropriated more
fashionable ideologies by wrapping them in their own explanatory models. Are we then to conclude that political societies' self-presentations are
always untrustworthy? Perhaps so, but when I write of ideology's functions, I do not refer to self-promotion in the narrowest sense. Ideology's
third function, that is, its license to rewrite history from inception to end,

[3] Edward Shils, "Charisma, Order, and Status," in his *Center and Periphery: Essays in
Macrosociology* (Chicago, 1975), pp. 259–60, 266–67.
[4] See, for example, Richard Faber, "Der kaiserlich-päpstliche Dualismus im Hochmittel-
alter," in *Staat und Religion*, ed. Burkhard Gladigow (Düsseldorf, 1981), pp. 79–81.

indicates we are dealing with more than a cluster of loosely packaged falsifications. Instead, we encounter what Karl Mannheim called "the total conception" of ideology.

Mannheim was extremely ambitious. He held that ideological structures could be mined to recover a society's "total mental structure."[5] As enchanting as that prospect may be, *Redeeming Politics* undertakes to discharge a more modest commission. We will not try to find out what whole societies thought. We are looking for enduring categorical structures that appealed to those ideologues who tried to influence citizens' thinking, structures that unquestionably influenced the formulation of Christian sociolatry.

Sociolatry once meant service to society, but most dictionaries have dropped the entry. In the case studies that follow, however, I have repossessed the word and modified its meaning. Sociolatry refers here to a type of ideology that associates salvation with political idealizations, symbols, and spells circulated to inspire loyalty, obedience, and service. Salvation, then, comes to depend on the perpetuation of the current distribution of political power or on citizens' support of some proposed redistribution. Frequently, Christian sociolatry makes Christendom's leading political figures (or leading dissidents) sacred messengers or substitute messiahs. Polemics against sceptics are laced with religious curses. After dramatic political conquests, sociolatry generally sports universalist pretensions; during political crises its claims are sometimes adjusted and counterclaims introduced. We will find that narrative (or ritual) decorum as well as historical context colored and conditioned sociolatry's triumphalist propositions and solemn condemnations, that sociolatry is a remarkably adaptable kind of ideology. But what is central to our definition is the patent assumption that salvation is corporate and, in some respects, political as well as eternal. To be redeemed, a community's politics must be ordered according to a divine plan, which ideologues are always ready to supply or revise.

Our story of ideologues and ideologies begins with the fourth-century historian and apologist, Eusebius of Caesarea, and with two Constantines, the one he commemorated and the one he invented. Actually, we could argue that the story of Christian sociolatry began with the New Testament, particularly with advice offered in St. Paul's letter to Christians in Rome. In the thirteenth chapter, the apostle enjoined believers to obey civil authorities because God had appointed them to keep things civilized until the second coming of Christ. That injunction has never ceased to generate controversy. Earliest exegetes found it difficult to reconcile the apostle's endorsement of the prevailing powers with politi-

[5] See Mannheim's *Ideology and Utopia* (London, 1936), pp. 49–53, 67–74.

cians' conspiracies against the new religion. Some interpreters preferred to underscore St. Paul's assurances that "every rule and every authority and power" would soon be destroyed (1 Corinthians 15:24).[6] That strategy, however, seemed obsolete by the early fourth century, when apologists for Christianity could be far more explicit than St. Paul about the empire's role in redeeming God's faithful followers: not long after the conversion of Constantine, the empire was a Christian empire. Eusebius soon transformed the first Christian emperor into a redeemer. And those changes arrest our attention in the first chapter because they determined the trajectory of Christian sociolatry from that time forward. Even today, the Constantine Eusebius constructed towers over the history of the Christian traditions.

Constantine's record of conquests was truly impressive, and the conquests together with the emperor's conversion to Christianity convinced apologists a new age had dawned. Subsequent disappointments, notably the invasion of Italy and sack of Rome early in the fifth century, posed problems for those intent on reviving enthusiasms identified with earliest Christian sociolatry. They had to redefine conquest to keep alive Eusebius's ambitions for a universal Christian empire, to sustain the illusion of a new age when the realities of rule and misrule seemed to shatter the dreams of their patrons and peoples.

The second and third chapters of *Redeeming Politics* discuss several revivals and redefinitions. The series starts with the responses of two fifth-century apologists, Paulus Orosius and Salvian of Marseilles, to the empire's humiliations and concludes with the predictions of a fledgling dynasty in England, eleven hundred years later, with promises that "florisshyng" Tudor roses would soon be planted in all the courts of western Europe. Our discussion is by no means exhaustive, but it shows how readily nostalgia for empire and the romance of conquest merged with hopes and plans for political and religious redemption. We will see how comfortably medieval visions and deceptions, which constitute the history of Christian sociolatry and a significant part of the history of human imagination, nestled in Constantine's shadow.

The fourth chapter reviews the story of Oliver Cromwell's New Model Army. It suggests that soldiers, just as generals or emperors, could lay claim to Eusebius's legacy, that Protestants as well as Catholics could settle in Constantine's shadow. Following the trail left by William Dell, one of the army's most influential preachers, we will survey the history of Puritanism at Cambridge and correlate Dell's spiritualism with the devel-

---

[6] For the early instances of Pauline exegesis, see Werner Affeldt, *Die weltliche Gewalt in der Paulus-Exegese* (Göttingen, 1969), pp. 86–90, 105. To sample contemporary arguments against the authenticity of the Pauline endorsements, consult Walter Schmithals, *Der Römerbrief als historisches Problem* (Gütersloh, 1975), pp. 191–97.

opment of Puritan sociolatry. From his parish, Dell wrote of the Holy Spirit's work in the world, yet he confessed he had not experienced it until he enlisted as chaplain in the New Model Army. The soldiers' discipline and the army's string of conquests persuaded him that he walked among saints, on the threshold of a new age. Dell and his colleagues believed their realm's redemption was at hand. When conquest gave way to the politics of compromise, however, the troops divided into factions, and we find that the Puritan preachers' democratization of Christian sociolatry depended on unanimity and solidarity easier to maintain while fighting than while debating over the fruits (or spoils) of conquest.

Emperors and armies, their conquests and apologists, parade through significant chapters in the story of redeeming politics. We should not forget, however, that churches were also in the business of redemption and very frequently in the throes of political controversy. Our fifth and sixth chapters retrieve Catholic and Protestant ecclesiologies to attest the versatility of Christian sociolatry and the ease with which clergy could adapt some of its themes to different claims for clerical rule.

The fifth chapter sketches the development of the imperial papacy during and shortly after the pontificate of Gregory VII. Gregorians were among the most resourceful impresarios of redeeming politics; their arguments for papal supremacy in the eleventh and early twelfth centuries profoundly influenced the history of Catholic and Protestant traditions. The sixth chapter lands us in the sixteenth century, in John Calvin's Geneva. It features Calvin's objections to the papacy's imperial pretensions, but we will concentrate on the imperious character of Calvin's redeeming politics. His doctrine of election virtually transformed his city into a church. He held that God appointed two ministries in Geneva, ordained preachers to inspire moral regeneration and magistrates to preserve civil order. The chapter investigates how and why the two became one, how and why the ministries became nearly indistinguishable in Calvin's rhetoric of reform and, after 1555, in the Genevan consistory's surveillance of public morality and political behavior.

Redeeming politics was conditioned by theorists' inclinations (and incentives) to idealize the political authority of soldiers, saints, emperors, magistrates, and popes. But should authorities' prestige be badly bruised, apologists either had to adjust or abandon their claims. We might expect that severe crises of confidence doomed Christian sociolatry; the final two chapters, however, demonstrate that sociolatry actually survived considerable adjustments and revived even among critics who ostensibly abandoned it.

Unlike several apologists mentioned in our second chapter, Augustine, bishop of Hippo Regius in North Africa, believed that the political crises of the early fifth century undermined ideals associated with Constantine and Eusebius. His monumental *City of God* is generally read as a formidable sentence on Christian sociolatry. I have collected evidence for a somewhat different interpretation of Augustine's treatise, evidence that also yields a fresh perspective on his career and his own redeeming politics. The empire's distress unquestionably tempted him to jettison some of sociolatry's prominent themes, but he revised others and reconstructed justifications for the current coalition between politicians and prelates. Augustine insisted that the Bible promised Christianity dominion over all culture and that such dominion was unthinkable apart from a Christian political culture.

To the most radical religious reformers in the sixteenth century, Christian political culture was an abomination. They were incensed when more moderate associates tried to win politicians' support for the reform of worship, theology, and church polity. They maintained that the Bible prohibited compromise, and even commerce of any kind, with the corrupt and corrupting world of politics. The eighth and last chapter explains how they came to that conclusion. It also reveals that the most violent critics of Christian sociolatry, who thought their colleagues' partnerships with political authorities locked the body of Christ in an unwholesome embrace with the body politic, were themselves unable to relinquish redeeming politics when they came to govern their own fugitive communities.

There are many contemporary analogues to the radicals' efforts to separate religion from politics, some apparently more successful than others. Often it is said that religion inhabits a universe where people are exclusively preoccupied with otherworldly powers. They may try to make those powers manageable, responsive to human need, or they may try only to make them philosophically respectable and responsive to human curiosity. Alternatively, citizens in that universe could choose to reconcile human societies to the inscrutability of their gods and to the unpredictability of divine intervention. Whatever the strategy, religion's universe is dominated by revelation. Questions of truth are either answered directly or tabled until additional disclosures enlighten religion's officials and theorists. Politicians, however, are thought to have settled in a different universe, where they grapple with questions of expedience and prudence rather than with questions of truth. Politics reconciles citizens to their corporate life and to tactics that harness wealth and power to each government's pursuit of the collective good (or to governors' pursuits of their own advantage). Whereas revelation determines the contours of religious life, reason determines the course of political life.

The contrasts are neat, commonplace, and cocksure. Nonetheless, having reiterated them in his paper on "the spiritual aroma" of political cultures, Raymond Firth immediately and justifiably became suspicious of their validity and usefulness. As others before him, however, Firth found it was easier to dispute make-do distinctions than to offer a more adequate grid.[7] The interpenetration of religion and political culture defies precise conceptualization. Boundaries between piety and practical affairs may be drawn, but not defended, without great difficulty. As often as some Christians rehabilitate familiar dualisms and contrasts, marking off the church's work from the government's goals, other Christians discover ways to dissolve the dualisms and present political societies or particular political decisions as divine and redemptive revelations.

The case studies in *Redeeming Politics* record some of those discoveries. Scholars tend to invoke the word *theocracy* when they encounter governments that register claims to divine sanction for their laws, leaders, and luck. I use the word *sociolatry* to denote an apologetic strategy that fuses statesmanship and Christian sociolatry. By exchanging an "ocracy" for an "olatry," however, I hoped to learn more and say more about the interpenetration of religion and political culture, to compile evidence that political idealizations and Christian traditions significantly influenced one another as well as the history of the human imagination. Not all the evidence is here; as I reread *Redeeming Politics* what most impresses me (and depresses me) is how much has been omitted. Byzantine caesaropapism, Hohenstaufen chronicles, Renaissance revivals of the ideal of empire, along with countless conquests and crises, should find space in more comprehensive reviews of political theology. Moreover, the limits of my commission and competence were quickly reached while I examined certain fundamental apologetic strategies and their settings, and detail was sometimes sacrificed to delivery. Omissions certainly will tell against *Redeeming Politics* unless we think of it as a modest proposal, prompting readers to reflect on the conflation of religious and political convictions and inviting them to qualify and revise as they measure the shadow Constantine casts over history and over the varieties of Christian political culture.

[7] Raymond Firth, "Spiritual Aroma: Religion and Politics," *American Anthropologist* 38 (1981): 583–84.

PART ONE

Conquest

Let every person be subject to the governing authorities
for there is no authority except from God, and those
that exist have been instituted by God.
—Romans 13:1

LONG BEFORE and long after St. Paul wrote to Christians in Rome, ruling elites associated their rule with divine will. They were understandably eager to tell this to the people they ruled; monuments, entertainments, public orations, and coins alluded to emperors' divine calling. About those people, little can be reported with certainty. Some of us today are tempted to think of credulous citizens as some form of ciliate life, swimming uncritically, even mindlessly, in political currents generated by clever apologists for autocracy and tyranny. But possibly citizens believed or feigned belief in statesmen's divine rights because they feared anarchy. Perhaps they believed because the idea of arbitrary authority in an ordered universe was unthinkable or because they resolutely wanted to create and spread order and to maintain political and moral discipline in an apparently disordered universe. Maybe citizens trusted pronouncements like St. Paul's simply because they were trusting people. "Let every person be subject to the governing authorities"; after all, God made them subjects, so there must be some reason for their subjection. "Remind them to be submissive to rulers and authorities, and to be obedient" (Titus 3:1). "Be subject for the Lord's sake to every human institution, whether it be to the emperors as supreme, or to the governors as sent by him to punish those who do wrong and to praise those who do right" (1 Peter 2:13–14). "For there is no authority except from God."

"For there is no authority except from God"! Arriving at this point, strict constructionists have little room to maneuver, no cause to equivocate, no place to hide. Even tyrants and persecutors "have been instituted by God. Therefore he who resists the authorities resists what God has appointed, and those who resist will incur judgment" (Romans 13:1–2). The apostle's very next sentence, however, suggests that his counsel might be conditional, "for rulers are not a terror to good conduct, but to bad" (Romans 13:3).

Monarchs and magistrates, then, who terrorized the faithful and pious were not "rulers" and "authorities." Had not Old Testament prophets scolded kings? Hosea even disclosed that Israel occasionally "made kings" without God's consent (Hosea 8:4). A king himself, David was believed to have urged rebellion when his colleagues, sovereigns on earth, conspired against their sovereign Lord: "Let us burst their bonds" (Psalms 2:2–3). And Thomas Aquinas agreed, citing the psalmist while lecturing on the thirteenth chapter of Romans: any ruler who acquired and exploited power to thwart divine justice did not possess authority "from God" or "instituted by God."[1]

Much depended on the ways motives, rule, and misrule were perceived, on how persuasively apologists presented their patrons and protagonists

---

[1] *Super epistolas S. Pauli lectura*, ed. Raphaelis Cai, 8th ed., vol. 1 (Rome, 1953), 190.

or on how persistently rebels expressed their disenchantment. In the fourth chapter, for instance, we find Oliver Cromwell's soldiers and "saints" confident that their king conspired against God and righteousness. Preachers announced that their army was divinely empowered to deliver the realm from its ungodly ruler. To confirm the commission, God sustained the soldiers' discipline, solidarity, and optimism; who but God could have choreographed their astonishing, unbroken series of conquests? Let everyone, then, be subject only to authorities whose conquests exhibited God's power and righteousness, only to those who rewarded the righteous and assured the redemption of obedient subjects.

Promises that obedient subjects enjoy eternally secure places in the heavenly kingdom remind us that Christian sociolatry did not altogether dissolve distinctions between the here and now and the hereafter. Instead, the rhetoric of redeeming politics forged connections between the two realms, only very rarely collapsing one completely into the other. For one thing, God's government of the hereafter was direct, but here God governed through deputies who delivered the church from its enemies, pagans from their superstitions, or populations from political confusion and civil war. Ostensibly these were political conquests and redemptions. Nonetheless, they were thought to prefigure and sometimes to hasten God's redemption of all created, worthy, and obedient souls.

In the fourth century, Eusebius of Caesarea made Emperor Constantine a model ruler and redeemer. Claims for subsequent sovereigns and militant saints were formulated in the shadow that Eusebius's Constantine cast across the history of the Christian traditions.

Chapter One

CONSTANTINE

WHAT WOULD have tempted someone in late antiquity to join a persecuted sect? Exorcisms and deathbed miracles may have mesmerized some who witnessed them. Inspirational preachers may have persuaded others who chanced to hear them in friends' homes or on the streets, for persecution was intermittent in the third and fourth centuries and did not always force Christians underground. All we really know is that conversions continued to swell the ranks of the new religion, despite legislation against its worship. Apologists for Christianity, however, realized that, if the Roman empire's rival gods and rival pieties were ever to be overtaken, if their own religion were ever to be awarded a permanent advantage, answers had to be found for one difficult question: Why would the Christians' God permit authorities to persecute Christians? If benevolent and powerful, this God must have had some secret reason for standing aside, so to speak, when imperial prohibitions were enacted or when vandalism against Christians, against their properties and their persons, and against their churches and sacred texts spread from territory to territory. It was not farfetched to suggest that persecution was punishment for Christians' sins and shortcomings, but bloodstained retaliation did not speak well of a God whose justice was thought to be tempered with mercy.

The problem was particularly complicated during the reign of Emperor Diocletian (284–305). According to the historian Lactantius, whose efforts to reconcile persecution and providence followed Diocletian's retirement, harassment had been bearable until Diocletian's deputies trumped up charges against leading Christian citizens. Thereafter, no Christian could escape the terror.[1] Its very severity, however, was a critical clue for both Lactantius and his fellow apologist, Eusebius of Caesarea. Christianity survived the campaigns for its destruction; with this in mind, apologists speculated that God had licensed one final offensive against worshipers in order to underscore the insuperability of divine will. History's most powerful scoundrels had done their utmost to suppress Christianity, yet with one stroke God had overcome the opposition, apportioned impressively painful deaths to persecutors (which the apologists embellished in their obituaries), and converted the whole empire. God, therefore, had

[1] *CSEL* 27: 179–90.

staged the misfortune and its miraculous reversal to prove to posterity his power over political culture.[2]

That one stroke was Constantine. After he became emperor, he collaborated with apologists to assure that an appropriate theology of victory was incorporated in their histories. Those accounts, though, still give scholars fits, for it is virtually impossible to sift the emperor from his apologists' stories. Fact, fiction, and wishful thinking blend in order to dramatize how all history had been redeemed and to illustrate how the new Christian empire's redeeming politics might spread its gospel as well as God's.[3]

Part of the mix bears repeating here, inasmuch as it traces the passage from persecution to privilege that begins with Constantine's father. Constantius was one of four regional rulers to whom Diocletian had given authority when he retired. He was responsible for the government of Gaul and Britain. He was, Eusebius tells us, the only tetrarch to have spared Christians and to have relaxed certain prohibitions against them, prohibitions that his colleagues ruthlessly enforced elsewhere. In 306, Constantius died, and without consulting any of the other tetrarchs, the army nominated Constantine to be its new commander. In the East, Galerius, who had achieved some authority over the imperial college, that is, over the other three tetrarchs, was helpless to prevent Constantine's succession.[4]

Galerius and the other two tetrarchs continued to persecute Christians, but Constantine refused to enforce most edicts against the new religion. In effect, he had declared his independence from the imperial college, although he took no initiative that would jeopardize his colleagues' control over their respective territories. He consolidated his government and undertook several expeditions against the empire's enemies across the German frontier. He allowed events in the Mediterranean districts to take their course, a course that eventually led to his intervention. Several months after his accession, the son of another tetrarch placed himself at the head of a mutiny in Rome. Galerius promptly repudiated the upstart. There happened to have been no vacancy to fill in this instance; a fifth tetrarch was politically (as well as semantically) intolerable. Maxentius, the usurper, defied his colleagues and recalled his father from retirement to share power and to defend Rome against the embittered tetrarchs. Se-

[2] See Jean Sirinelli, *Les vues historiques d'Eusèbe de Césarée durant la période prénicéenne* (Dakar, 1961), pp. 412–54.

[3] François Heim, "L'influence exercée par Constantin sur Lactance: Sa théologie de la victoire," in *Lactance et son temps*, ed. J. Fontaine and M. Perrin (Paris, 1978), pp. 67–70.

[4] *Eusèbe de Césarée: "Histoire ecclésiastique,"* ed. Gustave Bardy, in *Sources chrétiennes*, vol. 3 (Paris, 1958), 31 (8.13); *CSEL* 27: 201; and for much of what follows, review Timothy D. Barnes, *Constantine and Eusebius* (Cambridge, Mass., 1981), pp. 28–43.

verus, the first of them to invade Italy, was soundly defeated and captured. Constantine watched the conflict closely, but he had no wish to
commit troops until Maxentius's position weakened.

The first signs of weakness appeared during quarrels between Maxentius and his father in 308, and particularly when the latter tried unsuccessfully to seize authority from his son. Maxentius's taxation had all but
alienated citizens in Italy, who seemed ready to welcome a change in government, but Maxentius and his army continued to hold power. The
greatest threat to Maxentius and to Rome was Licinius, who succeeded
Galerius in 311. Like Constantine, Licinius noted with interest the problems Maxentius was experiencing. For his part, Maxentius perceived Licinius as a greater danger than Constantine, so he stationed an army in
Verona to protect the Italian peninsula against an invasion from the East.
Constantine, however, acted first. He descended from Gaul and found the
defenses near collapse. He overran the Piedmont with ease and crossed to
Verona to make short work of the army preparing to meet Licinius. Since
there seemed no need to hesitate, that is, to pause for Licinius, Constantine turned south to Rome.

Maxentius decided to risk a direct encounter rather than an extended
siege. Near the Milvian Bridge his forces battled those of Constantine for
mastery over the Occident, and Constantine completely crushed his opponent. For the next twelve years, he shared imperial authority only with
Licinius, and when his partner proved incorrigible, Constantine ended the
partnership and ruled alone for the remaining thirteen years of his life.

Christians were elated, for their new emperor was not simply more tol-
erant than his rivals; he claimed to have been converted to Christianity
during his campaign against Maxentius. Lactantius wrote as if the conversion had been a sudden one: as the decisive engagement approached,
Constantine was instructed in a vision to add the sign of the cross to his
soldiers' shields. The commander obeyed orders and the battle went his
way. Maxentius had issued edicts of toleration to assure the allegiance of
his Christian population, but apparently too late to attract divine assistance.[5]

According to Eusebius, Constantine's vision preceded his departure for
Italy. In Gaul, while planning his strategy, the emperor pondered the failure of conventional gods to protect their worshipers from military defeats. Moreover, Constantine considered that those same gods presided
over the very confusion he hoped to reorder. Eusebius reported that the
emperor's troubling analysis was interrupted by a revelation and by a set
of instructions quite similiar to those relayed on the eve of the battle for
the Milvian Bridge in the story told by Lactantius. In Eusebius's version,

5 CSEL 27: 223–24.

however, Constantine was given plenty of time to learn about his new religion.[6]

The contradictions between these two tales, one with its sudden and dramatic transformation and the other with its calculated and carefully confirmed conversion, need not detain us. We are not interested in establishing which details are authentic and which contrived. It is more important for our purposes that numismatic and documentary evidence corroborates the general impression given by both Lactantius and Eusebius: Constantine entered Rome in 312 with a genuine commitment to Christianity, and Christians imagined that their new Caesar had been sent by their God. Apologists reached back to the Old Testament to find analogies and prototypes. Maxentius's tardy and profitless efforts to court Christians were forgotten, and Rome's late ruler was cast as pharaoh in the apologists' recasting of the Exodus. The Tiber, it was said, swallowed Maxentius much as the Red Sea had ended the career of that earlier tyrant who stood between God's people and their liberator. Like Moses, Constantine received divine sanction and divine instructions for his campaign. Eusebius planted clues so that no one could miss his point. Constantine's conquests were of canonical consequence: the new emperor ushered in a new age. Bondage and persecution had prepared Christians for their new Moses and readied them for their new Zion.[7]

The character of Christian public opinion is harder to recover than the rhetoric of Christian sociolatry. We cannot know with confidence whether Eusebius's more intemperate remarks reflected other Christians' sentiments. Sepulchral reliefs in Arles and in Rome permit a provisional response, for the pharaoh's drowning was depicted with greater frequency in the fourth century than during any previous period. Apologists heralded a new age, and it would appear that a number of Christians were listening.

How did Constantine see things? We have mentioned his cooperation with encomiasts: he fed Lactantius facts and encouraged Eusebius's enthusiasms. He may not have populated his recollections of recent Roman history with the spiteful monsters that apologists created to dramatize previous persecutions, but he was no less happy than they were to see his rivals disappear. The emperor was an intensely ambitious man. He endorsed the comparison with Moses, he identified his good fortune with his Christian subjects' loyalty, and he appears to have accepted the chal-

---

[6] *LKK*, pp. 28–32 (1.27–1.32).

[7] *LKK*, pp. 21 (1.12), 26 (1.20), 34–35 (1.38). Also see Bardy, *Eusèbe* 3: 62–64 (9.9); and, for what follows, Erich Becker, "Konstantin der Grosse, der neue Moses: Die Schlacht am Pons Milvius und die Katastrophe am Schilfmeer," *Zeitschrift für Kirchengeschichte* 31 (1910): 162–63, 167–71; and Raffaele Farina, *L'impero e l'imperatore cristiano in Eusebio di Cesarea* (Zurich, 1966), pp. 95–103, 189–94.

lenge to convert his empire to Christianity as if the mission had been divinely delegated.

This is not to say, pace Eusebius, that the emperor was remarkably well
informed about his new religion. He was probably conversant with the
general content of Christianity, yet he was certainly impatient with the
quarrels over detail. He deplored the Christians' theological disputes, and
his inability to resolve them must have annoyed him. After all, by 325,
Constantine had reunified the empire and had silenced supporters of
failed tetrarchs, while disagreements that divided his new religion seemed
wholly beyond his power to compose. Notwithstanding the postponement of his baptism, church officials eagerly sought his intervention, and
since the seventeenth century, the emperor's admirers have presumed that
Christians' petitions attested his thorough acquaintance with the mysteries of his new faith. The petitions certainly provoked the emperor to med-
dle, but the point to remember is that his interventions would have made
him increasingly aware that his arbitration could bring no lasting consensus and permanent peace to the church. Although Constantine should
have been delighted with the apologists' infectious optimism and triumphalism, perpetual Christian quarreling no doubt made him cautious
with respect to some of their predictions for the new age.[8]

Caution did not make Constantine a lazy or negligent protector. He
did not outlaw pagan worship immediately, but his concerns and legislation gave Eusebius warrant for triumphalist pronouncements. And Eusebius gives us our first good look at Christian sociolatry. For the moment,
then, the question of Constantine's intentions may be put aside. To contemplate Eusebius's Constantine, which is our objective at this point, is
not to explore fourth-century imperial policy. To read Eusebius is to
watch certain projections and ambitions congeal and form a coherent ideology, a political culture for the new Christian empire, that became influential among church officials who shaped religious attitudes toward powers and principalities, for their own time and for the future.

Eusebius left us ample evidence of his enthusiasms. His court orations
packaged them for Constantine and his courtiers. His biography of the
first Christian emperor, which was composed after Constantine's death,
assembled anecdotes and court documents that echoed earlier hyperbole.
Eusebius apparently wished to commemorate the regime that, in his estimation, unambiguously marked a turning point in world history as well
as the fulfillment of God's promises to faithful and persevering Chris-

---

[8] For seventeenth-century scholarship, see Friedhelm Winkelmann, "Zur Geschichte des
Authentizitätsproblems der *Vita Constantini*," *Klio: Beiträge zur alten Geschichte* 40
(1962): 191–94. Also see Barnes, *Constantine*, pp. 272–75, and, for Eusebius's claims,
LKK, p. 128 (4.22).

tians. He believed that Constantine's conversion and conquests yielded empirical proof of the new religion's theological propositions.

The orations and biography are closely related, not simply to one another but also to the final chapters of Eusebius's history of the church. Ordinarily, that might be taken as a telltale sign of common authorship, yet Eusebius was not otherwise known to have transferred passages from text to text. The simplest solution is that he followed a procedure in his encomiastic accounts that he was otherwise reluctant to employ. But simplicity does not appeal to many critics who are justifiably irritated when Eusebius's "life" of Constantine is used to prop up controversial opinions about the emperor's career and Christianity. They suggest that the biography was fashioned or wholly remodeled long after the biographer and his subject had passed away. The biography is so central to our understanding of the development of Christian sociolatry that it will be necessary to take some stand on the issue of its composition.

Suspicions about Eusebius's authorship often rest on St. Jerome's catalogue of early Christian literature, for Jerome failed to include the biography in his list of Eusebius's works. But what critics believe to be an irresistible conclusion, supported by Jerome's silence and by some traces of textual tampering, is actually little more than an interesting yet remote possibility. Tampering and the inconsistencies it created in the narrative may be read more plausibly as Eusebius's own redactions. Silence during the fourth century should be explained as a token of the curious and unpredictable shelf life of political panegyric. Constantine's immediate successors might not have welcomed inflated accounts of their predecessor's achievements. All things considered, and in whatever way the critics' reservations are offset, the final word still belongs to Friedhelm Winkelmann, who surveyed most conceivable objections to Eusebius authorship more than twenty years ago. In his view, isolated interpolations and long silences do not obscure indications that the biography in its present form was the culmination of Eusebius's tribute to Christianity's first emperor.[9]

The tasks that Eusebius set for himself would have been more difficult had he not been received hospitably at court. Nevertheless, the bishop and biographer was not one of the emperor's closest advisers. He lived most of his life in Palestine, and he only met his ruler and subject several times. Courtiers, however, seem to have shared documents and information with him, and Eusebius's connections at court and with the emperor inclined him to minimize or to omit developments damaging to Constantine's reputation. His loyalties to other bishops probably disposed him to make little of the disharmony within the church. Notwithstanding these courtesies, it is unlikely that Eusebius composed his histories and orations

---

[9] Winkelmann, "Geschichte," pp. 187–243.

to promote his career. He was well advanced in age when he wrote his "life," and Constantine himself was no longer alive: the biography lavished superlatives on a dead and buried patron. Distortions appear because Eusebius, like Constantine, was more concerned with effect than detail. He appears to have been alert first to the church's interest and only then to his own. In the interests of the church, he reserved the new Christian empire a place of honor in his theology of history, and he tried to persuade imperial officials that Christian theology ennobled the new government.[10]

It could be argued that fourth-century Roman government had all the honor it needed, for Hellenistic theories of divine kingship were still in fashion. Without scandal, Constantine and his heirs could have claimed to be gods, had they not been converted to Christianity. That prospect so impressed Eusebius that he scripted an unusual disclaimer for the new emperor. In the biography, an unidentified Christian assures Constantine that he will rule with Christ in heaven, but the remark disturbs the emperor, who solemnly urges his votary to hold his tongue and, as the story goes, tells his admirer how satisfied he will be to live eternally as God's servant after his rule on earth is over.[11]

Constantine's modesty breaks the cadence of Eusebius's triumphalism. On the whole, Eusebius gave current notions of divine monarchy "an aggressively Christian content."[12] In one oration, he deposited Constantine in a grand chariot drawn by his deputies, his Caesars. Naturally, the emperor had uncontested possession of the reins, and the biographer editorialized and emphasized the emperor's complete sovereignty. According to Eusebius, God had planned the imperial autocracy so that government on earth might reflect celestial government. The faculty of reason, which allowed citizens to apprehend justice, goodness, and beauty, confirmed that the once godless empire had suddenly acquired with Constantine a truly godly government.[13]

Eusebius's virtual apotheosis of the emperor leavened the sociolatry of his orations, but what actually transformed political culture into a revelation were Eusebius's assertions about the ubiquity and universal rule of the divine Logos. The Logos was behind all divine instruction. Without it, natural reason could perceive nothing of lasting consequence. Nonetheless, in Eusebius's judgment, the Logos played principally a gubernatorial role in creation and in the conservation and redemption of creation.

---

[10] Sirinelli, *Vues*, pp. 489–90.

[11] *LKK*, p. 140 (4.48).

[12] Farina, *Impero*, pp. 270–78. Also see Francis Dvornik, *Early Christian and Byzantine Political Philosophy*, vol. 2 (Washington, 1966), 475–77, 611–14, 647–50.

[13] Eusebius, *Tricennatsrede an Constantin*, in *Die griechischen christlichen Schriftsteller der ersten Jahrhunderte*, ed. Ivar A. Heikel, vol. 7 (Leipzig, 1902), 201–2.

Nowhere was the Logos more active than in the field of politics, where it picked and protected its champions, destroyed their enemies, and perfected their sincere worship of the Christians' God. Of course, in all this, Eusebius had Constantine in mind. The emperor's intimate relationship with God was not a mystery to be admired *intra muros* and only in whispers. Eusebius explained that the Logos's political partisanship was a matter of public record and history.[14]

Rehearsing that history, Eusebius stipulated that the Logos propelled Constantine to victory over Maxentius and shielded him against Licinius.[15] Even Constantine's gratitude was a product of the Logos's prompting rather than a purely natural response to supernatural assistance.[16] The Logos also permeated the whole political culture, particularly since that culture had been converted. Eusebius was certain that the new Christian empire was the culmination of a historical process governed by the Logos from the very start. He held that God's spirit had precipitated political crisis and manipulated political conduct to prepare a great change in Christianity's fortunes. The task of the apologist and triumphalist was to circulate this good news, that is, to make history preach.[17]

History's sermon, as Eusebius relayed it, was characterized by contrasts that seem as perfectly a part of the genre as parables are part of the teaching of Jesus. Eusebius's statement that the reign of Constantine was unlike all that had gone before epitomizes the basic format. Predecessors had driven Christians from their homes, confiscated their properties, and ridiculed their faith. Constantine repaired as much of the damage as he could. Properties were restored. Churches were rebuilt. Dishonored by previous regimes, Christians were envied after the emperor demonstrated his indebtedness to their God. Persecutors had hounded the church's leaders, so Eusebius took special pleasure in reporting that Constantine sought their counsel. History spoke most eloquently of these momentous contrasts and reversals, and history, as Eusebius pointed out, was itself a principal beneficiary. Pagan officials often fiddled with the past and tried to erase the church's story by burning its documents. The new emperor commanded that surviving texts be copied and disseminated at public expense. He urged prelates to speak their minds, to convene synods, and to spread their doctrine. The contrasts indicated to Eusebius that a new era had dawned. He suggested that Constantine agreed, for how could a disciplined review of the record lead to a contrary conclusion? The Logos had arranged things too well.[18]

[14] Eusebius, *Tricennatsrede*, pp. 230–32.
[15] Bardy, *Eusèbe* 3: 115 (10.8).
[16] *LKK*, p. 95 (3.25).
[17] Farina, *Impero*, pp. 123–27, 166–69.
[18] *LKK*, pp. 68–72 (2.48-2.60), 80–81 (3.1).

In Eusebius's orations, the history lesson culminated with an analysis of specific structural changes in political culture, an analysis that furnished an additional set of contrasts. Eusebius averred that one need not travel back too many centuries to find barbarous conditions and political confusion perpetuated by incessant tribal warfare. Despite God's intention that humankind live harmoniously, borders were bloodied, remapped, and bloodied again. Petty jealousies were projected on deities and thereby dignified so they might develop into enduring animosities. Feuds needlessly flared into fighting, allegedly to keep militant gods happy. Eusebius blamed the blood and chaos on polytheism; the remedies were monotheism and world monarchy. Christianity and Roman hegemony developed nearly simultaneously—no accident, to Eusebius—and passions that set neighbor against neighbor were gradually tamed. But monotheism made halting progress and monarchy struggled against polyarchy until Constantine eliminated the other tetrarchs and reunified the empire decisively and, Eusebius thought, permanently. From that time, God's omnicompetence could not be doubted, and the empire's political coherence, if only in Eusebius's mind and orations, was forever wed to its religious unity.[19]

We need not itemize contrasts and claims to appreciate that Christian apology had hit upon a formidable reply to pagans who mocked the new religion's God for having abandoned his worshipers to persecution. Eusebius insisted that there had been a method behind the madness of infidels and tyrants: God ordained that the empire should reconcile all contentious peoples to its authority before its politics were redeemed by the emperor's conversion. As early as the third century, apologists identified the empire's political progress and its relative peace in some regions with the advance of Christianity. Origen once countered charges of political subversion by pointing out that Christians cooperated with Rome. Their prayers summoned divine assistance for the government, and their suffering instructed politicians in humility and fortitude. Naturally, after the final disarmament of Christianity's enemies, that is, after Constantine defeated Licinius, Christian apology was increasingly susceptible to triumphalism. The converted and reunified empire seemed a most complete revelation of the Logos, which had calculated precisely when and how a charismatic leader and a Christian political culture should enter history.[20]

Eusebean sociolatry has two focal points: Constantine and the redeeming politics of the Christian empire. The chance to write the emperor's

---

[19] Eusebius, *Tricennatsrede*, pp. 239, 248–50.

[20] *LKK*, p. 56 (2.19). For Origen, see *Origène, "Contre Celse,"* ed. Marcel Borret, vol. 4 (Paris, 1969), 344–48 (8.73), but also vol. 1 (1967), 360–62 (2.30). Also consult Erik Peterson, "Der Monotheismus als politisches Problem," in his *Theologische Traktate* (Munich, 1951), pp. 89–93, 103–5.

biography gave Eusebius a splendid opportunity to transform the manifestly successful general into a crusader much larger than life. The Logos not only selected its champion; it amplified his virtues. How otherwise, Eusebius wondered, could one account for Constantine's extraordinary magnanimity toward his enemies? He ordered his soldiers to refrain from molesting captives; and when such directives fell on deaf ears, he offered incentives for restraint from his own treasury.[21] The example was important for Eusebius because he also wanted to make a pastor of his indomitable crusader. The postscript to his biography's tale of the battle for Rome and against Maxentius demonstrates that nothing could be easier for Eusebius than to wheel from stunning military feats to his subject's exemplary clemency and philanthropy.[22]

Constantine's dedication to the relief of poverty and destitution seems too good to be true; Raffaele Farina was probably correct when he implied that the biographer surveyed the stories of Constantine's campaigns with one eye on the Gospels. Though enormously successful in war, Eusebius's Constantine was always more impatient to sign a truce than to conquer or reconquer territories.[23] Never was so invincible a warrior so irenic, and Eusebius was willing to transfer the emperor's instincts for reconciliation to the empire's chancery (for edicts and official correspondence owned that it was unwise to battle superstition with violence). Preservation of the realm's peace dictated some tolerance and prudence. Chancery documents professed the new regime's dedication to spreading Christianity throughout the empire; there could be no doubt that a new age had arrived. Universal enlightenment, however, would have to be postponed.[24]

The postponement did not distress Eusebius. Political culture was fraught with signs that the Logos had charged government with a mission and that Constantine's government was inclined to fulfill it. Chancery documents reasserted the emperor's intense interest in the church's welfare. Eusebius supposed that Christian worship would soon be a matter of public policy. He copied letters and decrees into his biography without much editorial comment because they seemed to him to echo his own conviction. They certainly ascribed the emperor's prosperity to his God's powers over history and political culture. Many of the chancery's instructions and specimens of Constantine's correspondence read like hymns of thanksgiving. The emperor was circumspect and thus reluctant at first to sweep the old cults from his realm, yet the rival religions could be combed from Roman civilization in time. Whole peoples, Eusebius said, would be

---

[21] *LKK*, p. 54 (2.13).
[22] *LKK*, pp. 34–38 (1.38–1.43).
[23] *LKK*, p. 52 (2.10); Farina, *Impero*, pp. 183–84, 196–98, 254.
[24] *LKK*, p. 72 (2.60).

attracted to the realm's official religion and confirmed in it by their emperor's example and by his regime's enactments. Laws, edicts, and exhortations would take their toll and would nudge the empire into its new age.
The imperial chancery was doing the work of dozens of itinerant preachers: it sent the gospel into every corner of Constantine's domain.[25]

One question of some significance permits us to chart our way back
from Eusebean sociolatry to history: Did Eusebius collect or compose his
chancery evidence? If the edicts and epistles were forged, earliest Christian sociolatry rested on enthusiasms that bore little or no resemblance to
official attitudes or government policy. But if Eusebius actually took
sheaves of prescriptions and proscriptions from the chancery and used
them in his biography, sociolatry was something of a collaborative effort.
The hoax, if there was one, was not clumsy. No serious doubts have ever
been raised with respect to the earliest edicts of restitution. Other mate-
rials, which, it was once thought, Eusebius manufactured, have recently
been accepted as genuine. Eusebius selected official documents to illustrate his history of the church. Adopting the same tactic in his biography,
he reinforced the rhetoric of Christian sociolatry and made the government his partner, one might almost say, his coauthor.[26]

Constantine's government, however, never really recruited prelates as
partners. The emperor welcomed the Christian clergy to his dinner table,
and he sought clerical counsel during his military campaigns. He kept
prelates as companions, much as credulous kings have kept astrologers
close at hand. Eusebius wrote candidly about his emperor's expectations:
were the prelates honored, their God's gratitude would be militarily and
politically advantageous.[27] Subsequently, Constantine relieved bishops of
their political responsibilities, but Eusebius was not alarmed by the imperial exemption. In fact, he thought it a generous concession, for the
burden of costly public service had been lifted without malice from the
backs of leading Christian clergy. His history of the church includes the
edict that Constantine circulated among African prelates soon after his
victory over Maxentius. The edict explained that expenses involved in
meaningful participation in political life were sure to distract priests from

[25] Eusebius, *Tricennatsrede*, pp. 199, 222–23; *LKK*, p. 126 (4.18).

[26] See Charles Pietri, "Constantin en 324: Propagande et théologie impériales d'après les
documents de la *Vita Constantini*," in *Crise et redressement dans les provinces européennes
de l'Empire*, ed. Edmond Frézouls (Strasbourg, 1983), pp. 67–69, 79, 84–87; Arnold Ehr-
hardt, "Constantin d. Gr. Religionspolitik und Gesetzgebung," *Zeitschrift der Savigny-
Stiftung für Rechtsgeschichte, romanistische Abteilung* 72 (1955): 170–72; W. Telfer, "The
Author's Purpose in the *Vita Constantini*," *Texte und Untersuchungen zur Geschichte der
altchristlichen Literatur* 63 (1957): 161–64; Farina, *Impero*, pp. 246–47; and, for an account of the nineteenth-century case against authenticity, Winkelmann, "Geschichte," pp.
197–99.

[27] *LKK*, p. 37 (1.42). Also note *LKK*, p. 32 (1.32).

their liturgical duties—upon which the regime's continuing good fortune was thought to depend.[28] By the time Constantine and his army had experienced the firstfruits of the emperor's conversion, only a fool or philosophe would have suggested that Christian liturgists be inconvenienced. Of course, the fact that church officials were excused from local civic service does not argue conclusively that Constantine thereafter chased other prelates from court, but if any appreciable numbers were present in the chancery and were influential partners, traces of their presence and influence have been effaced. Notwithstanding the theological affirmations that were coupled with privileges and prohibitions in an assortment of chancery documents, it appears that Constantine's administration achieved discipline and efficiency without the benefit of Christian clerical intervention. The best-known clerical counselor, Bishop Hosius (or Ossius) of Cordoba is the exception that proves the rule.[29]

Hosius was once said to have been among Constantine's retainers, even before the emperor declared for the new religion. Although evidence for that early association is flimsy, the assumption survived so long because Hosius's subsequent service, which is fully documented, was tremendously valued by his master. From 324, apparently, he was Constantine's chief liaison with the church. Eusebius and Athanasius placed him at the scene of major church councils in Alexandria, Antioch, and Nicaea. Hosius actually presided over the debates at Nicaea, and he was the first to sign the council's creed. While he pressed his prelatical colleagues toward a resolution of the Christological disputes, the emperor sat as a spectator in the gallery—no doubt the most conspicuous presence at the council. Hosius, however, was the government's agent. In a more modern frame of reference, he would be called the cabinet secretary in charge of ecclesiastical affairs. There is no reason to suspect that his portfolio contained business other than that pertaining strictly to the administration of the church, so his labors should not be construed as proof of clerical influence over all political culture. But his career can be cited with confidence to verify that clerical culture had become a part of political culture.[30]

Eusebius made a great fuss over Constantine's courtesies to the council fathers. At first glance, the emperor's attention and kindness may be taken as symptoms of imperial deference and submission, but Constantine in the gallery stands taller than Hosius at the rostrum. Constantine lavishly entertained many of the bishops at Nicaea, but before they de-

[28] Bardy, *Eusèbe* 3: 112–13 (10.7).

[29] See Clemence Dupont, "Les privilèges des clercs sous Constantin," *Revue d'histoire ecclésiastique*, 62 (1967): 731–36; but also review J. Gaudamet, "La législation religieuse de Constantin," *Revue d'histoire de l'église de France* 30 (1947): 32–38, 61.

[30] But cf. A. Lippold, "Bischof Ossius von Cordoba und Konstantin," *Zeitschrift für Kirchengeschichte* 92 (1981): 1–15.

parted he lectured them at considerable length and scolded them for dissensions and arrogance that threatened to divide *his* church.[31]

Constantine's solicitude was expressed on other occasions as well and in a number of different ways. He prohibited regional authorities from overruling decisions made by local ecclesiastical synods.[32] He intervened if controversies over remote episcopal vacancies dragged on and left churches without leaders. When negotiations stalled in Antioch, he nominated two fresh candidates and instructed the electors to stop making overtures to a third.[33] Examples of the emperor's decisive and fairly frequent mediation surface regularly in Eusebius's biography. Perhaps Eusebius only wanted to add some lively brush strokes to his portrait of the emperor as ideal pastor. Conceivably, he had no intention of documenting imperial mastery as well as imperial diligence. The examples, nonetheless, yield the impression that the government took a proprietary interest in the church, and Jean-Marie Sansterre doubts that Eusebius assembled his evidence casually. Sansterre speculates that the biographer deliberately placed the church so completely in Constantine's care to underscore the tradition of imperial supervision. According to this interpretation, Eusebius had no use for the Nicene provisions, so he emphasized the rights of emperors to review and possibly overturn the decisions of church councils.[34]

Whatever Eusebius's purposes were, his narrative certainly disposes readers to think that church and empire were integrated—and on the government's terms. Prelates made their choices at Nicaea, then the emperor turned them into law. With reference to this relationship, Eusebian sociolatry seems to tell us a great deal about history, but the literary programs of Eusebius's biography and orations are most important for our review of redeeming politics because they cast Constantine's shadow across the next centuries. All the same, the connections between sociolatry and policy are sometimes difficult to disallow.[35]

Should one wish to deal more precisely with those connections, with the character of Constantine's control and the extent of ecclesiastical autonomy, one drifts from sociolatry into a different area of interest. There, researchers commonly test administrative procedures to determine whether Constantine acted both as Caesar and as pope, and studies of caesaropapism usually produce pocketfuls of qualifications and extenuating circumstances that are periodically emptied and sifted in historical

---

[31] *LKK*, pp. 89–94 (3.15–3.22).

[32] *LKK*, p. 130 (4.27).

[33] *LKK*, pp. 116–17 (3.62). That third was Eusebius himself.

[34] Sansterre, "Eusèbe de Césarée et la naissance de la théorie césaropapiste," *Byzantion* 42 (1972): 554–86.

[35] Walter Ullmann, "The Constitutional Significance of Constantine the Great's Settlement," *Journal of Ecclesiastical History* 27 (1976): 10–12.

literature. Here, however, that method is very much beside the point. In the study of sociolatry, the identification of administrative procedures and the more or the less of imperial control take a back seat to our fascination with polemical and liturgical strategies that grafted the idea of sacred monarchy to assertions about the sacrality of history. Caesars become crusaders and pastors, churches are transformed into trophies, and cities are relocated narratively as symbols. What Eusebius did with Constantinople illustrates the point.

For Eusebius, Constantinople was a token of the new age. Not every citizen applauded Constantine's conversion. Some thought that fresh starts were dangerous. A later historian certified that many pagans feared that the emperor's apostasy might also lead to political misfortune.[36] The people of Rome, he claimed, were particularly outspoken; for generations, citizens and their senates refused to abandon pagan worship.[37] That historian, Zosimus, may well have overdrawn the pagan protest, but we know that Constantine was cautious when he visited Rome and that he visited rarely and briefly. He was hesitant about striking coins with Christian insignia in the city, though he showed no such reluctance elsewhere. Zosimus was probably right to have thought that the emperor was unhappy with the chilly reception accorded his new religion in the old capital. Constantine lost little time in hunting for a new home for imperial government. Six years after he deposed Licinius, he gave Christian triumphalists and heralds of a new age a new Rome, an ostensibly Christian capital in the East.

Eusebius must have been delighted. He had no brief for Rome, and the rededication of political culture could have acquired no better emblem than a new capital. He boasted that Constantinople had swiftly been purged of pagan worship, a boast repeated in other apologetic literature and, as we shall see, smuggled into Augustine's City of God. In Eusebius's story, the emperor's city on the Bosporus was tantamount to a votary offering. It is necessary again, however, to measure the distance between rhetoric and reality in order to focus and conclude this first sketch of Christian sociolatry.[38]

If we completely discredit the report in Eusebius's biography, we forfeit the capital's miraculous conversion but we also lose one of the first accounts of Constantine's new city. The city itself was no literary fiction or apparition. It was a daring enterprise, and dedication ceremonies in 330 were likely to have had an unmistakably Christian character. Onlookers acquainted with chancery edicts and exhortations would have expected the city's rapid conversion to the emperor's religion. Eusebius wrote as if

---

[36] Zosimus, *Histoire nouvelle*, ed. François Pachoud, vol. 1 (Paris, 1971), 52 (1.58).

[37] Zosimus, *Histoire* 1: 102 (2.29); 2 (1979): 328–39 (4.59).

[38] *LKK*, p. 104 (3.48); and *CCSL* 47: 160–61 (*DCD* 5.25).

the promise had been realized in a single sweep, but sociolatry, in this instance, was preemptive. It raced ahead of history and crossed from the practical to the quixotic. Constantinople's pagan temples were not systematically refashioned as churches. As Zosimus alleged, the emperor allowed pagans to build and rebuild their shrines within the precincts of his new city.[39]

Apparently, we are obliged to scuttle Eusebius's contention that Constantine tolerated no idolatry.[40] The alternative is to dream up decorative purposes for Constantinople's pagan shrines, unless we accept Gilbert Dagron's arbitration. Dagron suggests that Byzantine paganism was revived to the extent that it confirmed the emperor's apotheosis and increased the dynasty's chances for survival. The capital, according to this estimate, was not built and expanded for Christianity but rather for the emperor and the dynasty, and there is no denying that imperial authority occupied center stage even when Christian symbols were deployed. For example, either Constantine or his immediate successors designed the Church of the Holy Apostles in the new city as an imperial mausoleum and pilgrimage site. Two sets of six coffins honored Christ's first followers and flanked the entombed emperor. No chronicle of funeral arrangements has been preserved, and none can be reconstructed with certainty. Still, the design itself is a monument to the emperor's apostolic standing (or at least to his isoapostolicity) as well as an indication that the habits of Hellenistic divine kingship died hard.[41]

Since Eusebius made his emperor a crusader and an ideal pastor, it is no shock that thereafter Constantine, in encomiastic literature and in iconography, was paired with the apostles. Christian sociolatry may take such liberties. And no matter how swiftly or slowly Constantinople accepted its founder's religion, the new capital prospered as a climactic demonstration of God's government and as the capstone of the empire's redeeming politics. Paulus Orosius repeated Eusebius's inflated claims in the fifth century. Rome, he wrote, attained its position and power after centuries of hardship and struggle. God and Constantine made Constantinople Rome's equal in a matter of months. In sociolatry, if not in history, all things are possible.[42]

[39] Zosimus, *Histoire* 1: 104 (2.31).

[40] *LKK*, pp. 107–8 (3.54).

[41] *LKK*, pp. 144–45 (4.60). Also see Gilbert Dagron, *Naissance d'une capitale: Constantinople et ses institutions de 330 à 451* (Paris, 1974), pp. 401–9; Dvornik, *Philosophy* 2: 746–51; R. Janin, *Constantinople byzantine* (Paris, 1964), pp. 21–26; Joseph Vogt, "Der Erbauer der Apostelkirche in Konstantinopel," *Hermes* 81 (1953): 111–17; and Glanville Downey, "The Builder of the Original Church of the Apostles at Constantinople," *Dumbarton Oaks Papers* 6 (1951): 66–80.

[42] *CSEL* 5: 504–5 (7.28).

Chapter Two

CONSTANTINE'S SHADOW (I)

PAULUS OROSIUS had good reason to retell Eusebius's story of Constantinople's marvelous making and then to contrast it with the legends about Rome's uphill struggle for sovereignty in the Mediterranean basin. Invaders had just looted the venerable old capital. In fact, they infested much of the western empire, and Orosius was himself driven from Spain and forced to seek safety in North Africa. He found some consolation as he surveyed the empire's humiliation, for Constantinople remained standing even as Rome was brought to her knees. For Orosius, that was enough to confirm Eusebius's predictions of a new age. The old order that Constantine had rejected now seemed truly to have passed away. The new Christian empire was to be something quite unlike the empire that it was finally to replace, much as Constantinople had replaced Rome.

Rome was sacked in 410. By 418, Orosius was settled in North Africa. He agreed to assist Augustine, the bishop of Hippo, who was preparing a reply to critics of Christianity, particularly to their charges that the new religion was responsible for the old capital's sad fate. The critics complained that Constantine's apostasy precipitated the decline of time-honored cults and that the declining reputation of pagan worship, in turn, alienated Rome's gods and led to the ruin of Rome's empire. Augustine, as we shall see in another chapter, challenged this assessment, yet he did not simply recycle Eusebius's position. Rome's tragedy compelled him to modify Christian sociolatry substantially. Orosius, however, set a different course. His seven books of history, *Against the Pagans*, upheld Augustine's judgment that, contrary to the critics' views, the cults and gods of the pagans had never fashioned an invincible empire. But Orosius then came up with an unusual definition of conquest that helped him sustain the optimism generated by Eusebius and Lactantius.

Christianity's old conquest was still usable. The very fact that Christianity had prevailed after centuries of persecution seemed to tell against pagan nostalgia. If the pagans' gods had been so powerful, why had it proven impossible to suppress Christianity? Edicts had been formulated and unspeakable cruelties invented, yet the forces arrayed against the early churches were no match for the one God who, in due time, removed all rivals and for his chosen emperor, who similarly eliminated his competition. Orosius stressed not only the new religion's conquest and the empire's conversion but also the ease with which it purportedly had all been accomplished. If the pagans' gods had been vigilant and their cults sturdy before and during Constantine's campaigns, why had Rome's devotion changed so suddenly? Why was Constantinople won for Christianity so effortlessly? Why was Christianity irrepressible before Constantine and irresistible thereafter?[1]

Orosius went on to smear the pagans' pictures of their past. When they appealed to Constantine's apparent unwillingness to outlaw the old cults immediately, as if they wished to demonstrate that the emperor's conversion was neither sudden nor sincere, Orosius might have echoed Eusebius, who came to terms with the emperor's halting progress against idolatry by reminding himself and his readers that prudence often dictated procrastination. But Orosius never actually admitted that there had been irritating delays. He praised Constantine for his gentleness, for the considerate character of his orders, which, when they were issued, showed that the Christians' God worked more gallantly and graciously than the Christians' persecutors.

By calling attention to the contrast between the unsuccessful and ruthless tactics of pagan emperors and the successful policies of the first Christian emperor, Orosius indirectly encouraged perseverance during the crises of the early fifth century. Christians were experiencing a profound reversal, and it appeared as if matters would get worse before they got better. Barbarian tribes continued to chase Christians and others loyal to the empire from their homes. Distressed pagans apportioned blame for the misfortunes most menacingly. Orosius reminded the faithful that Christianity had been tested by more aggressive and more formidable enemies than those that now faced them. Their God had saved them once and would save them again.

Orosius, however, had to explain why Christianity's first political conquest and Constantine's redeeming politics had gone sour. He could have assaulted the problem with the customary battery of justifications; in fact, he did underscore the most common of them, the equation of persecution with divine chastisement. But he also gave the tragedy of his times an interesting twist, and having done so, he revealed how Christian sociolatry and triumphalism could survive the colder climate of the fifth century. Treaties had been broken, oaths violated, frontiers crossed, Italy invaded, and Rome sacked. Solid Christian citizens had been turned into pitiable and helpless refugees. The ruin seemed irredeemable, too terrible to be explained by the usual, pious pronouncements about persecution as punishment for sins. Orosius knew, of course, that God would ultimately rescue the empire and its new religion, and he wrote that he had already found signs of recovery, signs that were also clues to the master plan that

---

[1] *CSEL* 5; 354 (6.1).

made Christian suffering comprehensible. Orosius saw that some of the barbarian intruders were exchanging their weapons for ploughs and crosses. Others were sure to follow. God had apparently orchestrated the invasions to draw tribes closer to the Christian truths unpreached in their own territories. Rome's troubles were part of God's redeeming politics on a grand scale: Huns, Burgundians, Vandals, and untold others would eventually be conquered (and redeemed) by the empire's new religion and thus by the empire that they had come to conquer.[2]

It may not have occurred to Orosius that the same effect could have been produced by the empire's orderly expansion. Or perhaps he suppressed that possibility because he was compelled to comment on the facts before him. Of one thing we may be certain: facts and fictions were carefully crafted to fit with Orosius's two sturdiest convictions. Evidence was admissible if it matched Orosius's twin beliefs that God arranged all things for the best and that God would repair the damage done to the Christian empire. The beliefs themselves were braced by the record of God's cooperation with Constantine. Apologists also claimed that the very timing of Christ's incarnation suggested that God had ordained the empire as his special instrument for the world's redemption and conquest. Orosius agreed with Eusebius that it was no accident that Christ had come into the world just as Rome achieved uncontested supremacy and that this coincidence authorized apologists to square the details of subsequent political history with their theological predilections.

At one time, along the Mediterranean coast, small provinces had been ruled by forgettable sovereigns. Jealousies poisoned their relations. Laws and customs so varied that neighbors were strangers to one another. Then Augustus Caesar brought unprecedented peace and political coherence to the region in preparation for the Savior's appearance. Augustus incorporated great and small territories into his realm, in accord with a plan drafted, Orosius said, in heaven. And when the emperor ordered a census of citizens, the infant Jesus was enrolled, giving a sign that God at the very least sanctioned the conquests of Augustus. Having thus endorsed the empire when it was not yet Christian, God was hardly likely to abandon it after its government turned to Christianity.[3]

Orosius quarried his optimism from personal experience as well as from history. He traveled from Iberia to North Africa and then as far as Palestine. Wherever he went, one set of laws and standards operated; the same God was worshiped with the same rituals. People treated him hospitably, as though he were a comrade or a compatriot. All this seemed a remarkable blessing to the refugee from the carnage and chaos in Spain.

---

[2] *CSEL* 5: 554 (7.41).
[3] *CSEL* 5: 426–29 (6.22), 434–40 (7.2–7.3).

And all this was possible, he insisted, because Augustus and then Constantine had served admirably as God's deputies, and because the political order that the first had created and the second had redeemed was durable indeed.[4]

Durable but undoubtedly damaged! Orosius, in effect, responded to the crisis of his time by suggesting that to extend the empire's new religion was to mend the empire's political order. He acknowledged that there was no quick fix. Generations of internecine war might precede the decisive revelation that Christianity and monarchy were better than superstition and polyarchy. The soliloquy that closes Orosius's history even implies that God might continue to drive the barbarians into battle with one another in order to increase their longing for peace. It did not make for a pretty prospect, yet Orosius offered it so convincingly that it seemed the obvious price for redeeming politics. Even now Orosius's sense of divine providence and political crisis endows fifth-century turmoil and tragedies with a certain dignity. Christian sociolatry, in this instance, simply made conflict a precondition for the Christianization and reunification of Europe.[5]

Orosius did not convince all Christians that barbarian intruders would eventually make good neighbors. It was not easy to overcome long-standing prejudice. When barbarians first crossed into the empire and entered Christian literature, they were thought to be no better than beasts.[6] Actually, Orosius did little to improve their image. He only held out the promise that they would acquire civility once they wearied of war and accepted the new religion. Several decades after Orosius completed his history, Salvian of Marseilles composed his treatise *On the Government of God* and offered a significantly different interpretation of the barbarians' invasions and the empire's fate. For Salvian, the intruders had become the old empire's most robust and most reliable citizens. The Franks and the Saxons, often without the gospel, learned virtues that Christians had forgotten as well-regarded citizens of an imperfect and corrupting empire. Dissolute Romans fared badly alongside broad-shouldered Vandals. Salvian so admired the newcomers that he very nearly destroyed the imperial core of Christian sociolatry. He admitted that an alarming amount of anarchy had arrived with the Germanic tribes, but he also intimated that God had planned the disturbances so that the apostate

---

[4] CSEL 5: 281 (5.2). Also see Peterson, *Theologische Traktate*, pp. 98–101; Hans-Werner Goetz, *Die Geschichtstheologie des Orosius* (Darmstadt, 1980), pp. 117–25, 134–35; Benoit Lacroix, *Orose et ses idées* (Montreal, 1965), pp. 71–73, 199–210; and Johannes Straub, "Christliche Geschichtsapologetik in der Krisis des römischen Reiches," in his *Regeneratio Imperii* (Darmstadt, 1972), pp. 252–62.

[5] CSEL 5: 562 (7.43).

[6] For Ambrose's caricature, PL 16: 1081.

Christian empire might cease to believe its own triumphalist apologetic and waken to its apostasy.[7]

Orosius confidently looked ahead to the assimilation of barbarian settlers. Salvian implied that life among the Goths and Franks, as yet unconverted, was occasionally preferable to subjection to the empire's ruthless and depraved officials.[8]

Something must have happened during the decades that passed between the composition of Orosius's predictions and the formulation of Salvian's distinctions, something that shattered residual faith in the empire's endurance. Or we might speculate that what had not happened was more consequential, that barbarian intruders proved slow to trade their swords for crosses. In any event, Salvian was disposed to draw Christian political thought away from the standard faith in the empire's redeeming politics, and he had a ready answer to the question Orosius left dangling at the end of his analysis. Orosius, as we noted, assured Christians that their God permitted barbarians to overrun Roman territories and conquer the old capital in order to bring their tribes within Christianity's reach. But while Orosius failed to consider the possibility that the same result could have been achieved by the expansion of the empire and the conquest of the barbarians, Salvian explicitly addressed this issue by alleging that the empire had become unworthy of its new religion. Goths, Sarmatians, and Franks had lived along its borders for centuries, and they were offended by the empire's corruption and waste. To the extent that Christianity was associated with wicked and wasteful government, it was incapable of converting barbarians, whom Salvian narratively endowed with a rugged nobility.[9] Several passages in Salvian's *Government* seem to be on the verge of granting his noble savages a new order, a new empire, but Salvian recoiled from the conclusion that closed upon him when he observed that misery and perversion disappeared once the intruders seized a territory from its imperial masters. Nonetheless, his remarks on God's providence presented citizens with an interesting, if not a beguiling, prospect: Could the Germanic kings conceivably be God's new deputies? Might they be miniature Constantines, whose eventual conversions would lead to each tribe's redemption and finally to the rehabilitation of the Christian empire?[10]

The first great age of Christian political apology, however, was all but over. Phenomenal changes in each generation made the previous generation's explanations obsolete. During the fifth century, the so-called barbarians continued to trim the empire. The Vandals swarmed across the

---

[7] *CSEL* 8: 94–96 (4.17–4.18), 182–83 (7.19).
[8] *CSEL* 8: 110–11 (5.7).
[9] *CSEL* 8: 119 (5.10).
[10] *CSEL* 8: 136–37 (6.8).

northern coast of Africa. Goths grabbed Spain and southern France. Burgundians chased legions of Rome's mercenaries from the north. The reconstitution or reconfederation of empire seemed beyond the powers of any single tribal leader. Despite Orosius's promises, Catholic Christianity lost ground to the tribes' various pieties, paganisms, and Arian devotions. This is not to say that there were no dramatic conversions to the old empire's relatively new religion, but reversals often followed closely upon them. For instance, Ethelbert of Kent and the Anglo-Saxons he governed welcomed missionaries from Rome, and the pope was so taken with the idea that the politics of the Christian empire might be redeemed that he pronounced the remote sovereign a second Constantine. But when Ethelbert died in 616, his kingdom reverted to traditional Celtic religions. Southern Britain became so inhospitable that the bishops of London and Rochester fled to the Franks for safety.[11]

For two centuries, Germanic and old Roman cultures seemed everywhere to collide. But Gaul was one place where citizens of the shriveled empire and their strange new rulers collaborated. Barbarian chieftains replaced Roman emperors in the church's prayers, and Gallo-Roman bishops in the larger cities provided the developing *regnum Francorum* with able, regional administrators. The Merovingian dynasty was conspicuously successful in exploiting their territories' Christian elites, and it was not long before the tribe's worship took a turn toward the church.[12]

King Clovis converted to Catholic Christianity in 493. Fifteen years later, he effectively crusaded among the Arian Goths, many of whom subsequently accepted Roman Christianity. The church's officials saw their God's hand at the helm once again. Gregory of Tours, bishop and historian, thought Clovis's successes otherwise inexplicable, and his tale of the king's baptism suggests how well God steered the affairs of church and kingdom. According to Gregory, Clovis had wanted to be baptized for some time before the actual event, but the king feared public disclosure of his own piety would alienate his subjects, who were too fond of their idols to forgive his disaffection or accept his new religion. As the story goes, when the king finally worked up the courage to face his people, they preempted his announcement and urged him to lead them to salvation. Gregory's comments on the miraculous consensus preface his canonization of Clovis as a new Constantine, but we must not allow his triumphalism to mislead us. The Merovingian empire, although covered by a thin layer of Christian officials, long remained a collection of pagan war-

[11] *MGH, Epistolae* 2: 309, and Eugen Ewig, "Das Bild Constantins des Grossen in den ersten Jahrhunderten des abendländischen Mittelalters," in his *Spätantikes und fränkisches Gallien*, vol. 1 (Munich, 1976), 87–88.

[12] Rudolf Buchner, "Das merowingische Königtum," in his *Das Königtum: Seine geistigen und rechtlichen Grundlagen* (Constance, 1956), pp. 153–54.

rior societies. Conversion and political integration were slow processes culminating more than two centuries after Clovis, when the Franks acquired a new dynasty and a more formidable reputation for effective military expeditions.[13]

This development brings us into the age of the Carolingians, who displaced the Merovingians and then obtained papal endorsement for their coup. Rome and her bishops survived the centuries of uncertainty that followed the empire's dissolution in Italy, but just as the Carolingians were expanding their influence north of the Alps, the empire's old capital faced its greatest threat to date.

By 751, the Lombards from northern Italy had expelled Byzantine administrators from Ravenna. Until that time, the popes had maintained a precarious political existence by appealing alternatively to Constantinople against the Lombards and to the Lombards against the interests of the old empire. Impressive Lombard victories, however, changed the balance of power. The ducal officials in Benevento and Spoleto now listened exclusively to Lombard counsel, and Rome was all but encircled and besieged. The papal estates outside the city were soon taken, and the church had no choice but to appeal to the Carolingians for assistance.

Pippin, king of the Franks, twice crossed the Alps and forced the Lombards to give up their campaigns against Rome. His victories inspired a small revival of the universalist rhetoric of Christian sociolatry, particularly when the new Frankish dynasty promised to defend the church in return for papal legitimation. Fulrad, the politically influential abbot of St. Denis, proclaimed his Carolingian sovereign "king of *all* the faithful." When Charlemagne succeeded Pippin and added Bavaria and Saxony to his domain, the Franks seemed to be on the threshold of recolonizing Latin Christendom. *All* the faithful might soon have their new empire, a fresh political expression of their redemption and of their God's providential government. Eastern emperors had lost their hold on the West. The Byzantine garrison had been chased from Ravenna, and the Lombards, who had done the chasing, had been overawed and tamed by Carolingian armies. The course of events late in the eighth century invited apologists to reconsider and to recycle idealizations of political culture that had seemed inappropriate for so long.[14]

The idea of empire had a tremendous hold over the imaginations of Carolingian apologists. When Emperor Constantine IV was deposed in 797, and when kingmakers in Constantinople postponed naming a new

---

[13] *MGH, Scriptores rerum Merovingiarum* 1: 92–93; Ewig, "Bild," pp. 95–97; and Jan de Vries, *Altgermanische Religionsgeschichte*, vol. 2 (Berlin, 1957), 406–18.

[14] See Michael Tangl, "Das Testament Fulrads von Saint-Denis," reprinted in his *Das Mittelalter in Quellenkunde und Diplomatik*, vol. 1 (Graz, 1966), 540–55, and *KKP* 1: 174–76.

candidate, Charlemagne's friends reasoned that imperial power had been transferred or translated to the Carolingian court. Alcuin, an enterprising courtier and churchman, induced Pope Leo III to endorse the translation with an imperial coronation in Rome. In 800, during the Christmas celebrations, Charlemagne was crowned Holy Roman Emperor.[15]

As legend has it, the new emperor was taken by surprise. Einhard, his biographer, insisted that Charlemagne came to Rome merely to help the pope defend his political and pontifical power against defiant citizens of the city. Pippin, after all, had set the precedent for such expeditions. But the blush that Einhard added to his new emperor's cheeks is more hoax than history, for Carolingian courtiers had been making immodest claims long before their king traveled south. Papal coronation and consecration simply constituted de jure acknowledgment of the Franks' contention that God had raised up a new champion in the West to redeem the politics of Christian empire.[16]

If citizens or pontiffs ever required proof that their new emperor was a second Constantine, apologists could rehearse the conquest and conversion of pagan tribes. Nothing succeeds like success; the Franks, as faithful Christians and divinely favored conquerors, left nothing to chance after they subdued Saxony and baptized the Saxon chiefs. Charlemagne and his advisers composed a detailed list of regulations, proposing profound rather than cosmetic changes in Saxon worship. The document prescribed severe punishments for dissidents who revived tribal festivals and funerary practices associated with the indigenous cults.[17] Carolingian authorities, however, learned that it was one thing to dictate terms of surrender and another to enforce them. Armed uprisings in Saxony made it nearly impossible to complete the Christianization of the pagan territories. The pious pronouncements de partibus Saxoniae, therefore, stand as evidence of design rather than effect. Nonetheless, once we admit that the rhetoric of apologists customarily raced ahead of reality, design can safely be taken as the sum and substance of Christian sociolatry. Carolingian ambitions keep alive to this very day the Frankish sense of mission. What at first seems to be a set of fossilized edicts and prescripts formulated a vital ideal of imperial authority that, in the eighth and ninth centuries, bor-

---

[15] See Werner Goez, *Translatio Imperii: Ein Beitrag zur Geschichte des Geschichtsdenkens und der politischen Theorien im Mittelalter und in der frühen Neuzeit* (Tübingen, 1958); Wolfgang Wehlen, *Geschichtsschreibung und Staatsauffassung im Zeitalter Ludwigs des Frommen* (Lübeck, 1970), pp. 22–31; and Werner Suerbaum, *Vom antiken zum frühmittelalterlichen Staatsbegriff* (Münster, 1977), pp. 301–5.

[16] For Einhard's disclaimers, see *MGH, Scriptores rerum Germanicarum* 2: 458; but also note *KKP* 1: 255–63; Louis Halphen, *Charlemagne et l'empire carolingien* (Paris, 1947), pp. 124–33; and Helmut Beumann, *Ideengeschichte Studien zu Einhard und anderen Geschichtsschreibern des früheren Mittelalters* (Darmstadt, 1962), pp. 86–90.

[17] *MGH, Capitularia regnum francorum* 1: 68–70.

rowed models from the Old Testament to link Charlemagne's conquests and later Carolingians' more modest successes with God's providence. Even when Charlemagne promised to reduce government influence, that is, when he announced his intentions to deregulate (*superflua abscidere*), he confided that he had assumed the awesome responsibility for his subjects' righteousness and salvation, much as King Josiah had dedicated himself to the sanctification of Israel.[18]

Old Testament models for priestly kingship were popular before Charlemagne was crowned emperor in Rome. Afterward, apologists increasingly exploited parallels between their sovereign's conquests and those of Constantine. Chancery documents and numismatic evidence suggest that the Carolingian regime was intrigued by the comparison.[19] In 806, Charlemagne instructed his heirs to be vigilant benefactors of the church, to watch over St. Peter's city, to honor the clergy, and to safeguard ecclesiastical property. Like Constantine, he recognized that prelates were directly responsible for redeeming souls, but he urged his sons to remember their responsibility to maintain, reform, and redeem the church.[20]

The dividing line between rule and redemption, then, was never clearly drawn, and the thoroughness with which Carolingian officials supervised clerical affairs complicates matters for scholars who want to distill distinctions between church and state from the record of Carolingian administration. The new emperor unambiguously condemned church officials who appeared to have sacrificed discipline for profit. Even before his imperial title was conferred, his chancery told leading prelates, in effect, to scale down their households. One edict prohibited them from keeping kennels and hiring jesters, so they might seem more like God's solemn ambassadors than spendthrift and disreputable barons.[21] A memorandum offered rewards as inducements to clerical officials who seriously and successfully arranged for improvements in the education of local priests.[22] An exhaustive list of rules and regulations circulated in 789 with Charlemagne's "General Admonition," which announced that the king was as committed to the sanctity of his realm as Josiah was to the salvation of his ancient kingdom.[23] For Charlemagne, religious discipline and religious uniformity were politically essential; liturgical coherence and doctrinal consistency favored political solidarity. At the very least, regeneration of the Christian empire by the apologists gave the Carolingian

[18] *MGH, Capitularia regnum francorum* 1: 53–54, citing 2 Kings 2–3.

[19] Ewig, "Bild," pp. 102–4; and *KKP* 1: 272–84.

[20] *MGH, Capitularia regnum francorum* 1: 129.

[21] *MGH, Capitularia regnum francorum* 1: 64.

[22] *MGH, Epistolae Karolini aevi* 2: 532.

[23] *MGH, Capitularia regnum francorum* 1: 54–60.

government considerable credibility as it hustled to assimilate Saxons, Bavarians, and Lombards.

The church was a ubiquitous and energetic crier. Wherever they were read in the expanding empire, homiliaries assured subjects of their government's divine commission. Clerical court scholars composed chronicles that commemorated the conquests of their new Constantines, Charlemagne and his heirs. The Carolingians' redeeming politics heralded a religious renewal because rulers wished to be represented by unimpeachable prelates who would offer convincing testimony of their regimes' importance in God's providential arrangements. The church, of course, was too valuable an ally to be left to its own devices. The chancery dispatched deputies, known as *missi dominici*, to explain its provisions, disarm opposition, and assist the church's officials, who, in effect, were the court's precinct workers.

As age slowed Charlemagne, he delegated greater authority to his *missi*, but he insisted that the more intractable regional conflicts between prelates and laymen be resolved at court. In such disputes, his deputies were simply to gather information and take depositions.[24] The church, however, was not always happy with this procedure. The controversy in Tours shows that prelates were unafraid to play their one trump against the strong imperial hand when arbitration threatened their prerogatives.

In Tours, Alcuin had been charged with having incited a riot to protect the immunities of his church. One of the emperor's commissioners spent more than two weeks extorting evidence in situ, but the depositions were inconclusive. The commissioner, therefore, summoned witnesses to the imperial court, whereupon Alcuin forwarded a full account of the incident and a vindication of his actions. He also implored his friends close to the emperor to intercede on his behalf. Arguing for the inviolability of his church's privileges, Alcuin reminded both Charlemagne and his own partisans that former Frankish kings had confirmed the church's rights to give fugitives sanctuary, and he warned that the present sovereign would undoubtedly stain his reputation were he to exhibit less reverence than his ancestors for the church's privileges, immunities, and canons. The implication was that the emperor's arbitration must follow a pattern, that emperors were masters of the church only if they allowed tradition to dictate their decisions. Years later, Archbishop Hincmar of Rheims argued the point more forcefully when he told Charlemagne's grandson that he must be as humble and as submissive as King David if he expected God's approval and the clergy's obedience. The Franks' alliance with the church occasionally yielded these and other similar warnings to the effect

---

[24] MGH, *Capitularia regnum francorum* 1: 64, 67.

that imperial autocracy was conditional upon imperial conformity to God's will or to tradition, as the church might define them.[25]

Ordinarily conditions, when explicit, were cushioned with flattery, but the church was so scrupulous a custodian of the ideal of empire that prelates pulled no punches when they heard of schemes to partition the *regnum Francorum*. Charlemagne was the first to have suggested that strategy, but two of his three sons predeceased him. In the end, there was no need to make a choice between dividing the empire and dividing the family. Charlemagne's sole heir, Louis the Pious, ruled his territories and monitored ecclesiastical reform much as his father had, yet he was faced with the additional prospect of multiple heirs. Like his father, he made provision for each son to take a share, although Carolingian apologists objected to the plans. Their protests strayed close to sedition—not too close, but close enough to trouble Louis with the prophecy that God would not countenance a consecrated empire divided against itself.[26]

Louis died in 840, and his sons proceeded to dismember the empire and to compete with one another for larger portions of the prize. Universalist pretensions slipped from the rhetoric of each court's apologists, and by the tenth century, they were all but forgotten. Once, to patrol the *regnum Francorum* was to police an empire, a pitch that stretched from sea to sea. Later Carolingian chronicles reported matters and migrations as if one could pass into that kingdom from Burgundy, or as if one need only swim the Seine to be beyond the jurisdiction of the Frankish king. In other words, terms and titles that carried considerable freight for Merovingians and for the early Carolingians were meaningless by the time a new Saxon dynasty started consolidating and expanding its influence in Europe.[27]

The Saxons settled comfortably in Constantine's shadow, reviving the rhetoric of empire and journeying south every century or so to impose order on Italy. Increasingly, the apologists' blend of piety and politics prompted clerical resentment. The Saxon revival found few supporters in Rome and in France. Odilo, abbot of Cluny, even tried to cut Christianity loose from all imperial ideology by recalling that his religion had never respected boundaries, no matter how much territory they enclosed. Christianity, he said, reached populations that great emperors could neither

[25] *PL* 125: 854. For Alcuin's case and counsel, see *MGH, Epistolae Karolini aevi* 2: 396–98, 401–3. For relevant inferences from iconographic evidence, see Robert Deshman, "The Exalted Servant: The Ruler Theology of the Prayerbook of Charles the Bald," *Viator* 11 (1980): 390–91, 401–3.

[26] See the remarks of Agobard of Lyon, in *MGH, Epistolae Karolini aevi* 3: 160; but also note Wehlen, *Geschichtsschreibung*, pp. 119–20. For Louis's policy and plans, consult J. M. Wallace-Hadrill, *The Frankish Church* (Oxford, 1983), pp. 226–41.

[27] See Joachim Ehlers, "Die Anfänge der französischen Geschichte," *Historische Zeitschrift* 240 (1985): 26–29.

conquer nor control, notwithstanding their swords and statesmanship. When Saxon theorists spoke of their indestructible empire and foresaw their sovereigns' universal rule, they exhibited to Odilo only the curious results of their impaired vision.[28]

Briefly in the next chapter, and more exhaustively in the fifth, we shall take up the story of clerical opposition to the redeeming politics of the medieval Christian empires. Here, we shall leave Odilo with the last word because he certifies that Christian sociolatry had an enduring yet limited appeal. After Orosius and Salvian, apologists idolized Merovingian, Carolingian, and Saxon sovereigns as Constantine's heirs; none, however, could permanently ward off disillusionment.

[28] *PL* 142: 1032.

Chapter Three

CONSTANTINE'S SHADOW (II)

AFTER THE PONTIFICATE of Gregory VII, which will concern us in the fifth chapter, most bishops of Rome opposed theorists who identified either political or religious redemption with the rule of emperors or the regimes of lesser kings. But no pontiff mastered the politicians, their publicists, and the political situation of Europe as completely as Lothar Segni did when he assumed office as Pope Innocent III in 1198. Early in the thirteenth century, he turned belligerent barons into humble appellants. His intrigues gained him considerable say in the affairs of the empire. He prodded Philip II of France to acknowledge papal prerogatives, and he intimidated King John of England, whose reputation has never really recovered from the humiliation. Other princes swiftly and obediently responded when the pope called them to crusade. None of Innocent's successors could match his conquests, but the tragedy is that several tried. And the tragedy of one outspoken and unfortunate pope brings us to the fourteenth century and introduces our next encounter with those idealizations of empire drafted in Constantine's shadow.

The quarrel between Pope Boniface VIII and King Philip IV of France ended only when the king's agents forced his implacable adversary from Rome and held him captive in Anagni. Like Gregory VII and Innocent III, Boniface boasted the pope's supremacy, and his proclamation *Unam sanctam* (1302) is widely thought to be the best summary of papal hierocratic theory.[1] Unlike his predecessors, however, he was outmaneuvered before he could engineer many appreciable advances, and he died a prisoner of the king. After the short pontificate of Benedict XI, Clement V refused to come to Rome and took up residence in Avignon, closer to his French patrons.

Lombards and Tuscans were distressed by the fate of the papacy. They lost no love on the French, who were alternately trusted confederates and ruthless enemies. But if we were able to ask them and other Italians whom they blamed for the papacy's captivity, first in Anagni and then in Avignon, a sizable number would name the popes themselves and then deride the church's exaggerated fears of imperial intervention. One faction in nearly every northern Italian town argued that the arrival of the emperor

---

[1] *Enchiridion symbolorum definitionum et declarationum*, ed. H. Denzinger and A. Schonmetzer, 32nd ed. (Rome, 1963), pp. 279–81.

from the German lands was the first crucial step toward the recovery of political coherence south of the Alps. The popes might have summoned them, but they had not; now the papacy was paying the price. Emperors might have come without a papal summons, but several of them suspected that their power in Germany would have been in jeopardy had they preempted and alienated the church. Some Italians eager to have the emperor set things right assured German politicians that the popes' authority was limited, that bishops of Rome had no right to question or to impeach candidates who had been duly elected as emperors. God presided over the orderly passage of power in the empire without the advice and consent of the Roman church. Such was the line taken by Cino da Pistoia and by Cino's remarkable friend and fellow poet, Dante Alighieri of Florence, both of whom looked north for Italy's political salvation.[2]

Italians hoping for imperial intervention had one apparently unalterable advantage over their political opponents who feared that the emperor's presence in Italy would lead to the renegotiation of alliances and boundaries. Even if emperors were contemptuous of Rome's politics and indifferent toward the Avignon papacy, they believed that their positions were much more secure with papal coronation and consecration than without them.[3]

After Henry of Luxembourg was elected Emperor Henry VII, he and his advisers made plans to travel to Rome to receive the pope's blessings. Pope Clement V then resided in Avignon, as would his successors for the next seventy years, but he agreed to send legates to perform the requisite ritual. Naturally, Clement's cooperation was expensive: the emperor was asked to confirm the papacy in all its possessions and to make additional territorial concessions to the church. For much of the year (1310) the prince and his pope bargained, while Dante and others restlessly awaited the outcome. The emperor-elect reasoned that his journey would be too risky without complete papal approval, so he finally acquiesced to all Clement's demands. One condition, had it been faithfully observed, certainly would have diminished Dante's enthusiasms, for the pope virtually cuffed the emperor to a policy of nonintervention. He extorted from Henry a promise to retain the church's supporters in their municipal offices, no matter how unfriendly to the emperor their cities might seem.[4] Dante and Cino expected change. Clement V assured himself that Henry would change nothing, and only then did he order Italian citizens to wel-

---

[2] For Cino, see Michele Maccarrone, "Il terzo libro della *Monarchia,*" *Studi Danteschi* 33 (1955): 122–28.

[3] Michael Wilks, *The Problem of Sovereignty in the Later Middle Ages* (Cambridge, 1963), pp. 243–53.

[4] *MGH, Constitutiones* 4: 342, 401.

come this "king of the Romans" from Luxembourg and to see him safely through to Rome.[5]

If Dante knew of the agreement, he must have guessed that the emperor would be compelled to break it, because he wrote ecstatically about the great changes in Italy that would accompany Henry VII's march to Rome. He expected to be restored to Florence once the emperor had expelled the officials who had expelled him. But Dante was also persuaded that all Italy had reason for rejoicing.[6] His letters to fellow citizens were filled with rapturous phrases that compared Henry VII to the Old Testament prophets and to the New Testament's messiah.[7] He sent a letter directly to the emperor and told him that when he (Dante) first saw Italy's new political redeemer in Milan, John the Baptist's words mysteriously came to mind: "Behold the lamb of God who takes away the sins of the world."[8] Dante advised political authorities in Italy that the quickest path to peace was to accept the itinerant emperor's counsel and arbitration. Henry VII, he avowed, had come to their troubled cities to punish, console, correct, and forgive with the powers of Caesar *and* St. Peter.[9]

Since the emperor was unable to keep his promises to the pope and at the same time keep his own partisans happy, one insurrection followed another when he arrived in Lombardy. Dante's impassioned statements, some of the finest specimens of medieval Christian sociolatry, fell on deaf ears. Cremona was the first of several cities to declare against the emperor, but thirty miles to the north, the battle for Brescia was more costly. Brescia withstood a four-month siege that, much to Dante's consternation, kept Henry from his triumphant procession through Tuscany— through Florence and to Rome.

Dante blamed Florence, and he believed that the situation would much improve were the emperor to go directly to the Tuscan source of his Lombard crises. On this matter, Dante proved himself a shrewd analyst. Florence feared the emperor from the time he announced his journey, and Florentine officials began immediately to repair old alliances and to contract new ones. Ambassadors bounded back and forth between Florence and Avignon. In spring 1311, Bologna joined the league that Florentine officials had organized for the defense of the status quo against imperial meddling. This is not the place to write the history of negotiations and backroom agreements, but it is significant that Florentine citizens clan-

---

[5] *MGH, Constitutiones* 4: 376–78.

[6] *DAOM*, p. 541: "O Italia . . . rallegati."

[7] *DAOM*, pp. 559–60.

[8] *DAOM*, pp. 564–65.

[9] *DAOM*, pp. 544–45. In this connection, see Paul Renucci, "Dantismo esoterico nel secolo presente," *Atti del congresso internazionale di studi Danteschi*, vol. 1 (Florence, 1965), 325–26, 332.

destinely assisted the emperor's enemies in Lombardy and virtually sponsored Ghiberto da Coreggio, whose principal task was to seduce the emperor's vassals to rebel against "the king of Germany." It would seem,
therefore, that Dante was right when he counselled Henry VII that it was
useless to take on Lombard challengers one by one. As long as Florence
was free to assist insurgents, the emperor's army was saddled with an
endless assignment. Florentines might keep their perfect composure, dis-
dainful of the "king of the Romans," who was preoccupied successively
severing the Lombard heads of Hydra.[10]

When the emperor finally left Lombardy, he experienced further difficulties. He had to fight his way to Rome and then through the streets of
Rome where, despite days of bloodshed, his soldiers were unable to clear
the way to St. Peter's. Henry settled for a ceremony in the Basilica of St.
John in the Lateran (June 1312) and for the grudging participation of
several cardinals who would have preferred to have presided at the emperor's funeral. As it happened, Henry did die soon thereafter, but he
lived long enough to learn that his "papal" coronation solved nothing.
Lombard and Tuscan cities still defied him. With the aid of France, Naples, and Florence, other opponents were capable of keeping his army in
the field and at bay.

Henry's single undisputed triumph was a posthumous one, for which
Dante was wholly responsible. Dante narratively placed his emperor, who
had been unable to reach St. Peter's, on a throne from which no malcon-
tent, no pontiff, could remove him. In the *Divine Comedy*, the ill-starred
emperor rests regally in the most honored place in paradise, while purgatory and the inferno teem with his rebellious Italian subjects and proud,
unyielding popes.[11]

The *Divine Comedy* is Dante's revenge. He was convinced that his emperor's enemies cared more for their purses than for Italy's peace, that
greed and greed alone motivated the most influential advisers at the papal
court.[12] Emperors from the North, he said, had always been Italy's best
chance for political harmony. Their reluctance to travel south left their
vicars defenseless and made it easy for petty Italian tyrants to mismanage
their territories.[13] Dante considered Henry VII's firm resolve to travel to
Rome a happy end to imperial indifference and the grand beginning of a
new age. His job was to let citizens know of their impending political
redemption. After the emperor's death, however, Dante felt compelled to

[10] *DAOM*, pp. 568–71.

[11] *DADC, Paradiso* 30.133–48.

[12] In this connection, see Antonio de Angelis, *Il concetto d'imperium e la comunità soprannazionale in Dante* (Milan, 1965), pp. 192–93.

[13] *DADC, Purgatorio* 6.97–126.

inform citizens of the magnitude of their crime: the Italians had crucified their redeemer.

Dante's *Divine Comedy* can be mined for fragments of his political enthusiasms and censures, but his smaller composition *De Monarchia* more explicitly adapts Christian sociolatry to the fourteenth-century apology for empire.[14] The *De Monarchia* is an extended polemic against polyarchy that owes some of its themes to the government's propaganda. The emperor himself argued that authority was ungodly when shared or divided. Someone in his chancery was familiar with the tidy sequence that characterized previous apologies for universal rule: God invited Augustus to assemble all "nations" under one imperial regime before he sent Christ to invite humanity to repent its sins.[15] Dante repeated the argument that dignified imperial government, but he also tried to abstract his propositions about universal rule from contemporary controversies. He tried, in other words, to extricate political truths and political philosophy from the charges and countercharges that swirled about the emperor's arrival in Italy. He composed the *De Monarchia* while Henry VII battled his way down the peninsula, but the emperor's itineraries, alliances, and enemies were never mentioned directly. In reverse order, the treatise's three books rummage for historical and theological reasons to restrain papal interference in political affairs, furnish an exposition of old Rome's place in the history of Christianity, and index the practical justifications for the present emperor's authority and autonomy, that is, for the authority of the new Rome.

The new Rome was the empire once again made whole by Henry VII, the answer to Italy's political problems. Incessant warfare in Lombardy and Tuscany supplied Dante with textbook illustrations of polyarchy's unworkability. It was no secret that few neighboring cities and few feuding families within the same city could keep a truce for two consecutive decades. Still, Dante elected to omit references to Italy's political mischief; the *De Monarchia*'s first book set its practical justifications for universal government in the context of an Aristotelian meditation on human nature and human society.

The *De Monarchia* starts by contemplating the end for which humanity created happiness and intellectual advance.[16] Dante then stipulated that those ends could not be reached without peace and that peace in any one place was doomed unless conflict in other locations became extinct. Peace, therefore, must be universal, and the peacekeeper must be so formidable that arbitration instantly resolved contention. With this in mind,

---

[14] See Pino da Prati, *La politica e la filosofia nella "Monarchia" di Dante* (Sanremo, 1963), particularly pp. 35–41.

[15] *MGH, Constitutiones* 4: 802.

[16] *De Monarchia* is printed in *DAOM*, pp. 280–503.

Dante proceeded to argue his way from polyarchy to monarchy. If there were several peacekeepers and arbiters, contention among them was possible and there would be no lasting peace at lower levels. Only perfect contentment at the top could assure the elimination of jealousies, political anxieties, and violence (pp. 324–27). If humanity were to reach the ends for which it had been placed on the planet, one ruler must possess all power so that no desire for greater dominion perverted judgment and justice. God's creation could not make orderly progress toward its redemption unless a single, incorruptible, unimpeachable, and universal sovereign were awarded uncontested jurisdiction (pp. 336–41).

Dante held that there was no denying the philososphical case for his emperor's complete sovereignty, although he once hinted that absolute power might be shared without devastating consequences. Before that opinion turned the first book of the De Monarchia to rubble, however, Dante added that something that could be done equally well or better by one person ought not be done by two or three. Congestion and superfluity, he warned, "displease God and Nature" (pp. 354–55).

In calculating divine displeasure, Dante offered theological grounds for censuring polyarchy. The universe, after all, was well governed by its *one* master: God's government should be a model for imperial authority in human society (pp. 316–21). Dante alleged that those who failed to make the connection between celestial rule and terrestrial government had an underdeveloped appreciation for the cosmic order and a very imperfect understanding of human history, not to mention an incomplete interpretation of God's greatest revelation. God had waited until peace replaced polyarchy, until Augustus had expanded his empire, and only then had Christ come to redeem humanity (pp. 362–63).

Dante repeated the argument in a letter to his emperor, whose chancery hardly required the reminder. But the letter implored Henry to shake some sense into citizens in Italy, who seemed more obsessed with their cities' liberties than with their souls' salvation. Had Augustus not crushed rebellion, Dante volunteered, Christ would not have come.[17] The emperor from Luxembourg, however, was not equal to the task that Augustus had undertaken ages before. Soon Dante had to explain the imperial failure, whereupon he signaled that the recent disappointment was only a short chapter in the long history of intractable Italian resistance. Some emperors, like Charlemagne, were blessed with success.[18] Others, like Henry VII, were less versatile and less fortunate. All the same, Dante suggested that the political history of imperial Italy was also the history of salvation. He equated the Italians' appetites for freedom from imperial

[17] DAOM, pp. 564–67.
[18] DADC, Paradiso 6.94–96.

government with humanity's sinful bondage to base instincts, and he absorbed the uneven history of imperial policy and imperial conquest into a political theory that gave direction to Christendom's redeeming politics. For Dante, it followed from Augustus, from Charlemagne, and even from Henry VII, whose heroism was undiminished by his Italian failure, that a single world government was necessary for lasting peace and was a necessary precondition for the redemption of humanity.[19]

Dante could not change the fate of his own emperor, but he could and did give the case for world monarchy a compelling illustration by rewriting the history of old Rome's emperors. He wanted to cite precedents for imperial hegemony, yet he seems to have realized that, in some respects, he was on thin ice when he offered Roman conquests in late antiquity as prototypes for Carolingian and Hohenstaufen expeditions to Italy. The sticking point was that Roman successes generally predated the empire's conversion to Christianity. Moreover, in the fifth century, the venerable Augustine had attributed Rome's spectacular chain of victories to the Romans' ruthless pursuit of glory. Much of what Dante wished to say depended on a rehabilitation of the pagan soldiers whose industry and ingenuity made Rome an empire.[20]

All that Dante compressed into the second book of the De Monarchia reads like a reply to Augustine on the question of imperial motives for conquest. Dante's Romans were driven by a manifest zeal for justice that suggested to Dante that the Christians' God inspired those non-Christian warriors and rewarded them with remarkably good fortune.[21] Only a fool would think that God had no influence on pre-Christian history. The chronicle of Rome's dramatic deeds, narrow escapes, and stunning routs of enemy forces was no less a demonstration of divine solicitude than the record of the Hebrews' exploits. For Dante, the luck and valor of the Roman legions were actually miracles, distinct tokens of God's vigilance and intercession. He insisted that God had given the old empire its justice, its conquests, and its universal sovereignty.[22]

The second book's commemoration of imperial conquests gave readers in Avignon no cause for alarm. Theorists at the papal court contended only that authority had passed from the emperor to the pope when Constantine urged Pope Sylvester to watch over the western regions while he

---

[19] Brigitte Winklehner, "Die mittelalterliche Weltfriedensidee in ihrer Bedeutung für das politische Denken Dantes," in *Romanisches Mittelalter*, ed. Dieter Messner and Wolfgang Pockl (Göppingen, 1981), pp. 385–400.

[20] CCSL 47: 156 (DCD 5.19).

[21] DAOM, pp. 418–19.

[22] DAOM, pp. 383–87; and David Thompson, "Dante's Virtuous Romans," *Dante Studies* 96 (1978): 145–62. Also see da Prati, *La politica*, pp. 47–49; and Joan M. Ferrante, *The Political Vision of the Divine Comedy* (Princeton, 1984), pp. 15–16.

and the capital moved east. The document on which this contention was based was a forgery, yet it had not been exposed as such at the time Dante finished his second book and started the third. This book should have given readers in Avignon fits, for in it Dante challenged the authenticity of Constantine's commission. He vouched only that an ambiguous grant "was said to have been made," and he objected strenuously to theorists who used Constantine's grant to defend their pontiffs' rights to intervene in imperial affairs. Dante asserted that the very nature of imperial authority was to assist humanity in realizing the ends for which it was created and to please God. That could only be accomplished if emperors maintained peace, and peace, as we have heard, depended upon unity. An emperor's duty, then, was to unite, not to divide what had been united. If Constantine intended to partition his empire, as the forged commission implied, then he had forfeited imperial power. Since the intention and the forfeiture preceded the formulation of any document embodying them, the document was null and void.[23]

With respect to the commission, which is better known as "the donation of Constantine," the *De Monarchia* was limping along on some questionable assumptions, but the third book marches forward as if on legs of sturdy logic. Dante could not afford to be conciliatory, for the redeeming politics of empire would not succeed unless papal theorists in Avignon were silenced. It was necessary, therefore, to survey their other evidence for the church's rights to dictate political policy and either to take sovereignty from or to share sovereignty with the emperors of the new Roman empire. The church's rights and powers were thought to have derived from popular consent or from God. Some even declared that the church was its own source of political authority, an immodest proposition that Dante exposed as nonsense: a church that gives itself what it does not have gives nothing. As for the other possibilities, Dante first assaulted the appeal to popular consent. He denounced theorists who proposed such abstractions but who were unable to persuade a simple majority of Europeans to accept papal supremacy. Asians and Africans, he noted, seemed permanently beyond the range of papal government, and by their very independence, they invalidated the argument from consent. Dante finally reported that he had scanned both the Old Testament and the New and that he nowhere discovered that God had delegated political powers to priests and apostles. Instead, he found reasons to believe that God had forbidden the clergy to covet those very powers that medieval pontiffs subsequently claimed for themselves and their deputies. The *De Monarchia*'s penultimate pronouncement concludes the attack on papal theory with a dramatic declaration. There need be no clerical go-between, we are

[23] *DAOM*, pp. 476–77.

told, because God communicates directly with his imperial vizier, whose political prerogatives, therefore, are not subject to pontifical review.[24]

Presumably Dante knew how seditious he had become. Emperors and their courtiers still valued papal consecration and coronation. Circumstances forced them, from time to time, to embarrass particular popes, but the political tides of Dante's time had not turned against the papacy. While Dante and a few other theorists accused the church of unwarranted political interference, Henry VII was gambling rather recklessly to get to Rome to accept the church's blessings. Nevertheless, reservations about the *De Monarchia*'s radicalism have often been voiced, perhaps never more forcefully, however, than in a widely respected analysis of the treatise's third book written three decades ago by Michele Maccarrone. The case he makes against sedition emphasizes the *De Monarchia*'s polemical context. By associating Dante's composition with other theorists' deliberate use of overstatement and anticlerical slogans, Maccarrone advised that Dante's redeeming politics only appeared to imply absolute imperial autonomy. He explained, in order words, that Dante's rhetoric conformed to that of conventional antipapal protests and actually camouflaged Dante's more qualified and nuanced position.[25]

Maccarrone's approach is critical if we wish to measure the influence of Constantine's shadow on Dante's work, and Maccarrone's strongest argument draws upon the *De Monarchia*'s enigmatic last words, so we must spend some time at the end of the treatise before we press ahead.

After Dante stipulated that emperors received their authority directly from God, he seems to have changed his mind. As we might expect, he allowed that political arrangements for the world's peace and humanity's happiness in some fashion (*quodammodo*) provided for the salvation of Christians' souls. But then he conceded that in some matters (*in aliquo*) emperors had to defer to their pontiffs.[26]

The concession and conclusion are enigmatic because Dante appears to have divided sovereignty, notwithstanding the rest of the *De Monarchia*'s militant opposition to such division. Either we must question the extent of the treatise's opposition, as Maccarrone has, or offer a plausible interpretation of the final concession that will not alter substantially our reading of Dante's redeeming politics. The second option seems more attrac-

---

[24] *DAOM*, pp. 478–79, 490–93, 500–503. Also consult Bruno Nardi, *Dal "Convivio" alla "Commedia"* (Rome, 1960), pp. 238–43; Ernst Kantorowicz, *The King's Two Bodies*, (Princeton, 1957), pp. 456–64; Ferrante, *Political Vision*, pp. 113–14; and Gustavo Vinay, *Interpretazione della "Monarchia" di Dante* (Florence, 1962), pp. 10–12. For related arguments against the papal theorists' extrabiblical imagery, see Jacques Goudet, *La politique de Dante* (Lyon, 1981), pp. 199–200.

[25] Maccarrone, "Il terzo libro," pp. 117–18.

[26] *DAOM*, p. 502.

tive, and it can be explored in two ways. The first appeals to the political problems that prompted Dante's composition. Presumably, as Dante pondered the relationships between imperial and papal politics, Henry VII was still suing for papal support. Pope Clement V initially approved the emperor's plans to travel to Rome, but the pope's friends in France, Naples, and Florence labored to wreck imperial ambitions and, to that end, reminded the pope of the political importance of their patronage. Dante may have hoped that the emperor's first few successes against Lombard resistance would eventually have encouraged Clement to disregard Angevin overtures and to risk a more decisive commitment to the itinerant emperor. And if he were courting Clement, Dante could not have left subversive sentiments suspended from the last lines of the *De Monarchia*. From this perspective, then, the treatise's deferential conclusion was circumstantial. Dante added it to appease readers in Avignon and Rome otherwise displeased with the third book's assault on their arguments for papal supremacy.

This reading of the concession gains some weight when we turn from the *De Monarchia* to Dante's *Divine Comedy*, which was completed after Dante had abandoned all hope that help might come from Avignon. We find no concession there. His *Comedy* thrives on insult. He indicted the papacy for having perpetuated political chaos in Italy, and the speeches he scripted for St. Peter placed the blame for all Europe's wars at Rome's door.[27]

The *Comedy* goes beyond papal politics and raises doubts about the papacy's soteriological effectiveness. Previously Dante suggested only that the popes' authority to bind and loose sinners (that is, to condemn and to absolve) did not license papal interference in the affairs of Christian princes. At the time, he had in mind claims by certain pontiffs that Rome possessed the power, the right, and the responsibility to depose as well as to condemn disrespectful monarchs. The *Comedy* strips some papal censures and absolutions of all authority. We are told that Guido da Montefeltro languished in hell despite a full papal pardon. Papal curses, on the other hand, were inconsequential with respect to Manfred, king of Sicily, whom Dante deposited in purgatory. Manfred and other excommunicates await their redemption, and their very expectations are libels against the popes who damned them, for they prove that divine clemency was not hostage to papal whim. The *Comedy* itself proves that the *De Monarchia*'s concession was an ephemeral creature of circumstance, or it

---

[27] *DADC, Paradiso* 27. The *De Monarchia* was composed after the *Comedy* was begun but before it was finished—probably from 1312 to 1314. See George Holmes, *Florence, Rome, and the Origins of the Renaissance* (Oxford, 1986), pp. 235, 246, 257.

would if the *De Monarchia*'s final phrases were, in fact, a concession at all.[28]

That last provision introduces an alternative interpretation of the *De Monarchia*'s conclusion, one that places great stress on Dante's calculated ambiguity (*in aliquo*). Had Dante purposefully set out to malign papal theorists in Avignon and Rome, he could hardly have composed a less obliging editorial on their arguments for papal supremacy and imperial subordination. Recall that the *De Monarchia* reduces theorists' confidence in Constantine's donation to absurdity and insolently disposes of their other favorite claims and metaphors. Only then does the treatise seem to acknowledge the popes' rights to filial affection. The courtesy was an afterthought and perhaps an insult. It appears to have been a stage formula that, now as then, barely conceals Dante's lack of conviction. The most remarkable thing about Dante's concession is not that it gives the papacy so much more than the rest of the *De Monarchia* allowed, but that it gives so much less than papal clerocratic theorists wanted.[29]

With respect to Dante's idealization of imperial political culture, matters should stand as we have arranged them. In the *Divine Comedy*, God's government in paradise resembles imperial court life.[30] On earth, Dante implied, imperial government and undivided sovereignty reflected God's reign in heaven. Perhaps Dante considered himself another Orosius, whom he eulogized as a foremost "advocate of Christian times" and whom he assigned an enviable place in paradise.[31] Be that as it may, the *Comedy*, the *De Monarchia*, and the correspondence, which makes the emperor's descent into Italy messianic, are monuments to the "Christian times" of Emperor Henry VII.

A glance at another kind of monument concludes our work in the fourteenth century and suggests how narrative and the visual arts conspired to dramatize familiar themes. Dante pictured Henry VII as a Caesar and a surrogate St. Peter, but the emperor was received as neither and died in summer 1313 while campaigning against Tuscan insurgents. Soldiers carried his body to Pisa, one of the few Italian cities that remained loyal during Henry's ordeal. Tino di Camaino received the commission to design a wall tomb for the emperor in the right transept of the cathedral. From 1494 to 1921, repeated restorations took considerable liberties with the original design, and art historians still bicker about the proper reconstruction. In its present state, however, the tomb solemnizes in stone

---

[28] *DADC, Inferno* 27.67–136 for Guido; and *DADC, Purgatorio* 3.133–41 for Manfred. Also consult Ferrante, *Political Vision*, pp. 209–12.

[29] Giovanni di Giannatale, "Papa e imperatore in *Monarchia* III, 12," *L'Alighieri* 22 (1981): 57–60.

[30] *DADC, Paradiso* 25.40–45.

[31] *DADC, Paradiso* 10.118–20: "quell' avvocato dei tempi cristiani."

the *De Monarchia*'s meaning and the relevance of redeeming politics (if not for Tino di Camaino and his clients, at least for some knowledgeable restorers). Three panels of figures carved in relief decorate the console beneath Henry VII's reclining effigy. In all, twelve venerable sentinels guard the emperor's remains. Constantine's corpse was flanked by twelve coffins representing the apostles. Now Henry was accompanied by granite witnesses to his apostolicity, imagination's tribute to the apparent conflation of religious and political vocations that characterizes Christian sociolatry.[32]

Pontiffs, of course, entertained a very different idea about their emperors' religious callings: to put it very simply, emperors were called and should be compelled to obey their popes. Henry VII's successor, Louis of Bavaria, questioned the call and tried to deliver a deathblow to papal influence in imperial politics. In 1338, Louis persuaded the empire's electors to prohibit papal consecration of political candidates. As long as the Germans prized that troublesome custom, he said, their emperors-elect were no better than the Roman bishops' pawns.

The prohibition of 1338 was a small part of the new emperor's crusade against papal theory. Fierce counterattacks followed, but a small cadre of erudite partisans assembled at the Bavarian court and returned the fire from Rome and Avignon. Marsilius of Padua is probably the best remembered, but William of Ockham is a close second. The two apologists for empire cared little for understatement or innuendo. Protected by the emperor, they assaulted papal pretensions and defended their sovereign's right to rule without ecclesiastical interference. The point to be pondered, however, is that the emperor, his electors, and his ideologues inadvertently sabotaged their arguments for empire and for universal rule, and much the same could be said about Dante. It was imprudent to discredit papal consecration because political universalism in medieval Europe was moored to current notions of papal universality. Sink the dock and you sink the ship.[33]

The issue of papal consecration brings to mind the liturgies of Christian sociolatry and the fact that warrior aristocracies loved their rituals no less than modern parade-planners and parade-watchers. The principal liturgical expression of sociolatry's claims was the anointment of monarchs. Be it by pedigree, election, or force, a king's accession was usually followed by some ceremonial confirmation. Anointment, of course, had Old Testament antecedents, which Christian missionaries cited to convince Visigoths in the seventh century to incorporate that practice in their tribal

[32] Cf. Gert Kreytenberg, "Das Grabmal von Kaiser Heinrich VII in Pisa," *Mitteilungen des kunsthistorischen Instituts in Florenz* 28 (1984): 33–60.

[33] See Wilhelm Kölmel, *Regimen Christianum: Weg und Ergebnisse des Gewaltenverhältnisses und des Gewaltenverständnisses* (Berlin, 1970), pp. 539–40, 563–66.

rituals. The Merovingians do not appear to have been as cooperative, but the Carolingians quickly introduced royal anointment into Frankish political culture. Anointment thereafter was understood to bestow a quasi-sacerdotal or priestly character on new rulers and their regimes. Local bishops presided and thus assured their sovereigns that they simultaneously received divine blessings and divine duties. Pippin had his son Charlemagne anointed, so Pope Leo III did not think to repeat the ritual in 800, when he proclaimed the Frankish king an emperor. Sixteen years later, however, Pope Stephen IV traveled to Rheims to anoint Charlemagne's sole surviving son, Louis the Pious. Particularly when feuds and factions complicated succession, papal anointment was considered a distinct political advantage, although Carolingian prelates occasionally objected to Rome's apparent usurpation of what they said had once been an episcopal prerogative. By the eleventh century, many monarchs also resented Roman interference, and papal theorists were pressed to justify the liturgical endorsements that had given the papacy such political influence.[34]

No one disputed that liturgical recognition was tantamount to divine approval. Popes and their propagandists insisted that such approval was also the source of political power, a divine commission, as it were, that could only pass from greater to lesser authorities. Only popes, therefore, should anoint monarchs. The opposition replied that prevailing practices were based on a contrary assumption: cardinals, after all, consecrated popes; suffragans consecrated their metropolitans.

Episcopal complaints against the popes' liturgical politics were presented most indignantly in the *Tractates* known collectively as *The Anonymous of York*, although they are ascribed now to an archbishop of Rouen or to one of his deputies. The author somewhat playfully identified contradictions that fouled the papal case, but the defense of episcopal prerogatives was serious business, a matter of self-preservation. In Rouen, in the eleventh century, the archbishop's authority depended on the king's ability to forestall any papal renegotiation of diocesan regulations and boundaries. The *Tractates'* section on consecration emphasized that locally (and thus properly) anointed monarchs were obliged to shield their bishops from all libelous attacks, whether they originated among heretics in the vicinity or among theorists in Rome.[35] The argument shifted from the importance of the person who presided over royal consecrations to the important mission inherited by the person who was consecrated, the sacerdotal ruler. The anointed and consecrated monarch be-

---

[34] *KKP* 2: 287–89.
[35] For the *Tractates*, George Huntston Williams, *The Norman Anonymous of 1100 A.D.* (Cambridge, 1951), pp. 161–64, 171, 199–203; *MGH, Libelli de lite* 3: 678–79; and Kantorowicz, *Bodies*, pp. 42–61.

came the territorial church's supreme pastor. According to the *Tractates*, the sacred king even possessed the power to remit sins. It is no wonder, then, that the French still conceived of royal consecration as an eighth sacrament, long after the church in 1215 limited the number of sacraments to seven. Although the *Tractates* misrepresented liturgical history, the idealization of political power endured because citizens and courtiers wished to believe that their kings were empowered to convert many interests into one nation, much as ordination to the priesthood empowered candidates to convert many Christians into the body of Christ. For all this, however, it is not always easy to tease a "religion of nationalism" from an evident "religion of monarchy," but we shall take the problem and our interest in the ritual expressions of Christian sociolatry across the Channel to England and to the court of another Henry VII, the founder of the Tudor dynasty.[36]

In 1486, at the first signs of spring, Henry Tudor embarked on a journey, or progress, through several parts of the northern tier of his territory. Less than a year had passed since he had come to England to battle King Richard III for the crown, and his position was not yet secure. His partisans expressed confidence that generations of civil war had come to an end, but the former king's friends were unreconciled to their reversals. The northern reaches of the realm were filled with them, and King Henry was well aware that "they of thos parties be necessarye and according to their dutie most defend this land ayenst the Scotts," medieval England's perennial enemies.[37]

When the North of England was mutinous, all England was vulnerable. The new king, therefore, was quick to issue a general amnesty to his predecessor's supporters, but he needed a more comprehensive approach to assure that insurrections would be quashed before they had gathered much momentum. As the Tudors sent pardons to the North, they enclosed instructions to municipal authorities to round up and imprison vagabonds and other suspicious persons in the cities' streets and taverns.[38]

Pardons and police measures were parts of the Tudors' attempts to consolidate their conquests; and Henry VII agreed with his advisers that a series of public appearances would be prudent and politically advantageous. The Tudor trip to the North was less hazardous than the journey undertaken by our first Henry VII, Henry of Luxembourg, early in the

---

[36] For the religions "of nationalism" and "of monarchy," see Joseph R. Strayer, "France: The Holy Land, the Chosen People, and the Most Christian King," in his *Medieval Statecraft and the Perspectives of History* (Princeton, 1971), pp. 300–314. Also see Richard A. Jackson, *Vive Le Roi* (Chapel Hill, 1984), pp. 26–34.

[37] *York Civic Records*, ed. Angelo Raine, vol. 1 (Wakefield, 1939), 125–26.

[38] Raine, *Records* 1: 139–40.

fourteenth century, but the two are comparable because both monarchs were looking for liturgical legitimation. Henry of Luxembourg had been elected emperor, yet he believed his consecration in Rome would add authority to his government. Henry Tudor had seized his crown on the battlefield and been crowned in London, but he looked forward to local consecrations on the road north, ceremonies that would endorse his accession and knit his territories into a nation.

Henry VII expected citizens who had been conspicuously friendly with his former rivals to stage elaborate rituals to symbolize the strength and seriousness of their new loyalties. In this sense, the liturgies and pageants, which were usually associated with the "religion of monarchy," might contribute to the establishment of a national identity, and the North, as part of the new Tudor nation, would be more than a buffer state between England and the aggressive Scots. As it happened, municipal leaders, guild officials, and local prelates hastened to plan elaborate celebrations to entertain, flatter, and reassure their new king that his territories were at one in their admiration for his achievements and in their allegiance to his family. Masquerading as biblical patriarchs and medieval saints, citizens conspired to impress the royal visitor who had traveled north to impress them. The festivals were pleasantly diverting and politically hygienic; insofar as they named Henry as the realm's redeemer, the pageants remain splendid specimens of late medieval redeeming politics.

The ceremonies surrounding the royal entries generated and expressed collective sympathies for the new king's efforts to reunify his realm. Impresarios knew how to season their pageants with just the right amount of deference *and* civic pride. They wanted to demonstrate their cities' abilities to transcend the tensions that had divided England. They had to convey that citizens were eager to pay their respects to the new dynasty and, without overbidding their hands, they had to suggest that their cities were worthy of the new king's respect. Parades often started with a speech by someone impersonating the city's founder and patron. Ethelbert at Hereford, Bremmius at Bristol, and Ebrauk at York transformed legend into vivid proof of their respective cities' antiquity, honor, and endurance. It was as if the pageants' organizers wanted to remind the new monarch that his predecessors had come and gone, while their cities, insofar as they had prospered, stood as indelible testimonies to royal wisdom and generosity. The spectacles that followed, as a series of *tableaux vivants*, documents municipal prosperity and harmony. To be sure, the series of stages that comprised each thematically unified ceremony represented more than a costly charade designed cosmetically to conceal stubborn political problems. Shared work actually induced a sense of community and intensified pressures to place individual feelings and opinions in harmony with the community's ceremonial purposes. Some citizens dreamed up and others put together intricate contraptions simulating descents from heaven or blossoming Tudor roses. Drapers dressed the town's passages and pageant cars, while householders beautified their properties. The dramas and parades, which trumpeted the new king's virtues and the city's antiquity and honor, also exhibited the municipal solidarity achieved during planning and preparation as well as performance. In all, the pageants bound citizens to one another. They bound citizens and their king to each region's life and history—a life and history that transcended everyday experiences. And the rituals showed that citizens and their cities were bound to their new dynasty.[39]

For all this binding, one hierarchical relationship held firm. Other municipal pageants generated community solidarity and customarily dissolved for the day the barriers between one class of citizens and another. Royal entries, however, ultimately associated each city's solidarity with the king's consolidation of his realm and with the king's privileged place in political culture.[40] We have already suggested that the entries were equivalent to local consecrations and coronations. The cities' legendary founders solemnly conferred on Henry VII the symbols of their authority and then placed their cities' inhabitants in the new king's safekeeping. Other figures appeared to give Henry's responsibilities theological meaning. At York, "oure Lady" announced that Christ, her son, had "callid victoriously" a Tudor champion, whom she and her city were eager to acknowledge as their sovereign. The impersonator thereby encouraged the king and his citizens to consider his military conquest as proof of divine empowerment and divine election. A Worcester sentry was made to confuse Henry with King David; David himself appeared in York to surrender his "swerd of victorie" to England's new redeemer. Royal entries, therefore, were rituals of submission. In some instances, they were also occasions to remind the king of urban economic distress, but to the extent that optimism always dispelled the pathos and special pleading, royal entries were rituals of rededication.[41]

[39] For theoretical considerations, see Victor Turner's remarks on ritual formulations of *l'esprit collectif*, "The Center Out There: Pilgrim's Goal," *History of Religions* 12 (1973): 191–230, and *The Ritual Process: Structure and Anti-Structure* (London, 1969), pp. 194–203. For the pageants, consult Glynne Wickham, *Early English Stages, 1300–1600*, vol. 1 (London, 1959), 53–111.

[40] See Mervyn James, "Ritual, Drama, and Social Body in the Late Medieval English Town," *Past and Present* 98 (1983): 3–29 for "other municipal pageants"; and *Les entrées royales françaises de 1328 à 1515*, ed. Bernard Guenée and François Lehoux (Paris, 1968) for fifteenth-century French counterparts, particularly pp. 187, 255, and 300, where visiting French sovereigns were reminded of notable predecessors, Clovis, Charlemagne, and St. Louis.

[41] John Leland, *De rebus Brittanicis collectanea*, ed. Thomas Hearn, vol. 4 (London, 1770), 189–90 (York), 195–96 (Worcester), 199–202 (Bristol).

From the king's perspective, his tour may have had only the prosaic purposes of reclamation and self-assertion. Clifford Geertz tells us in unforgettable fashion that kings in most cultures travel through the countryside, attend festivals, accept gifts, and distribute honors to mark their territory "like some wolf or tiger spreading his scent."[42] Still, from a distance of centuries, the rituals of submission and rededication en route seem to be truly remarkable methods for extending Constantine's shadow. England was God's new Israel, and Henry VII was its new David.

Considerable imagination and diplomacy were required to glorify the new king's accomplishments and natural gifts and simultaneously to toast the dignity and dependability of cities brimming with his former enemies. By any measure, this was a miracle, and prelates were the principal medieval miracle-makers. When the citizens of York learned of King Henry's itinerary, they promptly petitioned their archbishop for assistance. He agreed to consult with a delegate from the city government, and one was dispatched immediately "to be sufficiently instructed." Subsequently, a local priest, Henry Hudson, was engaged to compose and to direct a pageant, and municipal officials compensated Hudson's parish for the time he would be lavishing on city business.[43] Several years later, the archbishop himself orchestrated entertainments for another royal visitor, Henry VII's daughter Margaret.[44] Prelates were closely involved with civic celebrations because many of them, by profession, were accomplished masters of ceremonies. The mass made theaters of all their churches. It was only natural that responsibilities for all rituals invoking supernatural sanction be placed in priests' hands, that the clergy take charge of the ritual redemption of municipal societies and the ritual sanctification of the realm's new regime.

If one is sceptical about the convergence of natural and supernatural, the celebrations and their designers will seem ridiculous. The costumes, winches, and literary allusions, the "peynted" pageant cars and the purple prose, will seem like gaudy "instruments of prestige propaganda," props manipulated in order to whip up and control emotions and to inflate influential egos.[45] We should not be shocked to find that the sublime in one age becomes ridiculous, disingenuous, or Machiavellian when a later and purportedly more scientific age examines it. We may be sur-

---

[42] Geertz's remark introduces his paper on "Centers, Kings, and Charisma: Reflections on the Symbolics of Power," in *Culture and Its Creators*, ed. Joseph Ben-David and Terry Nichols Clark (Chicago, 1977), p. 153. Also see William A. Christian, *Local Religion in Sixteenth-Century Spain* (Princeton, 1981), pp. 153–58.

[43] *Raine, Records* 1: 150, 153, 159.

[44] Leland, *Collectanea* 4: 275.

[45] See, for example, Sydney Anglo, *Spectacles, Pageantry, and Early Tudor Policy* (Oxford, 1969), specifically p. 106 for "prestige propaganda".

prised, however, to find at least one prominent early Tudor spectator sneering at the ease with which pageant-makers hoodwinked citizens and monarchs alike. The critic in question was Thomas More.

More's wonderfully Aesopian tale of a royal procession features a peasant visiting London for the first time. Wandering through the streets, More's rustic came across an excited crowd, yet he was unable to identify the cause of all the commotion until a bystander assisted him by pointing to the king. The peasant was instantly dispirited: How could that be the king, the object of such adulation, when he was merely a man in an embroidered garment?[46]

With that innocent observation, Thomas More and his featured speaker adroitly mocked both royal vanity and public fawning. The peasant's backwoods common sense unlaced the king's majesty and mystery as surely as his distant cousin's candor, in another tale, stripped an emperor of his new clothes.

But as clever and as contemporary as More and his peasant might seem to us, we must try to see that ordinary man in his embroidered garment as the crowd saw or apprehended him. Incontestably, More was a master at demythologizing, but myth commonly is the very bedrock of Christian sociolatry. If we turn to another royal parade, to the accounts of Catherine of Aragon's arrival in London in 1501, we could suggest that More had missed something quite crucial with respect to the integrative function and power of Tudor pageantry.

Catherine had come to England to marry Henry VII's son and apparent heir, Prince Arthur. The marriage contract marked a conquest of sorts, a Tudor diplomatic coup, inasmuch as previous English dynasties had attracted neither the attention nor the daughters of the continent's rulers for nearly a century. During her entry into London, Catherine learned that things had changed. As she made her way from London Bridge to St. Paul's Cathedral, she was lectured on the dynasty's grand work, and one particularly striking oration enables us to take the pulse of the entire proceedings.[47]

In one of the final scenes, "Prelacy" was presented as a man of prodigious learning, who compared the wedding that Henry had arranged for Arthur with the marriage that God had arranged for his son. Prelacy patiently explained that all distinguished theologians used familiar images to make Christianity's mysteries more intelligible. They talked of Christ

---

[46] See More's *Latin Epigrams*, ed. Leicester Bradner and Charles Arthur Lynch (Chicago, 1953), pp. 205–6.

[47] For Catherine's entry, *Chronicles of London*, ed. Charles Lethbridge Kingsford (1905; rpt. Dursley, U.K., 1977), pp. 234–48, and *The Great Chronicle of London*, ed. Arthur Hermann Thomas and Isobel Thornley (London, 1938), pp. 297–310. Also consult Anglo, *Spectacles*, pp. 53–97.

marrying the church at his father's behest, a marriage of considerable soteriological consequence, to say the least. In order to raise history to a higher register, that is, to dramatize the Tudor's redeeming politics, Prelacy then declared that the sovereign who had redeemed a realm formerly cursed with baronial wars and political chaos could be little less than a celestial lord. Henry VII had been "callid victoriously" and "preserved by dyvyn power certeygn." His negotiations for wedding alliances were providential in both senses of the term. Whereas theologians compared heaven's lord to a king who prepared a wedding for his son, Prelacy did not think it irreverent to reverse the simile. But the reversal and the virtual apotheosis of the Tudor dynasty made sense only in the context of the pageant, for pageant, as we have alleged, was an enchanted process in which place and time were transcended. Legendary figures, biblical patriarchs, and honored saints were brought to life to impart sacrality to the realm and its cities. What is more important, pageant created a uniquely harmonious community by enchanting those who prepared, acted, and watched. Prelacy, therefore, could exalt the king only because his pageant transfigured the people, the excited crowd in Thomas More's little fable. More joked about the hoaxes and the hyperbole that fattened the Tudor cult with bales of superlatives, but arguably his satire was not as clever as it initially appeared.

If we peer a bit further into the future of the Tudor dynasty, we can see that Constantine's shadow continued to stretch over Henry's diplomacy. His last celebrations marked the betrothal of his younger daughter to Charles, then heir to Castile, Aragon, Austria, and Burgundy, and later Holy Roman Emperor. The *Spousells* were printed in Latin as well as English so that citizens throughout Europe might learn of the latest Tudor triumph. The text recorded the festivities and boasted that "florisshyng" Tudor roses would soon "be so planted and spredde in the highest imperial gardeyns and houses of power" that the offspring of Henry's offspring would unite and rule all Christian lands.[48] The marriage itself never came off, but that is much beside the point. In Christian sociolatry, the principal function of redeeming politics and its universalist pretensions was to inspire rather than to program or produce.

[48] *The Spousells of the Princess Mary*, ed. James Gairdner, in *The Camden Miscellany*, vol. 9 (London, 1893), 32–33.

Chapter Four

PURITANISM AND CROMWELL'S NEW MODEL ARMY

APOLOGISTS often set their sovereigns in Constantine's shadow. They wished to inspire citizens' loyalty and obedience and to make sedition tantamount to impiety. If the political order and the divine order appeared identical, or at least consonant, protest might be averted because all would know that revolution put rebels' redemption at risk. But Christian sociolatry was not the exclusive property of ruling elites and their ideologues. When opposition parties and their preachers argued that rulers failed to embody sacred virtues and that the reigning order failed to enshrine cherished values and ideals, they occasionally adapted the themes of sociolatry to dignify their sabre rattling and justify their alternatives to offensive regimes.

In the 1640s, political protest was the religious and redemptive activity that virtually defined English Puritanism. For decades, Puritans had pressed for the reform of worship and church polity, but bishops and sovereigns had criticized and condemned the critics. Puritans came to think that substantial political changes were preconditions for any lasting religious reform. At first obliquely and then directly, religious regeneration and political regeneration were featured as the planks of the Puritan platform, the second likened to the first. The impulse to unite and discipline a holy commonwealth, the concern to rule by divine precept and with divine counsel what conquest had united, and the intention to redeem what godly conquerors united and ruled: these three enable us to place the Puritans' redeeming politics in Constantine's shadow.

. . .

In summer 1642, fighting broke out between the armies of King Charles I and those of his Parliament. At first, Parliament seemed to have all the advantages. It controlled the fleet and the treasury. It also controlled London, the realm's largest reservoir of recruits. Nonetheless, Parliament's contention that the war was waged against the king's sinister advisers and not against the king himself was a costly deception, for it all but prohibited sweeping offensives. Initial campaigns were conducted listlessly, as if Westminster's forces were merely marking time until the king came to his senses. Instead, Charles and his armies seized their chances: the royalists made considerable gains in the North; aside from several ports along the Dorset coast, their enemies found no sanctuary in the South and West.

The prospect of total and humiliating defeat tempted Parliament to pursue victory more aggressively. Its agents purchased a Scottish army by promising to reconstitute the English church along lines acceptable to their Presbyterian neighbors to the North. But the centerpiece of Parliament's more combative strategy was an army that seven counties had organized in December 1642 for the protection of East Anglia. Representatives of the Eastern Association met early in 1645 in Bury, twenty-five miles from Cambridge, to protest Parliament's plans for the redeployment of their local militia. They did not want their counties' defenses jeopardized, but Westminster had disregarded their objections. The army of the Eastern Association became the nucleus of Parliament's "New Model Army."[1]

The new modeling followed thunderous debates, not simply in East Anglia but in London as well. The war faction in Parliament and in the field wanted to launch a major offensive. When Parliament's forces under the command of the Earl of Manchester were slow to exploit their striking success at Marston Moor in summer 1644, the war faction campaigned for a new strategy and new leadership. Setbacks in the fall further provoked those who had grown impatient with the commander's tactics. Oliver Cromwell, then a cavalry officer, complained that Manchester's deliberate delays crippled the cause. At Marston Moor, he said, God revealed the war's inevitable outcome: "God made them as stubble to our swords." Cromwell pressed Parliament to hasten the results, and his enthusiasm infected some of the more irenic members of the legislature.[2] The army was soon "new Modell'd". Much to the dismay of moderates, however, Cromwell, his partisans, and his preachers captured the positions of greatest influence and authority. A moderate Puritan, Richard Baxter, lamented that, although command had actually been awarded to another, Cromwell's hold over "the new men" was unbreakable.[3]

Baxter reasoned that the war should be waged to reconcile Charles I with his Parliament and to remove the king's papist advisers ("delinquents" and "dividers"). He hoped to preserve the polity and practices of his Anglican church. Cromwell once invited him to enlist as chaplain to his officers, but Baxter refused and retired to Coventry when he perceived

[1] Clive Holmes, *The Eastern Association in the English Civil War* (Cambridge, 1974), pp. 216–19; and Mark A. Kishlansky, *The Rise of the New Model Army* (Cambridge, 1979), pp. 3–7, 26–51.

[2] *The Writings and Speeches of Oliver Cromwell*, ed. Wilbur Cortez Abbot, vol. 1 (Cambridge, 1937), 278, 302–11.

[3] *Reliquae Baxterianae*, ed. Matthew Sylvester (London, 1696), p. 49.

Cromwell's troops were "independents," persuaded of their sacred duty to overturn the kingdom's religious and political settlements. Independents, he charged, tolerated preaching from all quarters. After the defeat of royalist forces at Naseby, near Coventry, Baxter revisited the army and found infantry and cavalry alike had contracted the fevers that were formerly confined to Cromwell's troops. For the whole "new Modell'd" army, the war had become a crusade and, from Baxter's point of view, God's purposes had been wholly misconstrued.[4]

Baxter blamed himself. Had he accepted Cromwell's earlier invitation, he might have stayed the progress of radical ideas. After Naseby he tried to repair the damage. He joined the army and declared his own war against the "few fiery, self-conceited men" whom he identified as sources of "sectarian" ideas. But Baxter quickly learned that Cromwell's patience with unauthorized preaching encouraged laymen to mount the pulpit, though Parliament had outlawed such license. Common soldiers pronounced against episcopacy or infant baptism. Officers preached against the present political order. The New Model Army seemed to bristle with amateur theologians, and Baxter found himself "daily contending against seducers."[5] The task proved too much for him. He was hopelessly outnumbered, but what most galled him was that the New Model's officers at headquarters would hear nothing of his remedies. They were mesmerized by two radical preachers, John Saltmarsh and William Dell.[6]

We have to leave Baxter, who soon left the army. Because we wish to look at the development of Puritan sociolatry, we must concentrate on one of Baxter's two principal opponents. Saltmarsh is survived by a considerable collection of contemplative writing, but none of his sermons to the officers and troops of the New Model has been found. By contrast, William Dell's most celebrated sermons were quickly printed. Moreover, we shall find that Dell's early career, if trisected to distinguish his time at the university, his work in the parish, and his service in the army, gives us an excellent way to discuss separately three elements of Puritan sociolatry: its Puritanism, spiritualism, and millenarianism.

We soon return to the army to investigate the New Model's obliteration of boundaries that ordinarily divide politics from religion. But that investigation starts behind Cambridge walls and requires some rehearsal of developments that preceded England's Civil War.

William Dell entered Emmanuel College at Cambridge in 1624. Once

---

[4] Sylvester, *Reliquae*, pp. 50–51.

[5] Sylvester, *Reliquae*, pp. 52–54.

[6] Sylvester, *Reliquae*, pp. 56–57. Also consult C. H. Firth's still valuable study of *Cromwell's Army*, 3rd ed. (London, 1921), particularly pp. 331–33, and Michael Walzer, *The Revolution of the Saints: A Study in the Origins of Radical Politics* (Cambridge, Mass., 1965), pp. 12–13, 275–77.

the gates have closed after him, our story, to the extent that it is biography, stalls and disappoints. We are left outside the college with questions about Dell's early career and with a few informed guesses. Had he wished to deflect attention from himself to his college, Dell could not have planned matters more expeditiously. That he was settled at Emmanuel for at least seven years as a student and probably thereafter as a fellow of the college becomes less important than the college's conspicuous place in the history of English and American Puritanisms. Dell brings us to Emmanuel; Emmanuel College introduces us to Puritanism.

In January 1584, Walter Mildmay, then chancellor of the exchequer, received a royal charter for his new college in Cambridge. He established Emmanuel as a seminary, and he urged graduates to "water all regions of our land, yea of the whole earth, with a faith of purest doctrine and a life of most holy discipline."[7] The words "purest" and "discipline" become increasingly significant as we continue, and the universalist objectives will be amplified by the time we rejoin the New Model Army. For now, however, a selective summary of the college's history seems appropriate.

Mildmay coaxed Laurence Chaderton away from Christ's College and made him Emmanuel's first master. Chaderton was known to have preached openly against the Tudor church's fondness for statutes. However many ecclesiastical constitutions and laws of ecclesiastical polity were passed, he declared, it would remain impossible to legislate religious sympathy. Chaderton's divinity lectures encouraged students for the ministry to set aside the church's many rules and many of its rituals and to consult Scripture for liturgical guidance. His ultimate aim was to purify and simplify worship, and his new post at Emmanuel prompted him to develop "a higher strategy." Probably with Mildmay's backing, he laid plans to make the college and ideally the whole university a conduit through which learned Puritan preachers and Puritan reform might reach even the most remote corners of the realm. Neither Mildmay nor Chaderton was a radical, yet both were displeased with their queen's position on religious change. Elizabeth I insisted that the lower clergy and her parliaments take no initiative. If further reform must come, it must originate with the episcopacy, with the bishops whom she had designated as executors of the royal supremacy over the church.[8]

Time-honored immunities, to some extent, shielded Oxford and Cambridge colleges from episcopal supervision. This meant that college officials could experiment with simplified forms of worship, so Chaderton

---

[7] See Mildmay's preface to *The Statutes for the Government of Emmanuel College*, ed. Frank Stubbings (Cambridge, 1983), p. 26.

[8] For Chaderton's "higher strategy," see Patrick Collinson, *The Elizabethan Puritan Movement* (Berkeley, 1967), pp. 125–26, and particularly Peter Lake, *Moderate Puritans and the Elizabethan Church* (Cambridge, 1982), pp. 25–54.

and his fellows were able to make a promising start. But conservative Protestants were offended, and one of them filed a grievance. He accused college members of disregarding the Book of Common Prayer, yet he was upset most by the liberties they took with the sacraments: the men of Emmanuel apparently sat rather than kneeled at the communion table and they passed the loaf and cup from one to another as if they were gathered for a tavern meal.[9]

Several bishops responded to the challenge and the scandal. They warned college officials and tried to bully fellows and graduates, but there was little that the church could do about the college's contempt for religious formalism. Emmanuel took no pains to conceal its Puritan partiality for preaching over ceremony, and by the time William Dell matriculated, the college was one of the university's largest. Understandably, William Laud, first as bishop of London and then as archbishop of Canterbury, considered Emmanuel a critical obstacle to the realization of his own plans to end Puritan dissent.

Between 1630 and 1640, Laud's relentless opposition stampeded many of Emmanuel's fellows, former fellows, and graduates. Laud's attacks, therefore, ironically had the effect of spreading Puritan ideas. Thomas Hooker, John Cotton, Simon Bradstreet, John Harvard, and later Walter Mildmay's great-grandson William crossed the Atlantic. These men and other Emmanuel exiles profoundly influenced early American religious and intellectual history. In fact, Emmanuel is better represented by its fellows and graduates in registers of colonial New England's earliest Puritans than the whole of Oxford University.

William Dell must have known some of the exiles and many like them. Surely he learned firsthand why Cambridge had gained its reputation as the seedbed of Protestant and Puritan reform. Emmanuel's most recent innovations could have been cast as the culmination of a process that had started a century earlier. Before England broke with Rome, and while King Henry VIII was still numbered prominently among the old faith's best friends, Cambridge scholars used to gather at the White Horse Tavern near the university to discuss new ideas about piety and church polity, ideas just imported from the continent. One of the scholars, Thomas Bilney, was martyred; others, notably William Tyndale, Robert Barnes, and Hugh Latimer, survived England's conversion and are now known as the pillars of early English Protestantism. Thirty years later, and twenty years before the founding of Emmanuel, the university gave Puritanism its distinctly militant vocabulary. Late in the 1560s, fellows from several Cambridge colleges scolded church officials for their failure to rid English re-

---

[9] Cited in Stanford E. Lehmberg, *Sir Walter Mildmay and Tudor Government* (Austin, 1964), pp. 231–32.

ligious life of popish customs and to strip the reformed clergy of popish attire. Controversy erupted when William Fulke preached against those who prescribed kneeling at communion, particularly when he ridiculed vestments. It is not difficult to imagine how Dell and his colleagues at Emmanuel regarded Fulke and other pioneering Cambridge Puritans several generations after the vestarian question had troubled the scholarly community. Cambridge was haunted by heroes of Protestantism and Puritanism.

The best-remembered Tudor Puritan at Cambridge was Thomas Cartwright. In 1570, he refused to relinquish his opinions about the further reform of the church and was deprived of his posts at the university. Cartwright and his understudies believed that specific alterations, simplifications, and purifications of worship would be inconsequential unless the English church were "unbishoped" and wholly restructured. (One subversive cleverly left his or her mark on the title page of Matthew Parker's official biography, *The Life of the Seventieth Archbishop of Canterbury*: "The numbre seventy is so compleat as it is great pitie ther shold be one more."[10]) Cartwright's campaign illustrates the Puritan disposition; his nemesis, John Whitgift, then master of Trinity College, Cambridge, gives us a general idea of the conservative reactions with which Dell and Emmanuel's Puritans would still have to contend sixty years later.

Cartwright and the Puritans charged that there were no precedents in Scripture for the English church's archdeacons, bishops, and archbishops. Whitgift countered that "the name of a pastor doth comprehend both archbishops and bishops," and he branded his Cambridge enemies as fools whose discreditable enthusiasms impelled them to associate the end of papal influence in England with the end of episcopacy.[11] Surely, he chided, university men should be capable of discriminating between popish bishops, whom John Calvin reviled, and their English bishops, who derived their authority from the civil magistrates and whose courts served to maintain civic order.[12] Much of Whitgift's debate with Cartwright, in fact, was a contest for bragging rights to John Calvin. Frequent church holidays and festivals reminded the Cambridge Puritans of Catholicism, and Cartwright leavened his arguments against feast days by reminding colleagues that Calvin nowhere introduced or sanctioned them. Whitgift replied that Calvin's silence was not tantamount to condemnation and that it was not inconceivable that practices could commendably be introduced into England though they were not tested first in Geneva.[13]

According to those Puritans who wanted to simplify the liturgy, Ca-

[10] Quoted in Collinson, *Puritan Movement*, p. 146.
[11] *The Works of John Whitgift, D.D.*, ed. John Ayre, vol. 2 (Cambridge, 1852), 99–101.
[12] Ayre, *Whitgift* 3 (1853): 433–34.
[13] Ayre, *Whitgift* 2: 587–89.

tholicism's great mistake was to dictate the material context of worship in every detail, that is, to introduce "commendable" innovations and then sanctify them with decretals and church constitutions. To a point, Whitgift agreed, yet he could not fathom why these Puritans would object to the efforts of their reformed church and its bishops to set certain standards when Scripture's silence, and Calvin's as well, could lead only to anarchy. Scripture, for instance, had not specified the exact manner in which communion should be celebrated, but that did not authorize liturgical confusion. Whitgift was convinced that the church had the right and the duty to legislate uniformity in doctrine and in religious practice. His detailed, nearly interminable, refutation of Cartwright reflects his determination to leave nothing to chance.[14]

Whitgift did manage to have Cartwright expelled from the university. As archbishop of Canterbury, Whitgift continued his battles against Puritanism, and he was particularly wary of sedition in parishes served by Cambridge graduates. Queen Elizabeth and her government endorsed the archbishop's efforts, and the last decades of the sixteenth century were relatively quiet. At Cambridge, complaints were occasionally registered against kneeling at communion or against the use of crosses during baptism, but no challenges comparable to Cartwright's rocked the schools. In 1609, what could have become a resurgence of outspoken opposition was quickly suppressed when the government overturned the election of a Puritan master of Christ's College. At Emmanuel, as noted, experiments were tried, perhaps nervously. But, in all, college authorities were unable to prevent the church's drive for conformity from reaching beyond traditional college immunities and into college chapels.[15]

William Dell was still at Emmanuel in 1636 when the king's council disallowed the university's exemptions from archiepiscopal visitation and correction. Archbishop Laud lobbied long and hard to eliminate the university's immunities. With the right to investigate and to punish, he might more easily remove the rubbish of radical ideas from college studies and college chapels. Had he not been distracted by other tasks, Laud could have integrated university investigations with his other campaigns for religious conformity in England, campaigns that, for our purposes, may be reduced to two strategies. With the first, he attempted to gut Puritan theology; he and his colleagues were preoccupied by their theological refutations of predestinarian Calvinism. With the second, Laud tried to re-

[14] Ayre, *Whitgift* 1 (1851): 112, 236–37.
[15] See Lake, *Moderate Puritans*, pp. 259–61; Elliot Rose, *Cases of Conscience: Alternatives Open to Recusants and Puritans under Elizabeth I and James I* (Cambridge, 1975), pp. 122–23; Mary Fulbrook, *Piety and Politics* (Cambridge, 1983), pp. 102–29; and Stephen A. Bondos-Greene, "The End of an Era: Cambridge Puritanism and the Christ's College Election of 1609," *Historical Journal* 25 (1982): 197–208.

place the pulpit with the altar as the principal focus of worship. The Laudian reform, therefore, entailed reemphasis of free will and of the Eucharist. In the first instance, doctrinal assertions were braced against careful patristic scholarship. In the second, medieval liturgical practices were reintroduced. Together, the strategies suggested to angry Englishmen that English Catholicism was making a comeback. From 1623, royal pardons for English Catholic recusants confirmed suspicions that Stuart kings and their governments were likely to collaborate with Laud, turn Romeward, and muzzle Puritan preachers.

Laudian pamphlets mocked predestination, which was in some ways an easy target. The doctrine could mean that God had prearranged every historical detail from the saving of souls to the loss of one's keys. Puritans, however, generally had a more nuanced understanding of God's providence. They explained that election was predetermined but that preachers must assist the elect to shape a calling, a freely willed response to divine grace. For Puritanism, the pulpit was critical. From pious Puritan sermons, God's chosen people must learn what commitments to family, ministry, and public order enabled them best to show forth God's grace, which had been given to them without any prevenient merit on their part. They must also learn from their preachers how to exhibit and advance God's plan for a Christian commonwealth in England.

One sees how closely Puritans linked pulpit and predestination, and that connection gives us our first glimpse of Puritan sociolatry. Puritan sermons reminded the elect to be ever vigilant against complacency as well as against popery.[16] England's most earnest Christians were chosen to receive God's grace, but the gift required them to reform their behavior and their church. Laud's initiatives terrified those earnest Christians, who thought themselves well rid of Rome, and the Laudian reform edged Parliament closer to conflict with the king. Puritan preachers frequently appeared before the House of Commons to warn legislators of the danger. In 1641, late in December, Stephen Marshall told Parliament, which had been called into session to refinance the government's foreign adventures, that God had assembled them for very different reasons. Marshall held that Parliament had been called, in the higher sense of the term, to overhaul England's ecclesiastical order. He stressed the deplorable condition of the preaching ministry. On this count, he quoted Laud's predecessor, Archbishop George Abbot, who had observed that England's pulpits were in the possession of men who would "not be thought fit hog-heardes to keep swine." But Marshall, who was not keen on episcopacy, observed that Abbot and his associates had not corrected the problem and that

[16] John F. Wilson, *Pulpit in Parliament: Puritanism during The English Civil Wars, 1640–1648* (Princeton, 1969), pp. 56–57, 168–89.

Laud was unlikely to propose acceptable remedies. God, therefore, summoned Parliament to repair the damage. Marshall warned that piecemeal policies would not satisfy Parliament's heavenly master. Playing Puritan prophet, he presented England's legislators with a simple choice: either total reformation or utter desolation.[17]

Having completed his studies at Emmanuel, William Dell was passing his first year in the North Bedfordshire parish of Yelden when Marshall (another Emmanuel alumnus) delivered his ultimatum to the House of Commons. Marshall and his Puritan colleagues at Westminster were busy redeeming politics. They had little time for the finer points of predestinarian theology, but Dell enjoyed the quiet of his rural parish and pondered some of the problems posed by Puritanism's unusual mix of activism and determinism.[18]

The predestinarian position was still susceptible to misinterpretation. If divine grace were irresistible and if God prearranged the distribution of grace, there seemed to be little room left for human agency. The call-and-response format of Marshall's sermon would have been out of place, for if the call were genuine, the response would have been assured. Nonetheless, Marshall's remarks and Puritan activism required a deliberate and freely willed choice (reformation rather than desolation).

Dell had the leisure to reconcile Puritan statements on God's predestination with the urgency of Puritan preaching and to reinterpret Puritan militancy as a sign that saving grace had empowered Puritans to reform their church and save their world. The only treatise that survives from Dell's years at Yelden, perhaps the only one he wrote, happens to be an excellent specimen of the Puritan spiritualist adaptation of predestinarian Protestant theology. Entitled *Christ's Spirit—A Christian's Strength*, it ascribed divine election and human initiative, call and response, to Christ's Spirit without minimizing Christians' responsibilities to document or prove their regeneration with their deeds. It supplies a spiritualist raison d'être for redeeming politics.

Dell started by suggesting that sincerity and good intentions were the Spirit's work in and with believers. They were signs that grace had been given freely by God, and they were conditions for the further work of sanctification and salvation. Such further work and the continuing collaboration with the Spirit depended upon inspired preaching. To be sure, the sermon was the word of man, not God; Dell insisted, however, that God breathed life and "fire" into the composition and delivery. Saving work

---

[17] See Marshall's *Reformation and Desolation* (London, 1642), pp. 7, 46, 50–52.

[18] With respect to "the ambiguity of activism and determinism," see David Zaret, *The Heavenly Contract: Ideology and Organization in Pre-Revolutionary Puritanism* (Chicago, 1985), pp. 154–58. For a review of Dell's career in Bedfordshire, consult Eric C. Walker, *William Dell, Master Puritan* (Cambridge, 1970), pp. 39–72.

in the pews began in the pulpit. If restrictions were placed on preaching, if rituals superseded the sermon, "a dead ministry" would deaden worship. It mattered little how many rituals were layered atop each other, how many licenses or how much learning authorized preachers possessed, or how colorfully ministers were clothed. The Spirit's work ceased unless the Puritans' manifestos were preached.[19]

In the Yelden treatise, Dell alleged that Puritan sermons displayed God's powers not simply to animate and convert listeners but also to inspire the elect with righteous indignation against policies that retarded their church's reformation. Dell advised the government to remove impediments to free preaching, and he warned church officials that their fondness for legislation obstructed spiritual progress. Legislation, he said, reinstated the old covenant of works. Officials like Whitgift had been busy with "the order and ordering of the church," as if the Holy Spirit were idle in heaven. As a result, Christians were buried beneath an avalanche of laws and regulations. Dell held that legislation made it all but impossible for Christians to experience directly the liberation that started with the inspired ministry and the inspired sermon.[20] He was not ready with specific remedies. Puritan spiritualism, at this point, was stronger on diagnosis, but *Christ's Spirit* and subsequent compositions contained a provisional prescription: "Ceremonies are best laid down and old customs best laid aside by the efficacy of the Spirit."[21]

For Dell, this "efficacy of the Spirit" was associated with conversions and the spiritual conquests of Christians in the pews, yet his language and his conflation of divine and human agency were easily accommodated to the fieldwork of the New Model Army when Dell joined its ranks. After all, *Christ's Spirit* was a treatise about empowerment, with the accent on power. In the full title, Dell called it "a plain discovery of the mighty and invincible power that all believers receive through the gift of the Spirit." The Spirit was continually active in the elect. It supplied Christians with new strengths and virtues to battle lust and corruption. The treatise concluded with hints that the human will was nearly "overpowered" by the Spirit, which battled the "bias" of the flesh and virtually made human nature "conformable" to the divine. Before Dell left Yelden, his Puritan spiritualism was prepared for war.[22]

In Dell's view, all the elect possessed the Spirit's power. Any of the faithful should be able to preach and prophesy to the others. Decades earlier, Tudor Puritans had thought of prophesying as an exclusively clerical practice. Actually, it then amounted to little more than unrehearsed,

---

[19] *The Works of William Dell* (New York, 1916), pp. 37–39.
[20] Dell, *Works*, p. 25; but cf. pp. 255–56.
[21] Dell, *Works*, pp. 405–7.
[22] Dell, *Works*, pp. 32–33, 50–52.

collaborative exegesis of select scriptural passages, but Elizabethan officials found the practice objectionable and suppressed it. By 1640, more
radical Puritans were claiming that lay prophesying was one of the distin-
guishing characteristics of a truly reformed church. The edifying exhortations that resulted seemed to many seventeenth-century Puritans to be
certain signs of the Spirit's presence and power. At Yelden, Dell denounced restrictions on preaching and prophesying as popish conspiracies. Later he joined other military chaplains who complained that lawmakers immodestly tried to dictate terms to God's Spirit when they issued
prohibitions from Parliament against unauthorized or "mechanik"
preaching in the New Model. Dell's theological ideas and political predis-
positions were perfectly tailored for the Puritan army. Before we turn to
the army, however, let us spend a moment more on the argument for free
preaching, inasmuch as Dell steered his case for pulpit and lay prophesying toward some startling conclusions.

The argument was that individuals empowered by the Spirit should be
free to preach as the Spirit moved them. When the need for church order
was given priority over the free or open pulpit, Dell thought that religion
was compromised for the sake of convenience and convention. Parliament tried to prohibit "mechanik" preaching because lawmakers' concerns with discipline and good order outweighed patience and piety. Dell
could imagine no better sign that Parliament's faith had failed. He believed that the Spirit would care for its own, care for the soldiers' regeneration and the army's unity and solidarity. And when the Puritans' war
against king and Parliament ended, Dell retained his trust in the Spirit, to
which he attributed all the army's conquests. He continued to oppose
restrictions placed on preaching. Having returned to Cambridge as master of Caius College, he attacked schoolmasters who insisted that education was prerequisite for ministry. He must have taken academic qualifications for ordination as another set of standards designed to channel
God's power and God's Spirit, for the controversy was sparked by a colleague's statement that studies rather than inspiration imparted the most
useful knowledge of Scripture. Dell replied that learning was more likely
to turn impressionable candidates from their callings, "from the gospel to
heathenism." Colleagues who were eager to saddle the Spirit with tests in
order to measure candidates' intelligence and memory perfectly demonstrated, from Dell's perspective, how impenetrable education had made
the heads of educators. "To the little ones" (*parvulis*), religious truths
were self-evident and easily mastered because the Spirit had imparted understanding. The wise, on the other hand, were made foolish. Colleges,
Dell let out, were paying small fortunes for books that the apostles would
have burned.[23]

[23] Dell, *Works*, pp. 511–12, 519, 545–47.

Dell's contempt for the colleges almost certainly reflects his distress at the contrast between scholars at Cambridge and soldiers of the New Model Army. Arrogance at the university prompted and perpetuated divisions. In the army, the Spirit blessed the elect with an invincible certainty, a common feeling that made no room for factions and petty jealousies. "Plain, simple, meek" Christians agreed instinctively on all important matters, or so Dell remembered. The Spirit "knit together" an army of saints. Reading the structural differences between armies and academies in theological terms, Dell returned to the university after the wars to flog his colleagues with this theme, as if the Spirit's work and its military conquests were all the elect need know. University learning was nothing next to the Spirit's power, which won battles and seemed to prescribe a pattern for the new political order.[24]

At Yelden, Dell sketched the Puritan spiritualist position and thus laid the foundation for Puritan sociolatry. But in the dedicatory epistle published with *Christ's Spirit*, he confided to his patroness that he had not yet seen much of the Spirit's power.[25] That changed when he joined the New Model. Dell took the army's unity and Cromwell's conquests as unmistakable signs of spiritual empowerment. The third of our three segments of Dell's career brings us to his military service and most ecstatic sermons. In his view, this phase seemed to bring him to the dawn of a new age and to a great change in the course of history.[26]

From start to finish, the English Civil War was a religious war. The Puritans wanted the realm's religion changed radically. In fact, their proposals were so radical—the abolition of episcopacy, the purification of worship, the free pulpit—that both sides anticipated how severely their adoption would jolt the existing order and replace it with something entirely different, with either the reign of Christ or the reign of the Antichrist. Predictions of that stripe, then, made it easy to report each battle as if it were a decisive millenarian conflict, as if the cannons of God's elect were changing the course of history. Preachers in the New Model Army learned quickly the great power of apocalyptic imagery. Cromwell's soldiers, exhilarated by their successes at Marston Moor and Naseby, welcomed millenarian assurances that their enemies' destruction was imminent. Their chaplains, however, were infuriated by the halting progress of the Puritan revolution in Parliament, so they intimated that Satan's forces were not only royalists in the field but also complacent or cautious legislators at Westminster. Parliament periodically lapsed into acrimonious

---

[24] Dell, *Works*, pp. 191–92, 486–87.

[25] Dell, *Works*, p. 11.

[26] In this connection, see Leo Solt, *Saints in Arms* (Stanford, 1959), pp. 19–20, 25–42, and Bernard Capp, "*Godly Rule* and English Millenarianism," *Past and Present* 52 (1971): 114–16.

debate, which was evidently inconsistent with pious and spiritual government. The New Model, on the other hand, had achieved discipline and
unanimity without "due deliberation." It was obvious to some Puritan
army chaplains that their troops, and not their legislators, were the bearers of God's new kingdom and the authentic practitioners of Puritanism's
redeeming politics.[27]

The army proved to its chaplains that it was guided and governed by
God's Spirit. William Dell alleged that the soldiers' solidarity as well as
the New Model's string of military successes were irrefutable signs that
the "kingdom in the spirit," about which Isaiah prophesied, had finally
come. Particularly striking was that kingdom's liberty, that is, the liberty
of each soldier-citizen to speak or preach his mind. Elsewhere rules and
regulations were imposed to safeguard religious uniformity, but Dell re-
joiced that when soldiers were free to become preachers, and when
preachers were free from restrictions on their preaching, the Spirit elicited
unanimity without requiring conformity. Unity without conformity, in
fact, was the Spirit's gift to the army and to England. Soldiers acknowledged the diversity in rank and in talent, yet they realized that their collective success and "perfection" necessitated cooperation. Dell believed
that the Spirit fashioned the army's extraordinary order and had blessed
the army with good fortune, all to instruct Puritans how to govern their
new age. Parliament, however, was unwilling to see things that way and
was certainly unprepared to take lessons from a few deluded army chaplains.[28]

One of Dell's colleagues, William Erbury, brazenly put Parliament's
intransigence in millenarian perspective. He allowed that Westminster
had taken God's purposes some distance toward their realization. Lasting
dissension in Parliament, nonetheless, prevented Puritan legislators from
stepping unaided into the new age. Erbury noted that the New Model
Army had conquered its own divisions as well as the realm's royalists. He
canonized the soldiers, making them saints in whom God's Spirit reigned
and through whom God would redeem Parliament and all English politics.[29] Dell earlier suggested much the same thing in his Marston sermon,
*The Building, Beauty, Teaching, and Establishment of the Truly Chris-
tian and Spiritual Church* (1646). He repeated the theme that he originally formulated at Yelden: whoever tried to legislate religious sympathy

[27] See John Morrill, "Religious Context of the English Civil War," *Transactions of the
Royal Historical Society*, 5th ser., 34 (1984): 155–78, and for apocalyptic imagery, Paul
Christianson, *Reformers and Babylon: Apocalyptic Visions from the Reformation to the
Eve of the Civil War* (Toronto, 1978).

[28] Dell, *Works*, pp. 81, 95–96.

[29] Consult Erbury's *The Lord of Hosts: or God Guarding the Camp of the Saints and the
Beloved City* (London, 1648), pp. 7, 10, 13, 26–32.

and religious conformity exhibited irreverence as well as impatience. How foolish and impious to preempt the Spirit's "building" and "teaching"! Disagreements in Parliament merely indicated to Dell "what wild and woeful work" legislators did when they quarreled over the shape of worship. Dell implied that the Spirit had abandoned the Puritan Parliament, and he reissued his own assurances that the Spirit directly guided the "saints" in Parliament's army.[30] The most expert arbiters were helpless to compose the disagreements that troubled Westminster, and as long as such Puritan assemblies were racked with controversy, how could Isaiah's prophesy be fulfilled: "*All* your sons shall be taught by the Lord"? By contrast, "love and amity, peace and unity" made the New Model seem sublime. Dell concluded that the army and not its Parliament was ready and able to turn the world "upside down," to usher in the new age of the Spirit.[31]

As it happened, informers from Parliament were present at Marston when Dell delivered his scalding sermon. They returned to London and alarmed those legislators who believed that Dell had targeted them for turning. Several weeks later, Dell was summoned to Westminster to answer charges based on the reports of his Marston sermon. The whole episode, however, is difficult to assess. The Marston sermon, as we have it, was published after Dell's ordeal, and he may have doctored it to reassure investigators that no harm had been intended. The indictment said that Dell had accused legislators of conspiring with the king against their own army, but the published sermon contains no such complaint. Were the informers mistaken or did Dell delete the accusation when he prepared his remarks for the printer? Similar incongruities complicate the task of interpretation, but one charge against Dell is confirmed by all that we know with respect to his service as chaplain. Parliament's indictment reported that Dell preached against anyone who dared to impose rules on the New Model's saints. Dell definitely believed that the army's soldiers were part of a new political order, over which the old order's representatives exercised no authority. Empowered by the Spirit, the saints were harbingers of the new age and could judge without justices, legislators, and kings the best ways to hasten its arrival.

In November 1646, four months after the charges against him were dropped, Dell again appeared before Parliament. He had been asked to preach on the reformation of the church, yet he used the opportunity to reply directly to the charge of antinomianism that surfaced during the

[30] Dell, *Works*, pp. 98–101.

[31] Dell, *Works*, pp. 104–5, 109. Also see, in this connection, Christopher Hill, *The World Turned Upside Down* (London, 1972), pp. 70–78; Geoffrey F. Nuttall, *The Holy Spirit in Puritan Faith and Experience* (Oxford, 1946), pp. 134–49; and for what follows, Walker, *Dell*, pp. 64–71.

Marston investigation and frequently seasoned polemics against the New Model's preachers. Critics had said that Dell advocated lawlessness. In his sermon, published as *Right Reformation*, he responded that "the ancient light" had recently dawned in the army; should Parliament's rules and laws tend to obscure it, the laws and not the light must be sacrificed. It made no sense, he insisted, to talk of antinomianism or lawlessness when the New Model's discipline and unity so plainly demonstrated the Spirit's government. "The ancient light" was the Spirit's politically regenerative power and the mediator of God's laws, against which no earthly power would prevail.[32]

Dell never forgave Parliament for trying to suppress "mechanik" preaching. He regularly preached or wrote that there would be no room in England's "new kingdom of the Spirit" for those who wished to legislate silence.[33] The new age dawning in the army would change the whole complexion of government. The church would be purged of its constitutions and its superfluous ceremonies. The Spirit would give to all the world's councils the solidarity that made the New Model, in Dell's eyes, a perfect emblem for the age to come. This, in a nutshell, was the dream that galvanized Puritan sociolatry. It dissolved along with the chaplains' optimism about the army, although particles survived in arguments for the free pulpit and in Dell's later campaigns against Cambridge scholars. The story of how enthusiasm changed to disenchantment may more properly belong to our chapters on sociolatry and crisis, but a brief epitaph seems appropriate here.

William Dell and his colleagues learned to their displeasure that the New Model's solidarity (and spirituality) depended ultimately on the king's ability to stay in the field. Once Charles I was cornered and captured, and once the soldiers took to discussing his fate and the future of government, disagreements flared and vituperative debates shattered the saints' consensus. Dell retired before things turned ugly, but William Sedgewick voiced the chaplains' disappointments and berated the troops. All the army's conquests, he said, were exposed to Antichrist's counterattacks, and Sedgewick was surprised at how swiftly the soldiers succumbed to them once "malicious projects for selfe safety" were proposed for discussion. Many of the New Model's preachers expected their inspired soldiers to be saints in war *and* in peace, but the problem was that

---

[32] Dell, *Works*, pp. 115–16. For allegations of antinomianism ("the lawless spirit of enthusiasts"), see Samuel Rutherford's *Survey of the Spiritual Antichrist* (London, 1648), particularly pp. 202–4, 208–10, 224, 239. For roots in the continental reformation, consult Theodor Sippell's still valuable interpretation of "William Dells Programm einer 'lutherischen' Gemeinschaftsbewegung," *Zeitschrift für Theologie und Kirche*, Ergänzungsheft 3 (1911): 21–25, 72–73, 115.

[33] Dell, *Works*, e.g., pp. 142–43, 338–40, 562–63.

unanimity was better preserved by fighting than by debating. "You began in the Spirit," Sedgewick mourned, "and end in the flesh."[34]

The debates became especially bitter when Parliament tried to disband the regiments in 1647. The army would not obey as long as the soldiers' wages were in arrears. Cromwell's son-in-law and collaborator, Henry Ireton, formally requested legislators to address themselves to the salary grievances before they sent their soldiers home. Ireton's tone, on the whole, was respectful, but he specified that Parliament must also grant troops a general amnesty for having dared to set conditions on their obedience.[35] An army council was appointed to carry negotiations forward, but as it turned out, the soldiers' representatives extended their grievances into recommendations for the reconstitution of the realm's government.

The soldiers argued that Parliament had been in session too long. They proposed that it should adjourn, but only after making provision for greater popular participation in triennial elections. Several "levelers" among the troops wanted to reap more considerable political profits from the king's disaster and the New Model's conquests: soldiers and officers generally agreed that indefinite sessions of the realm's legislature brought no benefit to its population, but only some were ready to subscribe to the levelers' radical proposals for expanding England's electorate.[36]

Cracks in the army's consensus continued to develop, and by the late summer of 1647, men who had once fought so well together at Naseby and Marston Moor were fighting among themselves. At the time, the troops had retired to Reading to await Parliament's response and see how London's citizens would react to the army's protest. If London defended the legislators at Westminster, the New Model's remonstrance could have little effect on Parliament. The levelers, however, suggested that the soldiers' real enemies were the officers, who asked too little of the government and who, as entrenched aristocrats, were likely to compromise too much to preserve their privileges and power. Ireton resented the accusations. He denied the army's council had been more solicitous of the king's prerogatives and Parliament's rights than protective of the soldiers' and citizens' liberties.[37] But Ireton had given his critics ammunition, particularly when he tried to restore the king to parliamentary custody, from which other soldiers had taken him.[38]

Whether Ireton was in league with members of Parliament or simply wanted to appease those who construed the king's kidnapping as a scurrilous provocation, his frequent appeals for orderly reform antagonized

[34] See Sedgewick's *Justice Upon the Army's Remonstrance* (London, 1648), pp. 1–4.

[35] *Puritanism and Liberty*, ed. A.S.P. Woodhouse (London, 1938), p. 402.

[36] Woodhouse, *Puritanism*, p. 407.

[37] Woodhouse, *Puritanism*, p. 93.

[38] See Kishlansky, *Army*, pp. 230–37.

more radical colleagues. Soldiers elected from the ranks to the army's council, "agitators" as they were aptly called, complained that Ireton's talk of order was gibberish that poorly camouflaged the true feelings of the New Model's patrician officers. At an October council meeting convened at Putney, the agitators interrupted deliberations with their caustic observations. The council seemed to them to be close to making some unacceptable compromises with tyranny. "And if ever a people shall free themselves from tyranny, certainly it is after seven years' war and fighting for their liberty."[39]

At Putney, Ireton proposed that the vote for future members of Parliament be limited to propertied citizens. As expected, agitators charged that he elevated "a private prejudice" above his obligations to pursue a more promising settlement for the realm his troops had conquered. Ireton replied that God's Spirit had abandoned the army, that soldiers were prey to their own petty and ill-informed opinions.[40] But before the conversation could be contaminated by insult and recrimination, Lieutenant Colonel William Goff realized that the council meeting was in trouble. His efforts to avoid the crisis bring to mind the idealization of the New Model Army that was so central to Puritan sociolatry. It seems as if Goff tried to repossess the substance of those inspiring sermons that had prepared the troops for battle when he proposed that the present war of words be suspended for prayer and soul-searching. ("I would speak," he said, "because God hath called forth my spirit to unity.") Officers and agitators alike, however, were unwilling to countenance delays. Politics at Putney had put an end to the redeeming politics of the New Model Army.[41]

[39] Woodhouse, *Puritanism*, p. 89. Also review Woodhouse, p. 18, and, for a good sample of agitators' interruptions, pp. 107–24.

[40] Woodhouse, *Puritanism*, p. 70.

[41] Woodhouse, *Puritanism*, pp. 40–42.

PART TWO

Clerocracy and Conflict

For in [Christ] the whole fulness of the deity dwells
bodily and you have come to fulness of life in him, who
is the head of all rule and authority.
—Colossians 2:9–10

OF ALL CONQUESTS imaginable in this world, Christ's victory over death could be called the most momentous, not only because the enemy seems insuperable but also because Christ and his apostles in each generation invite everyone to share the triumph. Occasionally, accepting the invitation meant endorsing those apostles' claims to political authority, subscribing, that is, to clerical rule or clerocracy. Claims to political authority in such instances absorbed political office into the church's ministry. They related rule to redemption and promoted levels of religious organization capable, in theory, of making Christendom or some part of it a republic of the faithful (*res publica fidelium*). The claims, however, were sometimes registered with repellent vigor. Moreover, emperors, armies, and their apologists expressed ambitions to rule the Christian commonwealth and expected clerical commendation for their labors. They agreed with the theorists of clerocracy that Christ was "the head of all rule and authority"; they denied that Christ's representatives in the clergy were therefore empowered to supervise affairs of state.

The development of clerocratic claims, which recirculated the themes of Christian sociolatry, made conflict in Constantine's shadow inevitable. And conflict, in some centuries more than others, to be sure, affected that development.

Chapter Five

THE IMPERIAL PAPACY

LEGITIMATING IDEOLOGIES scandalize some readers by associating emperors and armies with redemption. Notwithstanding Old Testament models, it seems irregular, if not irreverent, to speak as if brutal warriors and guileful politicians possessed sacred authority. A church, of course, is a more recognizable repository for the sacred and a more conventional route to salvation. After Pentecost, Christian churches instructed the faithful about God's promises and imparted the grace necessary to obtain what God had promised. Some church officials joined political interests and ambitions to those clerical responsibilities. And why not? As the apostles' heirs, they acquired the power to bind and loose, to condemn and absolve sinners; the consequences of their judgments reached well beyond the grave. If their powers so obviously exceeded those of the world's governments, which rewarded and punished only the perishable parts of man's estate, it seemed reasonable that prelates should govern governors, rule rulers, and determine the shape of Christian political culture.

In Matthew's Gospel, it was St. Peter who received the commission to bind and loose (16:18–19). The bishops of Rome claimed to be Peter's executors, for according to tradition, he was the first of their number. The argument was disarmingly simple but not uncontested. Centrifugal forces in the church favored the existence of rival episcopal centers. Bishops, barons, and emperors resisted Rome's efforts to draw political implications from the Petrine commission. Often during the thousand years that followed St. Peter's death in Rome, his successors governed only their city and their few estates outside its walls. Even that realm was reduced by skirmishes with near neighbors and by family feuds. Occasionally the bishop of Rome governed only a single fortress. But for theorists who insisted that Rome's bishop, as St. Peter's heir, was the patriarch or pope (*papa*) of the universal church, the realm of their prelate-prince was never smaller than the vast territories of Christendom.

Apologists for papal supremacy got a late start. Organizational needs persuaded each of the earliest Christian communities to allow some local authority to coordinate liturgical practice and delineate doctrine, but coherent episcopal government developed only gradually. Each church soon had a bishop. The more ambitious bishops orchestrated the evangelization of provinces that stretched miles in every direction from their churches. The less ambitious looked to them for leadership and, when summoned, they assembled in synods to discuss issues central to the maintenance of unity and the identification and suppression of significant heterodoxy. Obedience to a single regional authority was exacted and offered for the sake of religious uniformity. Moral imperatives were eventually added to utilitarian justifications: it was not only expedient to keep order, it was morally and soteriologically sound to uphold discipline and practice obedience. With arguments of this kind, several episcopal centers came to dominate Christendom by the third century. The bishops of Antioch could count on the attendance of most Syrian prelates at their synods. The bishops of Carthage were acknowledged leaders of the North African clergy. The bishops of Rome expected obedience from all Italy. Luigi Scipioni is quite right to speak of such ecclesiastical centralization as the "monarchialization" of episcopacy.[1] It would take another eight centuries, however, before the "imperialization" of the papacy became the critical concern of Christendom's prelatical and political leaders. The bishops of Rome battled episcopal colleagues for exclusive rights to the Petrine commission and challenged the verdicts of regional synods. Intermittently popes also tried to put pressure on politicians and influence the distribution and redistribution of political power. All this culminated in the eleventh century, during the pontificate of Gregory VII (1073–1085).

The tenth and early eleventh centuries were particularly dark ages for Rome. Skirmishes between influential families in the city preoccupied pontiffs, most of whom were hostage to the interests of one or another of the factions. While their popes were distracted by local hostilities, northern European barons increased their control over their regions' ecclesiastical affairs. They and their retainers closely monitored the churches' congresses to be sure that official pronouncements conformed to the policies and prejudices of their governments. Sovereigns and squires nominated bishops and invested them with the symbols of spiritual as well as temporal lordship. More often than not, bishops thereafter were submissive, if not spineless; popes were peripheral.

The papal recovery was prompted by Emperor Henry III in 1046. Other emperors had previously crossed the Alps to rescue the Roman church from intruders; Henry came to save it from its popes. A disputed papal election had thrown the Italian churches into confusion. Claimants refused to reach a settlement. Accusation and insult spared no reputation. For the sake of order, the emperor convened a synod of bishops soon after his arrival, advocated the deposition of Pope Gregory VI, and chased Gregory's rivals from the field before having his own candidate named

---

[1] Luigi I. Scipioni, *Vescovo e populo: L'esercizio dell'autorità nella chiesa primitiva* (Milan, 1977), pp. 218–20.

pope. Subsequent reforming popes cleaned house in Rome and reasserted their right to discipline Catholic clergy everywhere. Gradually they turned on their northern European patrons and asserted papal independence and papal supremacy.

Since clerical corruption was a serious embarrassment and an occasion for baronial interference in the church's affairs, reformers reemphasized Rome's long-standing opposition to the exchange of favors or money in connection with ecclesiastical appointments, promotions, and elections. Persons buying or selling offices were guilty of simony and increasingly likely to find themselves removed from office (if the buyer) or excommunicated (if the vendor). During the pontificate of Leo IX (1049–1054), the papal campaign against simony gathered momentum, in part because one of Leo's chief executives, Cardinal Humbert of Silva Candida, closed some loopholes that permitted it. Incumbents charged with simony said they had purchased only the estates, rents, and revenues associated with their offices, that is, the temporalities. Humbert ruled that the financial benefits of office and the office itself were inseparable. He alleged that greed had seduced intelligent incumbents to defend silly distinctions between what was for sale and what was not. Greed enslaved simoniacs to the devil, and what was worse, according to Humbert, the simoniacs sold the churches in their care into slavery to their new master.[2] Humbert spent a large part of his career combating the devil's work. He traveled through Tuscany consecrating reformers because corrupt bishops would not. He probably composed the antisimoniacal clauses in papal charters that guarded the elections of abbots and priors against unwelcome intervention.[3] Even after Pope Leo's death, Humbert scolded powerful laymen and clerical officials for having given or gotten money in return for influence in their churches' balloting and general business. Simony, he said, was heresy, whoever practiced it. Emperors figured prominently in Humbert's gallery of rogues because they and their accomplices traded or withheld properties and privileges to sway elections and pressure incumbents.[4]

Humbert's appeals and arguments were echoed by the monk Hildebrand, perhaps the most influential voice at the papal court after Humbert's death and during the 1060s. As early as 1059, he advocated sweeping reforms in an address at the pope's Lateran palace. The document that recorded the deliberations that followed intimated that Hildebrand had by then been made an archdeacon, but rapid advancement actually came

[2] MGH, Libelli de lite 1: 149, 191–92, and Gerhart Ladner, Theologie und Politik vor dem Investiturstreit, 2nd ed. (Darmstadt, 1968), pp. 56–58, 137–38.

[3] Consult Werner Goez, "Reformpapsttum, Adel, und monastische Erneuerung in der Toscana," in Investiturstreit und Reichsverfassung, ed. Josef Fleckenstein (Sigmaringen, 1973), pp. 227–28.

[4] MGH, Libelli de lite 1: 217.

later.[5] His meteoric rise prompted envy and suspicion. Enemies suggested that his promotions were stained with simony. Twenty-five years later, and ten years after he became pope, they charged that Hildebrand had intrigued to succeed Leo IX but that he and his agents were unable to manage their plots and payments. Denied the prize, the ambitious monk allegedly pensioned off a lesser official and started his quick climb to the bishop's chair.[6] But enemies and friends agreed that Hildebrand served the papacy energetically during his ascent. As legate, arbiter, and adviser—settling disputes, issuing prohibitions, perhaps accepting bribes—he was an indispensable deputy. Prelates petitioning Pope Alexander II during the last year of his pontificate were wise to send copies to Hildebrand, whose counsel was critical and frequently decisive.

Hildebrand succeeded Alexander in 1073 and took the name Gregory VII. His pontificate started on a promising note: he received dispatches signaling that the Greek churches might be ready to accept papal supremacy. Twenty years before, Cardinal Humbert had offended the patriarch of Constantinople during one of his missions, and the strained relations that resulted virtually silenced all talk of Christendom's reunification. By 1073, however, the East had reasons to seek reconciliation. Seljuk Turks had captured most of Asia Minor, the region that provided eastern emperors with their best brigades. Constantinople desperately needed military assistance, and Gregory VII realized that Constantinople's crisis was Rome's opportunity. He urged princes in western Europe to recruit and send troops; he offered to lead them himself. Since the new western emperor, Henry IV, had just made the usual professions of loyalty to the papacy, Gregory seemed free to contemplate a grand papal triumph in the East. "I shall go," he wrote theatrically to Henry, "and I shall leave the church to God and to you."[7]

Despite the emperor's oaths, the imperial government in the West was pliant only to a point, and the pope reached that point the moment he resumed Humbert's campaign against simony and lay influence. Had he wanted to comply with papal prohibitions, Henry IV could not. Compliance was certain to be taken as a sign of weakness, and decades of decentralization and civil war had already weakened the emperor's position. Barons still loyal to Henry would not tolerate papal interference in the affairs of *their* churches. When put to it, the emperor was simply unwilling to preside over the dissolution of imperial prerogatives. If he provisionally enrolled on the roster of Rome's princely subjects with his oaths and pledges of obedience, it was to get and not to give away what he

    [5] Giovanni Battista Borino, "L'arcidiaconato di Ildebrando," *Studi Gregoriani* 3 (1948): 481–82.
    [6] *MGH, Libelli de lite* 2:379–80.
    [7] RG 2.31.

wanted, namely, absolute control over the religious life and political destiny of his empire. Gregory VII soon suspected as much. He questioned whether Henry's varnished expressions of submission concealed ill will and impious ambitions. The pope warned that, although he might easily be gulled by sweet sentiments and phrases in imperial correspondence, St. Peter read the emperor's letters with special discernment (*subtili inspectione*). As if peering over the pope's shoulder, the apostle would weigh Henry's explanations and promises. And St. Peter would certainly defend his see and punish imperial deceit.[8]

It requires no special discernment to detect the spark that ignited the conflict between pope and emperor. Both Gregory and Henry aspired to greater influence in the Lombard plains and particularly in Milan. Earlier in the century, the papacy was asked to referee a contest between local Milanese reformers and leading clergy. Pope Stephen IX sent Hildebrand to collect information and subsequently to arbitrate. Hildebrand and other legates, at length, overcame Milan's reluctance to submit to Rome or to any settlement arranged by Rome, and the archbishop finally accepted terms rather more than less favorable to the reforming interests. In 1070, however, the archbishop resigned his post as part of an agreement worked out with representatives of the emperor. An imperial candidate, Gottfried, was named but not elected to succeed him. Outraged citizens, however, kept Gottfried from his cathedral, and when the old archbishop died in 1071, they refused to elect or confirm the emperor's nominee. Erlembald, the city's principal power broker, disregarded local pressure for a free election and listened only to Hildebrand, who proposed Otto, a second candidate for the archiepiscopal office.[9]

Otto was no more popular than Gottfried. A mob intimidated the pope's choice and forced him to renounce under oath any attempt to advance his candidacy. Although Gregory VII invalidated the oath soon after he assumed office, he was unable to fill the vacancy in Milan during the first three years of his pontificate. He wrote to encourage Erlembald, but the deadlock in Milan persisted until the emperor introduced a new candidate and demanded his acceptance.[10] Pope Gregory VII vigorously objected. The emperor, however, had already ignored the church's sanctions against advisers who engineered Milanese initiatives, so the pope knew the imperial chancery had little respect for the church's censures. But before Rome could intensify efforts to rally the Italian aristocracy against its German masters, Emperor Henry IV summoned German and Lombard bishops to a synod at Worms in 1076.

Thirty years before, Henry IV's father had called a similar synod to

[8] *RG* 3.10.
[9] *MGH, Scriptores*, 8: 24–25.
[10] *MGH, Scriptores*, 8: 99, and *RG* 1.26.

depose Gregory VI, then bishop of Rome. The son expected to imitate his
father: condemning a pope and completing a coup should have been no
more difficult in 1076 than it had been in 1046. The bishops at Worms
composed a comprehensive indictment, accusing the pope of having assumed his office unlawfully (*invadere*) and then of having exceeded his
commission by arrogantly formulating regulations and prohibitions for
the entire church. Rumors reached Worms that Rome was on the verge
of open revolt against Gregory VII. The synod's reproach just might give
insurgents the prompting necessary to seal the incumbent's fate. Nonetheless, the emperor had hoped to extort a document with more teeth. No
formal deposition was passed at Worms, although the bishops did not
brake far from the precipice. They abjured their obedience to Rome and
called upon the pope to step aside.[11]

Pope Gregory VII took immediate action. He excommunicated the dissidents before the ink on their indictment had dried. Italian and German
Christians must therefore choose between their supreme pontiff and their
outlawed emperor, and as things turned out, Gregory had a stronger hold
on Rome and on princes and prelates elsewhere than Henry had on his
empire. A number of prelates present at Worms defected soon after the
synod adjourned. German authorities, who had only reluctantly consented to Henry IV's succession, used the papal countermeasures and the
excommunication as excuses to reconsider and advance another candidate for imperial power. They invited Gregory to Germany to help them,
and the pope was happy to oblige.

The emperor realized that he was unlikely to win the civil war in Germany unless he settled his quarrel with Rome. The only way back to complete sovereignty in Germany lay through a papal pardon, so Henry
rushed to intercept Gregory VII as he was traveling north. In the snows
of Canossa, Henry performed a humiliating penance before the pope,
who thereupon was faced with a difficult decision: forgive the delinquent
yet apparently contrite emperor or forge ahead to give the church's blessings to his enemies and their new emperor.

We might say that, at this critical moment, the pope's political instincts
failed him, but then we know, as he did not, that absolving Henry IV
would have disastrous consequences for his pontificate. The pope was a
priest as well as a politician, and a priest's obligation was to return the
stray to the flock, to welcome the prodigal, to pardon the penitent. Gregory VII forgave Henry and returned to Rome. Deprived of a critical advantage, the insurgents in Germany struggled for several years but even-

---

[11] *MGH, Constitutiones* 1: 106, 109–10, and Harald Zimmermann, "Würde Gregor VII
1076 in Worms abgesetzt," *Mitteilungen des Instituts für österreichische Geschichtsforschung* 78 (1970): 127–31.

tually surrendered to their emperor. Having stooped and groveled at Canossa, he had reconquered his subjects and by 1080, he was again harassing Rome's legates and obstructing Rome's plans for reform. Gregory VII responded with a second excommunication, but the emperor no longer feared baronial insubordination and widespread German submission to papal decrees. He confidently assembled his bishops at Brixen, deposed Gregory, and named Archbishop Wibert of Ravenna as the new pope (the antipope).

The old pope needed new allies. His relations with the Normans who ruled Sicily and much of southern Italy had been uneven. Periodically he warned them to keep their distance from the papal estates, but from 1080, he courted them and urged them to storm Ravenna and rid the peninsula of the emperor's scoundrels and their impostor pope.[12] No decisive military offensives resulted, but the war of words between proponents of papal supremacy and apologists for empire was ferocious. In Rome, accusations and justifications were invented to impress the unlearned (*imperitus multitudo*), but most arguments for an imperial papacy were addressed to bishops and courtiers who might then persuade their sovereigns to support Gregory VII and his successors. The enmity between Gregory and Henry, more than any other single factor, induced theorists to take the case for Rome's leadership seriously. The age of the Gregorian reform and its aftermath constitutes the great age of papal sociolatry because papal supremacists transformed arguments for papal preeminence in the church into arguments for the popes' prerogatives to distribute and redistribute political power.

Remembering that Gregory VII had been willing to hand the church's helm to Henry while he led the crusade to Constantinople, August Nitschke suggested in 1956 that the pope had originally hoped for some coalition between church and empire. Nitschke and others, then, were inclined to blame Henry for the break. According to this reading of affairs, extravagant political pretensions cultivated in Constantine's shadow goaded reforming popes and their publicists into formulating sweeping counterclaims for papal primacy.[13] Actually, the emperor's theorists hinged the presentation of their patron's jurisdiction on a simple

---

[12] See Bonizo of Sutri's *Liber ad amicum*, which couples reports of Gregory's deposition and the Norman negotiations, *MGH, Libelli de lite* 1: 612–13. Also note *RG* 6.5b, article 7; 7.14a, article 4; but especially *RG* 8.7. See H.E.J. Cowdrey, *The Age of Abbot Desiderius: Montecassino, the Papacy, and the Normans in the Eleventh and Early Twelfth Centuries* (Oxford, 1983), pp. 138–50; and for previous Norman alliances, Josef Deer, *Papsttum und Normannen: Untersuchungen zu ihren lehnsrechtlichen kirchenpolitischen Beziehungen* (Cologne, 1972), pp. 126–33.

[13] August Nitschke, "Die Wirksamkeit Gottes in der Welt Gregors VII," *Studi Gregoriani* 5 (1956): 168, 189.

denial of the pope's: the bishop of Rome, they said, had no special responsibility for the course of European politics. An excellent specimen of the imperialist argument, the *De paenitentia regum*, bedevils the papacy with its own history. The compiler packed the short treatise with excerpts from papal correspondence purporting to show the church's submission to previous political regimes. Passages from Scripture were displayed to prove that submission was agreeable to God. At one point, the *De paenitentia* cuts to the heart of Rome's position on the Petrine commission by repeating the advice from one of St. Peter's letters. Christ may have implied that the church should follow St. Peter's (and Rome's) lead, but Peter explicitly instructed Christians to "be subject for the Lord's sake to every human institution, whether it be to the emperor as supreme, or to governors as sent by him. . . . Honor all men. Love the brotherhood. Fear God. Honor the emperor" (1 Peter 2:13–17). The compiler did not think it necessary to explain or editorialize. Other sayings were included with the summaries of biblical stories, from tales of David's kingship to those of priests' concessions in apocryphal literature. The *De paenitentia* smugly assumes that the church's own narratives and canons placed the emperor's position beyond dispute.[14]

Papal theorists insisted that their antagonists' biblical and historical scholarship was wanting. Manegold of Lautenbach, for example, admitted St. Peter had countenanced submission to the state. Scriptural evidence left him no alternative, yet he also charged that the emperor's exegetes had forgotten the apostle's unspoken assumption. Honor the emperor, to be sure, but only on condition that the emperor honors the church. Christians' submission to the secular government might accompany or follow (but it must never precede) the government's submission to the church and its leaders. Answering the *De paenitentia*'s citation of Pope Gregory I, whom Gregory VII particularly admired, Manegold maintained that the first Gregory had deferred to imperial judgments only after Byzantine emperors had acknowledged the superior authority of papal decrees.[15]

Manegold wrote confidently of Gregory I's predicaments and diplomacy, yet with serious misconceptions. At the start of Gregory's pontificate (590), Aquileian bishops refused to acknowledge his leadership, the Lombard queen was attached to heretical doctrines, and imperial officials in Constantinople discouraged Rome from taking initiatives that might jeopardize what was left of Byzantine influence. Italy was a colossal mess.[16] Gregory I regularly had to convince the Lombards that he was in

[14] *MGH, Libelli de lite* 3: 609–14.
[15] *MGH, Libelli de lite* 1: 389.
[16] Consult *MGH, Scriptores rerum langobardicum*, pp. 90–103, and Georg Hauptfield,

league with the emperor and then convince the emperor's agents that as pope he could count on the Lombards' loyalty. But when the Lombard queen finally agreed to have her son baptized according to the Roman rite and abandoned heretical Christology, her chief adviser prevailed upon her to befriend the pope's Aquileian enemies. Gregory I had complained to Constantinople that his efforts to end the schism of the northern Italian bishops had been unfairly restricted. In passages that appealed to Manegold and other Hildebrandine apologists when they defended Gregory VII's defiance of the German emperor, the first Gregory impressed upon the Byzantine imperial court that the Petrine commission gave him, not the emperor's deputies or the emperor himself, the power to govern the church.[17] But Gregory I was resigned to bargaining the papacy back into the life of the Italian church; he wanted to see old barriers fall, not new ones built, and he understood that sustained polemic would create fresh wounds, formidable obstacles to papal policy, and greater handicaps for his successors. Grand master that he was, he knew his chesspieces, especially the relative values of bishops and queens. He accepted what there was of the Lombards' acquiescence. Northern bishops went their way for another century, until the Lombard king, Cunipert, forced a reconciliation with Rome. And after a coup in Constantinople had scrambled Byzantine politics, Gregory I promptly assured the new empress of St. Peter's steadfast support. Politics made the first Gregory a versatile, flexible pontiff; centuries later, polemics made him an unbending autocrat.

Manegold supplied, rather than recovered, the contexts of Gregory I's remarks as well as the contexts of other texts used by antipapal theorists to prove previous papal subservience. Eleventh-century apologists for the imperial papacy protested interpretations that compromised their case for Rome's management of the universal church and direction "of all rule and authority." Manegold's contexts amounted to little more than a conditional clause. The intricacies of papal statesmanship were irrelevant. If politicians declared their obedience to Rome, the pope endorsed political regimes. When only the endorsement survives, readers must assume the prior declaration. With a single hypothetical condition, Manegold thus reduced bundles of the opposition's citations to smoke as if they were straw.

The opposition's Old Testament passages, however, were somewhat less combustible, so Manegold took a different approach. Instead of supplying terms, conditions, and contexts that patriarchs and prophets had not thought to elaborate, he cut the Old Testament from the canon. The

---

"Zur langobardischen Eroberung Italiens," *Mitteilungen des Instituts für österreichische Geschichtsforschung* 91 (1983): 87–94.

[17] See, e.g., *MGH, Epistolae*, 2: 405.

only way to deny that Solomon's deposition of Abiathar (I Kings 2:26–
27) was a precedent for Emperor Henry IV's deposition of Pope Gregory
VII was to deny that the Hebrews' scriptures had anything to teach a
Christian political culture. Manegold suggested that Christ's revelations
made the Old Testament obsolete. Why would anyone want to revive the
cast-off customs of Hebrew monarchs?[18]

Not all of Rome's retainers were as ready as Manegold to remove the
Old Testament from their arsenal; its books were stocked with stories of
princes contemptuous of priestly authority and punished for their contempt. Many of the testimonials and tales had no bearing on the eleventh-
century papacy's redeeming politics in church and empire, yet what could
be more suggestive of prelatical dignity than the eighteenth chapter of
Deuteronomy, which ordered all laymen to yield the firstfruits of their
fields to their priests? Even some of the passages that seemed inconsequential could be transformed by agile allegorical exegesis into evidence
for the church's authority over government and for papal preeminence in
the church. One need only see that oxen referred to princes or roofbeams
to popes. Among papal exegetes, Bruno of Segni was the most diligent in
mining deeper meanings in those stretches of Scripture that appeared poetic and obscure rather than polemical and prophetic.[19] While Bruno and
his colleagues gathered and decoded biblical texts, canonists collected
rules and opinions published by previous popes and councils. Their purpose was to demonstrate that papal centralization was nothing new. Incontrovertible propositions about the pope's place as supreme arbiter regularly punctuated the church's history. Anselm of Lucca and Bonizo of
Sutri labored to reassert the tradition of papal leadership so that Gregory
VII's pronouncements and ultimata might claim continuity with the past.
Even exuberant Gregorians would not have cheered the pope's originality. Each pope was part of a developing consensus, the cumulative weight
of which was evident in the canonists' collections of rules and decrees and
in the current pope's judgments, which were frequently substantiated by
specimens derived from them.[20]

Historian Karl Morrison holds that "there was little, conceptually, in
the [Gregorian] reformers' thought that had not been anticipated in state-

[18] *MGH, Libelli de lite* 1: 409.

[19] For Bruno's *Expositiones*, see, e.g., *PL* 164: 345–58 (Exod. 29), 467–70 (Num. 5), and
511–12 (Deut. 18). Also see Réginald Grégoire, *Bruno de Segni: Exégète mediéval et théo-
logien monastique* (Spoleto, 1965), pp. 191–214, and I. S. Robinson, "Political Allegory in
the Biblical Exegesis of Bruno of Segni," *Recherches de théologie ancienne et mediévale* 50
(1983): 69–98.

[20] See Horst Fuhrmann, "Das Reformpapsttum und die Rechtswissenschaft," in Fleckenstein, *Investiturstreit*, pp. 201–3, and Karl Morrison, *Tradition and Authority in the Western Church, 300–1140* (Princeton, 1969), pp. 307–8.

ments of ninth-century popes. In the spirit, and sometimes in the words, of Nicholas I, they argued that Rome was the custodian and interpreter of true doctrine, and that popes conveyed the means of salvation to the rest of the world through the hierarchy." Gregory VII would have been pleased with the appraisal. Originality and novelty, now regarded reverently, were more like libels in the eleventh century, as they were in late antiquity when popes Boniface I and Leo I affixed the demand "nothing new" (*nulla novitas*) to their arguments for papal primacy. Gregory VII insisted that his decrees on obedience and clerical morality were consonant with those of the church's previous synods and echoed those of previous popes. Greybeards in his administration could attest to similarities between his pontificate and that of Leo IX, between his intentions and those of Humbert. Probably Gregory would have been fondest of comparisons with Gregory I, whom he often quoted. Still, appeals to the tradition of papal monarchy could not camouflage the new departure that has ever since marked the seventh Gregory's pontificate as "the greatest turning point in the history of Catholic Christendom." Notwithstanding their homage to predecessors, Gregory VII and his apologists harbored what Morrison called "loftier aspirations . . . to universal juridical competence." In St. Peter's name, they claimed the right to preside over political as well as ecclesiastical hierarchies. At the very start of his pontificate, Gregory told the king of Aragon that Christ made St. Peter a prince over all the world's kingdoms. Six years later and one month after he had excommunicated Emperor Henry IV for the second time, the pope informed the king of England that he and St. Peter were each king's true keepers.[21]

Brief memoranda of this kind appear in the pope's detailed discussions of business. He seldom spelled out systematically his grand theory of papal rule; perhaps it was less a theory than a grim reminder that Rome was responsible for the world's redemption and peace. Gregory reminded himself of his pontifical duties, presenting them to some advantage as he bargained for political assistance and influence. In 1075, he worried that relations between Denmark and Rome had cooled, so he wrote to King Swen to improve them. He told Swen that Christians should be united, one to another and all to the pope, through Rome's universal government (*ex universale regimine*). In his remarks on regional affairs, Gregory carefully dropped a reference to the king's mortality: princes as well as paupers succumb to a final leveling. Ostensibly, the pope was only urging

[21] *RG* 1.63 (Aragon); 7.23 (England); *PL* 20: 778 (Boniface); 54: 424, 709, 955 (Leo). For Morrison's sound assessments, see *Tradition*, pp. 280–82, 290–91, but also note Erich Caspar, "Gregor VII. in seinen Briefen," *Historische Zeitschrift* 130 (1924): 12–13. For an evaluation of "the greatest turning point," Gerd Tellenbach, *Church, State, and Christian Society at the Time of the Investiture Contest*, trans. R. F. Bennett (Oxford, 1948), pp. 162–68.

Swen to govern piously, but by pairing great and small in this world, diminishing the great, Gregory also made the king one of the many subjects of a prelatical prince with influence in the next world. The letter to Denmark concludes with an offer. If Swen will give the Roman church an army captained by one of his sons, the pope will give the Danes a new kingdom to conquer and rule. Gregory probably had his troublesome neighbors in mind, the Normans who were then occupying southern Italy, but he might also have contemplated an expedition across the Adriatic Sea. At any rate, Gregory considered it perfectly appropriate to transfer rulers as imperiously as he and his predecessors and pontifical colleagues translated suffragan bishops.[22]

If Gregory was selling the rights to the Norman territories in Italy in 1075, he definitely abandoned the idea five years later. He could not afford to anger warriors to the South when faced with hostile armies in the North. Moreover, his plan to rid Italy of emperor and antipope comprised alliances with the Normans, so Gregory consented to renew grants of land made by previous pontiffs and agreed to tolerate for a time the Norman possession of cities taken without papal permission. For their part, Jordan of Capua and Duke Robert Guiscard pledged to support and subsidize papal policy and made themselves vassals with formal oaths of fealty.[23]

Few medieval vassals displayed the constancy of Jane Austen's heroines, but oaths and feudal obligations were generally regarded as sacred. They guaranteed the political and social order as long as they were observed. Power and respectability attended feudal lordship, and the loss of either would not be taken lightly. Gregory VII reacted immediately when he thought that he had lost a vassal in 1074. King Solomon of Hungary apparently accepted his kingdom as a fief from the German emperor, but the pope asserted that long ago one of Solomon's predecessors had given Hungary to the Roman church and that Emperor Henry III subsequently endorsed the transaction. Rome enjoyed a special stewardship that Solomon, according to Gregory, was powerless to repeal. Unlike many other feudal lords, however, the pope could not count on raising an army quickly. He was often separated from delinquent vassals by vast stretches of alien territory. Yet he had several advantages over all other feudal lords: he could employ spiritual sanctions and he had some claim to authority in the international institution, everywhere influential, the church. If it was not yet clear in 1074, it certainly was obvious in Gregory's struggles with Henry IV that the pope could hardly press for princes' obedience

[22] *RG* 2.51.
[23] *RG* 8.1a, b, c, 8.7.

and add bite to the bark of apostolic rebuke until he had increased his control over his church.[24]

To increase papal control over the church, Gregory had to follow the hazardous road to reform. He held regular synods in Rome to enact disciplinary measures and to draw friends and enemies to his side, the former to be encouraged and the latter intimidated and corrected. He dispatched legates to communicate and enforce decisions reached at his synods, to convene local and regional councils, and to oversee ecclesiastical elections. If irresolute bishops and abbots failed to promote reforms, legates were to seize the initiative. If elections produced disputes, legates were to compose them. In 1077, in Aquileia, the region that Gregory I had tried unsuccessfully to subdue, prelates and laymen challenged the decision of the seventh Gregory's emissaries. The pope had hard words for the dissidents. His legates, after all, were St. Peter's deputies. Aquileian defiance, he promised, would be met with "the sword of St. Peter" and "the javelin of apostolic censure."[25]

Before we hear more about Gregory's weapons, we might glance quickly at the development of legatine (and papal) authority in the church. One example should suffice, for Pope Boniface I was not untypically resourceful when he inherited authority from Pope Zosimus in 418. Zosimus confused matters seriously when he reversed his predecessor's judgments and then reversed himself during negotiations with North African prelates. He left affairs in Gaul equally snarled when he tried to limit the power of lay officials over church appointments. The principal problem for the Roman church was that it was Roman, that is, geographically fixed. From Zosimus's errors, if from no other sources, Boniface learned that ecclesiastical disputes far from Rome could only be resolved by recommendations and restrictions that were sensitive to local conditions and customs.[26] But it was easy to acknowledge the difficulty; harder to handle church business *in remotis*, to delegate authority to reliable local bishops, and to defend them when other prelates in the region questioned their competence and commissions. At the start of Boniface's pontificate, the heaviest shelling was in the East, where Rome and Constantinople were battling over church vacancies in Illyria. For decades, the bishops of Thessalonica had represented Rome as vicars, legates permanently in residence in Greece. The patriarchs and councils of Constantinople resented the arrangement; papal meddling seemed to them an innovation and direct insult. A controversial episcopal election in Corinth brought simmering antagonism to a boil and compelled Boniface to de-

---

[24] *RG* 2.13.

[25] *RG* 5.5.

[26] *PL* 20: 760. Also see Erich, Caspar, *Geschichte des Papsttums von den Anfängen zur Höhe der Weltherrschaft*, vol. 1 (Tübingen, 1930), 344–60.

fend Bishop Rufus of Thessalonica in terms particularly relevant to our review of Gregory VII's redeeming politics.[27]

Boniface had consulted Rufus before confirming the election of Bishop Perigenes in Corinth. Objections were raised because Perigenes had been elected to another see before coming to Corinth, but the pope suspected the protest had been planned by the patriarch of Constantinople to give him an excuse to overrule Rome. Before the patriarch could take effective action at a regional council, the pope rushed word to Rufus that the council could not challenge the vicar's judgment. Boniface also warned the Illyrian clergy in a separate letter that the vicar, just as the pope, exercised powers granted by Christ to St. Peter. Vicars, on behalf of the bishop of Rome, screened *all* local quarrels, discredited or sanctioned *all* ordinations and consecrations, and convened *all* regional councils. If the patriarch of Constantinople and prelates summoned to his forthcoming council were to defy the bishop of Thessalonica, they would defy the bishop of Rome. If they defied Rome, they seceded from St. Peter's church. Boniface assumed the patriarch and his council would boast that they had simply severed the papal head from an otherwise healthy body of Christ. The pope announced that their action and boast would only demonstrate that they had cut themselves off from Christianity.[28]

Boniface's letter to the Illyrian clergy was a masterful compilation of arguments that had circulated in previous papal correspondence. Anticipating Constantinople's reply that papal primacy was unprecedented as well as unwanted, Boniface crafted a historical consensus with his material, much as descendants build a family tradition with the heirlooms in their attics. Insolence in the East, however, did not end. The patriarchs of Constantinople were unimpressed by the assertions of the bishops of Rome. Rufus's successor in Thessalonica, Anastasius, encountered indifference and opposition a dozen years after Boniface's death. Papal leadership and vicarial authority were hotly contested then and consistently thereafter, both in Thessalonica and throughout Christendom. Ironically, the contests contributed to the stock of arguments for papal preeminence as the case for Rome's supremacy was augmented and refined every time it was tested against dissidents' charges. When the issue emerged in discussions of eleventh-century church order, Gregory VII could proclaim in no uncertain terms that his legates, though inferior in rank to resident clergy, could depose them. In 1078, two legates were empowered to investigate complaints registered against the archbishop of Vienne. The next year, Gregory asked one of the two, Bishop Hugh of Die, to sift

---

[27] For details, see Charles Pietri, *Roma Christiana: Recherches sur l'église de Rome, son organisation, sa politique, son idéologie de Miltiade à Sixte III (311–440)*, vol. 2 (Paris, 1976), 1107–30.

[28] *PL* 20: 775–78.

accusations against the administration of the archbishop of Rheims. The pope told his legate to pronounce the verdict required by righteousness "without hesitation" if the allegations survived the archbishop's efforts to acquit himself before a local council. In the same letter to Hugh, but with reference to another accused prelate, Gregory associated his legate's work with his own, explicitly allowing several hands to wield "the sword of St. Peter."[29]

But the sword of St. Peter was still Rome's to unsheath. Only the pope, as St. Peter's heir and as the church's ultimate arbiter, could distinguish between the righteous and unrighteous, between those who trusted that the church made God's will manifest and those who trusted in their own cleverness and cunning (*calliditas*). The pope alone, then, had final custody of the single weapon that could throw the self-reliant into disorder (*confundet*), make the affluent destitute and the powerful powerless.[30] Pronouncements of this kind, promises to allies and threats to enemies, reflect the triumphalist as well as universalist pretensions characteristic of Christian sociolatry. Nonetheless, Gregory VII's swords and javelins did not amount to a coherent political theory comparable to that of Pope Gelasuis I (492–496), now famous for his use of "swords" as metaphors for the regal and sacerdotal authorities that jointly ruled the world.[31] Gregory brandished his weapons, as he once said, to declare to Christians what righteousness required. Declarations accompanied by demands and threats might not produce immediate compliance, but they were formulated to prompt sinners to reconsider their offenses. The sword was part of the pope's pastoral or teaching office; it instructed and corrected as well as punished. It brought offenders back to their senses and back to the church.[32]

Grave administrative difficulties arose when resident bishops and archbishops withheld their cooperation. That was why Gregory commissioned his legates to assemble local clergy in councils and sometimes to approach secular authorities for assistance in disciplining particularly incorrigible church officials. For example, the pope calculated in 1075 that many German bishops were likely to be contemptuous of Rome's efforts to reform the church. Gregory's pontificate was still in its infancy; remote authorities had not expected a vigorous renewal of the papal campaign against simony. Gregory, therefore, wrote directly to Duke Rudolf of

[29] *Epistolae Vagantes of Pope Gregory VII*, ed. H.E.J. Cowdrey (Oxford, 1972), p. 79 (1079); *RG* 6.2 (1078); 2.55a.

[30] *RG* 6.14.

[31] Consult Walter Ullmann, *Gelasius I (492–496): Das Papsttum an der Wende der Spätantike zum Mittelalter* (Stuttgart, 1981), but also note Alfonso Stickler, "Il *Gladius* nel registro di Gregorio VII," *Studi Gregoriani* 3 (1948): 89–103.

[32] *RG* 2.15; 9.33.

Swabia, urging him to disregard his bishops' protests (or silence) and to prevent simoniacs from taking or retaining their positions in the church by force if necessary (*etiam vi si oportuerit*). If disobliging prelates cursed his intervention, Rudolf must insist that he was acting in obedience to the pope and tell them to apply to Rome for any further explanation.[33]

Whether Gregory VII turned to princes for help or turned to them for hindering reform, whether he offered them the sword's hilt or blade, two basic principles governed the pope's overtures (or outrage). He borrowed the first from Ambrose, the bishop of Milan, whose defiance of Emperor Theodosius in the fourth century was the prototype for Gregorian defiance. Corrupt or contrite, emperors, said Ambrose, were "within, not above, the church."[34] The second principle was Gregory VII's extrapolation from the first. He put it most succinctly in late 1080, when he explained to King Philip I of France that sovereigns' states as well as their souls were in St. Peter's power: "Beatum P[etrum], in cujus potestate est tuum regnum et tua anima."[35]

Papal sociolatry is unthinkable without Gregory VII's two principles. Their articulation should remind us of the rhetorical flourishes in his letters to the kings of Aragon, England, Hungary, and Denmark. Perhaps we can now see more clearly, however, that Gregory's political presumptions and the redeeming politics of the imperial papacy developed from and with Gregory's attempts to assert his control over church discipline and church order. But to this point, the three most dramatic expressions of that development have been held in reserve. We have yet to discuss Gregory's second excommunication of Emperor Henry IV (1080), his lengthy justification for that action composed for Bishop Hermann of Metz in 1081, and the curious document inserted in Gregory's papal register and widely known as the *Dictatus papae*.

The excommunication took the form of a prayer to St. Peter and St. Paul, whom Gregory asked to confirm Rome's judgments against the emperor. The document incorporated an account of Gregory's difficulties with the Germans, featuring the first excommunication and the pardon at Canossa. The pope took care to defend himself against charges that he wielded the sword of St. Peter and issued excommunications merely to promote the church's political interests. He insisted that he reacted only (and judiciously) to Henry IV's opposition to church reform. By preventing the convocation of reforming councils after he was absolved at Canossa, the emperor vividly demonstrated his disobedience. His wholesale rejection of papal leadership endangered the church in Germany; Christians estranged from the pope were doomed to disorder. There was no

---

[33] *RG* 2.45.
[34] *PL* 16: 1018; *RG* 4.2; 8.21.
[35] *RG* 8.20.

alternative, save to relieve the emperor of his office (*illi regiam tollo*), to forbid his German and Italian subjects from following him. With this injunction, the excommunication dismantles partitions between church and state, for Gregory VII not only deposed one monarch, he named his successor. Henry IV was deposed because he was "proud, disobedient, and deceitful." Rudolf of Swabia, "humble, obedient, and trustworthy," was awarded the "power and dignity of rule." Then Gregory concluded with an appeal to Peter and Paul, "most holy fathers and princes," to make their authority known to the world by authenticating the pope's pronouncements, by hastening Henry's downfall and Rudolf's accession. Gregory implicitly acknowledged the unusual character of his request. Christendom, he said, was familiar with St. Peter's power to depose wicked bishops and appoint worthier successors. Christendom also agreed that the church could bind and loose, condemn and pardon, the souls of sinners to lasting effect. If Peter as prince and his papal deputy were so influential in spiritual matters, which carried such great weight, how could it be doubted that they exercised final authority in secular matters which were of less consequence?[36]

But there was doubt. The archbishops of Cologne and Trier remained in the royalist camp after the second excommunication. To woo German prelates from their emperor, Gregory made a concerted effort to convince them his arguments against Henry and for papal primacy were sound and solidly based in the history of Christianity. That was the purpose of Gregory's second letter to Bishop Hermann of Metz, which was really a message for the German episcopacy. The letter's reach, however, extended far beyond the current crisis. It was cited in dozens of canonical collections and copied into numerous polemical treatises and chronicles. It gave spirit and swagger to subsequent expressions of papal sociolatry. The letter to Metz has been called the most important contribution to twelfth-century polemical literature. Possibly more than any other document in the history of medieval Christianity and in the arsenal of papal supremacists, Gregory's long letter was responsible for the church's emancipation from secular authorities. We must be careful not to exaggerate the degree of freedom actually obtained, as we shall see. But it is difficult to overstate the influence of this particular document and its thoroughgoing debasement of secular politics. In the thirteenth century, when the church finally ceased to canonize kings and emperors, theorists were likely to credit Pope Innocent III's efforts and edicts, but Innocent's pontificate (1198–1215) and achievements can justifiably be retold as the afterlife of the redeeming politics of Gregory VII's imperial papacy.[37]

[36] *RG* 7.14a.

[37] *RG* 8.21; Donald Weinstein and Rudolph M. Bell, *Saints and Society: The Two Worlds of Western Christendom, 1000–1700* (Chicago, 1982), pp. 201–2; I. S. Robinson, "The Dissemination of the Letters of Pope Gregory VII during the Investiture Controversy," *Jour-*

The assault on secular government in the letter to Metz included an account of previous pontiffs' reactions to tyranny. The emperors' apologists wished to derogate from the pope's authority by classifying Gregory VII's excommunications as innovations, so Gregory named other popes who had demanded submission to Rome. He singled out the first Gregory for threatening disobedient monarchs and magistrates with dismissal. He mentioned that Pope Innocent I had excommunicated Emperor Arcadius and that Bishop Ambrose similarly penalized Emperor Theodosius. Pope Stephen II, he said, not only released the Franks from their oaths to the Merovingian king in the eighth century; he designated Pippin, the first Carolingian, to succeed him. Gregory VII's condensed history of pontifical curses (and courtesies) must have left his more fastidious and scholarly allies with much to lament and correct. Nonetheless, he gave the past that critics had denied them to his efforts to exact obedience from the church's politically most powerful subjects.[38]

Just as it gathered momentum, Gregory's history lesson was interrupted by his imaginative countermaneuver against apologists, like the author of the De paenitentia regum, who assumed that a king's calling was more honorable than a pope's. Gregory stated unequivocally that political ambitions and assorted arguments for secular sovereignty derived from the worst human impulses. The courts of kings were the devil's playgrounds; virtue's chances for survival there were negligible at best. Christ despised the unregenerate kingdom of this world, and only the church's supreme pontiff, Gregory suggested, could infuse statesmanship with piety and morality. Only the pope could redeem Christendom's politics. Unredeemed, unsupervised, and undisciplined, political strategies maintained and spread the devil's rule along with that of kings and emperors. According to Gregory, the eminent Constantine understood the problem in precisely that way and consequently subjected himself to his bishop's decisions.[39]

Constantine was exceptional. Rome's gallery of good emperors contained only four others: Theodosius, Honorius, Charlemagne, and Louis the Pious. By contrast, nearly one hundred popes could be numbered among the world's holiest men—as long as Gregory VII was doing the numbering. Popes, he explained, had not aspired to their high office; they were chosen. And they remained humble after they acquired power, un-

---

nal of Ecclesiastical History 34 (1983): 193; and John Gilchrist, "The Reception of Pope Gregory VII into the Canon Law," Zeitschrift der Savigny-Stiftung für Rechtsgeschichte, kanonistische Abteilung 59 (1973): 70–73.

[38] To sample Gregory VII's oversimplifications, compare RG 8.21 (p. 554, lines 3–8) with Max Kerner, "Die frühen Karolinger und das Papsttum," Zeitschrift des Aachener Geschichtsvereins 88/89 (1982): 5–41.

[39] RG 8.21 (P. 53, lines 8–14; p. 559, lines 5–9).

like politicians and princes, who either climbed ruthlessly to the top or succumbed shamelessly to pride and to their worst instincts once, like Saul, they were unexpectedly picked to rule. The savagery of Gregory's attack was unremitting. Only simpletons, he suggested, could think that secular power, having seduced so many, was greater than priestly power. Princes themselves tacitly recognized that the reverse was true when in extremis, they entrusted themselves to priests. What laymen on his deathbed ever sent for a government official and applied for political absolution? Since consolation, forgiveness, and eternal rewards were the church's to dispense, and since the papacy was the purveyor of the church's ministries and reform, the church and its pontiffs must surely have the competence and divine commission to distribute and redistribute rewards of lesser value. The destiny of immortal souls turned on papal pronouncements. Popes could forbid the administration of saving sacraments in a particular church or diocese or throughout a vast territory. Gregory VII trusted that anyone who studied the matter (*sciolus*) and weighed the immortal soul against the perishable state would agree that pontiffs outranked kings. The consequence, never far from the comparisons formulated in the second letter to Metz, was that the fate of kings and kingdoms, on occasion, was Rome's to deliberate and decide.[40]

The letter to Metz and the second excommunication unfurled propositions deposited in previous papal correspondence. Gregory's admonitions, threats, and promises come no closer to resembling a theory. The twenty-seven proposals contained in the *Dictatus papae* are quite different. The claims are unaccompanied by argument and exposition; they look like titles in search of texts. Most of the topics would have been familiar to apologists acquainted with the history of Rome's insistence on papal supremacy, for instance, with Pope Damasus's contention that the Roman church was never mistaken and could never err. The staccato presentation of papal infallibility and superiority, however, makes the document seem daring, its author perhaps a bit impulsive. And several titles reinforce that impression, particularly the eighth, which alone would qualify the *Dictatus* as the premier document of the imperial papacy. It precedes short remarks that echo Gregory's other claims to receive homage from all princes and depose emperors; in effect, it calls upon emperors to surrender their imperial insignia. The eighth article declares that only the pope has the right to appear before his subjects as an emperor.[41]

---

[40] *RG* 8.21 (p. 555, line 10 to p. 557, line 10).

[41] *RG* 2.55a; Horst Fuhrmann, "*Quod Catholicus non habeatur, qui non concordat Romanae ecclesiae*: Randnotizen zum *Dictatus Papae*," in *Festschrift für Helmut Beumann*, ed. Kurt-Ulrich Jäschke and Reinhard Wenskus (Sigmaringen, 1977), pp. 269–73; and Percy Ernest Schramm, "*Sacerdotium* und *Regnum* in Austausch ihrer Vorrechte," *Studi Gregoriani* 2 (1947): 421–22, 436–48, reprinted in *KKP*, vol. 4.

The arrogance of such statements tempts us to assume that Gregory VII was never afflicted by self-doubt. We know he was capable of battering assaults on prelates and princes. We would not be surprised to learn that he wrote to the Irish nobility and church officials that all "principalities and powers" were subject to his pontifical will, that they should and would kneel at his feet. But Gregory compromised far more often than he conquered. Sometimes he called out the strokes, urging allies to apply the lash, yet in some crises he found himself friendless. Infrequently he could even speak of himself as a victim. In a mesmerizing letter to Abbot Hugh of Cluny, which seems out of place among the register's bustle of business and recrimination, Gregory confided his fear that involvement with secular affairs had so scarred his soul that he was unworthy of having his prayers answered. Gregory's sadness may have been feigned in 1075 to endear him to his pious correspondent, but I tend to think his sorrow sincere. Ten years later his grief was greater and with good cause.[42]

Gregory VII's abortive efforts to unseat Emperor Henry IV during the 1080s led to his own defeat and dislocation. Henry negotiated his way through Italy, over or around forces in league with the pope, and Rome capitulated in 1084. The emperor installed Archbishop Wibert of Ravenna as Pope Clement III, while Gregory celebrated Easter in the fortified Castel Sant'Angelo, well within earshot of the antipope's festivities. The Normans soon took Rome and rescued Gregory, but their murderous revels left several precincts in ruin and so incensed the citizens that the pope, who was blamed for the rescue and revelry, was compelled to depart with his rescuers. Hearing of Gregory's misfortune, the archbishop of Canterbury was not particularly eager to pillory the "de-Romed" pontiff, but he was unable to suppress the suspicion that God had turned on Gregory and used the emperor to retaliate against the imperious attitudes of the imperial papacy.[43]

Gregory VII died in exile in 1085. After the short pontificate of Victor III, Otto of Ostia accepted the papal office as Urban II in 1088. Increasing optimism in Rome was partly based on the emperor's troubles in northern Italy. His son and Lombard subjects had rebelled against him, and he was virtually a captive in his castle near Verona. Optimism among Gregory's friends was also founded upon the new pope's reputation as an ardent campaigner for reform. It has since been said that the true measure of Urban's success was his power to persuade European nobility to undertake the first crusade against Islam in the East. His dedication to the development of a curial organization in Rome, however, proved to be a

---

[42] *RG* 2.49 (to Hugh); Cowdrey, *Epistolae Vagantes*, p. 138 (to Ireland).
[43] *PL* 150: 548–49.

more lasting monument to his decade at the church's helm and a valuable asset to subsequent pontiffs. In his survey of medieval history, Horst Fuhrmann admitted that "compared with the rationalistic bureaucracy of the papal central administration, the itinerant kingship of Germany looks primitive."[44] But administrative improvements could not long forestall the revival of imperial influence in Italy. After his father's death, Emperor Henry V reasserted both German sovereignty in Lombardy and the emperor's claims to present candidates for important ecclesiastical offices. Rome's counterproposals early in the twelfth century were actually concessions. The papacy grudgingly acknowledged that emperors, although laymen, could cast the deciding vote when the church's elections were deadlocked. Effectively the papacy also admitted that emperors could veto elections by refusing to invest elected and consecrated candidates for episcopal sees with the bishop's regalia. To intrepid supporters of the imperial papacy, the various concordats with Europe's princes seemed a wretched setback that no amount of rhetoric could disguise.

There is, then, no way to gloss developments during the early decades of the twelfth century as strides toward the realization of Gregory VII's ambitions. The political climate was unfavorable. But some truth bristles in Franz-Joseph Schmale's statement that the eventful pontificate of Innocent II (1130–1143) was "the final and decisive victory" of Gregorian ideas. Innocent's administration illustrates remarkably well the persistence of Rome's universalist pretensions under circumstances that kept the church's "universal patriarch" from Rome. It also illustrates the lack of any positive correlation between rhetoric and reality.[45]

Innocent II was driven from Rome immediately after his election in 1130. Details are difficult to establish because contemporary reports of his election and that of his rival were drenched in vinegar—animosity toward one or the other of the candidates distorts every narrative. Nonetheless, it appears as if some highly placed prelates conspired to keep news of the previous pope's death from their colleagues and from the powerful Pierleone family, which aspired to control the papal curia as well as the city. The conspirators elected and enthroned Innocent in secret. Their opponents responded by making common cause with Peter Pierleone, who assumed office as Pope Anacletus II and promptly invalidated the furtive Innocentian election. Speaking for Innocent, Arnulf of Lisieux complained that Anacletus had purchased his promotion, but Pierleone popularity in Rome and the timely declaration of support from the Norman king of Sicily, Roger II, should have made such simony un-

---

[44] Horst Fuhrmann, *Germany in the High Middle Ages*, trans. Timothy Reuter (Cambridge, 1986), p. 76.

[45] Franz-Joseph Schmale, *Studien zum Schisma des Jahres 1130* (Cologne, 1961), pp. 291–94.

necessary. Whether paid for or otherwise, Roman reaction against the Innocentians made the city unsafe for Innocent from 1130 to 1138. During that time, he did return once with imperial troops, only to realize that he could not remain unmolested without a sizable garrison in the city, a garrison that the emperor was unwilling to commit for his protection. As long as Anacletus lived, Innocent and his resourceful chancellor Haimeric were safer in Pisa, where they eventually set up an alternative papal court. From Pisa, Innocent excommunicated both Anacletus and Roger. He boasted that all Italy endorsed his election, but he had no army to extend his jurisdiction south of the Lombard cities loyal to the emperor. Syllables were his only soldiers, and words were unable to overcome intense Roman resistance to his papacy.[46]

Most of Innocent's words, however, were not really intended for Rome. He and Haimeric attempted to shrug off their rivals' possession of the papal palace by emphasizing the pan-European character of their own interests and support. They looked on Anacletus as a usurper, a local tyrant of no consequence; the imperial papacy, they intimated, had moved with Innocent to Pisa. Anacletus, of course, also lobbied for northern European endorsements. His family's international banking connections gave him a distinct advantage, so Innocent decided to travel north and recruit prominent clergy in every region to press his case before their colleagues and sovereigns. His apologists were sensitive to readers' sympathies and patriotism when they retailed stories of Anacletus's misconduct. Arnulf of Lisieux charged that while Peter Pierleone was a papal legate in Brittany and Aquitaine, he extorted funds from French prelates so that he could travel in luxury and purchase sexual favors. Arnulf closed one inventory of offenses against the French by abruptly addressing St. Peter, as if the apostle had a ballot to cast in the disputed election. Would you, Peter, or your sinless friends, have tolerated the damnably debauched apostolate of Anacletus of Rome?[47]

Arnulf's dramatizations of dishonesty and his caustic commentary may have swayed some, but Innocent's striking success in France was probably due to the patient work of two abbots, Suger of St. Denis and Bernard of Clairvaux, who negotiated behind the scenes to assure a favorable outcome. Louis VI of France declared for Innocent, as did Henry I of England. Bernard prevailed upon the German king (and future emperor) not only to express his support but also to make symbolic gestures of feudal

[46] PL 179: 39. Also see MGH, Libelli de lite 3: 100 (for Arnulf), and Mario de Bergamo, "Osservazioni sulle fonti per la duplice elezione papale del 1130," Aevum 39 (1965): 58–61.

[47] MGH, Libelli de lite 3: 94–95.

submission to the papacy and then lead an expedition to restore the Innocentians to Rome.[48]

Thanks to Bernard and Haimeric, who probably engineered "the
northern strategy," regional church councils as well as rulers endorsed
Innocent II. For their part, the Innocentians made good on their claims
about the international character of their pope's ecclesiastical government. Pisa became the nerve center of the northern European church.
Lawyers converged on the city with appeals; cardinals from France and
Germany assembled along with Italian colleagues to hear them and deliberate. When Anacletus died, Innocent brought his court and curial tribu-
nals to Rome, pardoned the Norman king whom he had excommunicated, and enfeoffed him with the island of Sicily. If we relied on solemn
ceremonies and ritual gestures, Innocent II's imperial papacy would seem
to be some recompense for Gregory VII's trials. After all, the emperor
(Lothar III) to the North and the Norman monarch to the South were
the pope's bondsmen. But one dispute far from Italy showed the limita-
tions of Rome's redeeming politics as well as the astounding presumption
of its apostolic ideology.[49]

From the time of Pope Urban II, crusaders had been capturing cities
and carving out kingdoms for themselves in the region we now call the
Middle East. When Innocent reoccupied Rome in 1138, aristocrats from
the Loire valley, from Normandy, and from other European regions
reigned in such exotic places as Edessa, Antioch, Tyre, and Jerusalem.
Places that for centuries had known of Latin or Roman Christianity only
the little that pilgrims, as tourists, had disclosed were suddenly flooded
with pilgrims of a very different sort, who had every intention of remaining, ruling, and importing their Roman liturgies and laws. They also imported their controversies over papal supremacy, for Rome found it difficult to introduce discipline and to assure that the popes' candidates were
settled in important posts in the crusaders' kingdoms. Their distance from
Rome enabled local churchmen and lay authorities to shuffle bishops
from see to see without asking for papal advice or confirmation, to act as
if the Orient were exempt from papal supervision.

Several twelfth-century popes damaged their case, virtually inviting opposition when they were invited to arbitrate local quarrels. While the city
of Tyre was still under Muslim rule, the patriarchs of Antioch and Jeru-

[48] Morrison, *Tradition*, pp. 335–36, and Aryeh Graboïs, "La schisme de 1130 et la
France," *Revue d'histoire ecclésiastique* 76 (1981): 588–89, 605.

[49] For "the northern strategy," and the Innocentian victory, see Werner Maleczek, "Das
Kardinalskollegium unter Innocenz II und Anaklet II," *Archivum Historiae Pontificae* 19
(1981): 70–77, and Schmale, *Studien*, pp. 86–90, 230–31, but cf. Pier Fausto Palumbo,
"Nuovi studi (1942–1962) sullo scisma de Anacleto II," *Bulletino dell'instituto storico italiano per il medio evo* 75 (1963): 96–99.

salem competed for authority over churches considered within the jurisdiction of the archbishop of Tyre. Pope Paschal II judged in favor of one
claimant but the next year in favor of the other. Pope Honorius II, soon
thereafter, added to the confusion by reversing his predecessor's second
decision.[50] The situation worsened by the time Innocent II had secured
Rome, for in 1135 the fight for Tyre's suffragans became a fight for Tyre,
which an army from Jerusalem captured that year. Antioch expected its
interests to be honored; ancient records proved Tyre had long looked to
Antioch for leadership. But the army then in Tyre had been recruited in
districts tended by the patriarch of Jerusalem, who, without waiting for a
new round of negotiations and papal directives, named his own candidate, Fulcher of Aquitaine, to preside as archbishop of Tyre.[51]

Had Fulcher been content with his appointment, the crisis might have
ended there, at least for a time, although the patriarch of Antioch refused
to surrender several of Tyre's dependencies. But Fulcher bickered with his
patron in Jerusalem and tried to transfer his allegiance. He assumed he
could easily obtain Pope Innocent's cooperation. Years before, when
Aquitaine had endorsed Anacletus, Fulcher had resigned his episcopal see
in protest, so he deemed that Innocent now owed him a favor. He planned
to go to Rome to take payment and receive papal confirmation of his
archiepiscopal appointment in person. The patriarch of Jerusalem suspected secession, but he was unable to prevent the journey. Nonetheless,
when Fulcher arrived in Rome, he discovered that he had miscalculated;
the pope's long conflict with Anacletus had left him with many outstand-
ing obligations. As it happened, Fulcher's enemies in Jerusalem had been
inveterate Innocentians during the schism, and the pope repaid them by
instructing the new archbishop of Tyre to honor his debt to his patriarch
and original patron. Innocent sent a polite letter to inform Jerusalem and
Antioch that the case was closed, but Fulcher continued to stir up trouble.
Innocent then issued a thunderous pronouncement, a revealing fragment
of papal hierocratic theory, that ordered Tyre to profess unconditional
obedience to Jerusalem and Rome. Borrowing from previous papal decrees, Innocent insisted that Rome, as St. Peter's see, was the foremost
church in all Christendom, "the mother of all others," from which St.
Peter ruled through his popes while he maintained his critical position at
the gates of heaven. If Fulcher and his new friends in Antioch defied the
pope and thus insulted St. Peter, those gates would be forever closed to
them.[52]

[50] PL 163: 304; 166: 1279–81.

[51] I follow the account in book 14; chaps. 11–14 in William of Tyre's *Historia rerum in
partibus transmarinis gestarum*, reprinted as part 1 of vol. 1 of the *Recueil des historiens des
croisades, historiens occidentaux* (Paris, 1844), pp. 621–27.

[52] PL 179: 347 ("Prima et mater omnium").

Nothing unforeseeable here. Throughout the early Middle Ages, the papacy annexed requirements for Christians' salvation to its ambitions to govern the church and, as the imperial papacy developed, to its plans for the government of Europe. Innocent II's letter to Antioch, Tyre, and Jerusalem simply reiterated Rome's position on papal supremacy. What makes the reiteration a memorable spectacle, and what makes Innocent's letter the perfect document with which to conclude our chapter, is the fact that Rome's apostolic ideology was recycled and recited for the benefit of apostolic churches in Syria and Palestine. St. Peter was in Antioch before he came to Rome; Antioch claimed him, as did Rome, as its first bishop. Still, Innocent thought himself justified in parading Peter as a weapon to force Antioch to submit to the papacy's ruling. Even if one supposed that St. Peter's martyrdom in Rome privileged papal decisions, should it not have seemed insolent to tell the patriarch of Jerusalem that Rome was "the mother of all"? From one holy city, St. Peter departed this life, but from the other, Christ. The question of impertinence is itself impertinent, the invasion of one perspective by another. But we may speculate whether eleventh- and twelfth-century perceptions of Rome's redeeming politics as intrusive and impudent did not contribute to papal frustrations. Perhaps all we are entitled to say with certainty is that the imperial papacy trusted in the truths of Christian sociolatry. Evidently, however, imperial pontiffs rather consistently overbid their hands. Innocent's statements, for instance, were unavailing. It could be argued that his decisions and tenacity only served to precipitate the next round of controversies over papal politics in Palestine.

Controversies followed, one after another, for centuries. Apologists for empire and publicists for autonomous states revived Aristotelian politics, resurrected Roman law, and sometimes retreated into Constantine's shadow, provoking strident reactions from papal theorists. Within the church, critics of hierocratic theory suggested that God's will might be better revealed by church councils (regional as well as ecumenical) or in congregational consensus than by papal pronouncements; on that score, papal protests covered and recovered familiar ground. Occasionally, when anticlerical sentiments sparked debate, greater emphasis was placed on scandal than on statecraft and on "what righteousness required." That each controversy incorporated previous propositions and added something new—a fresh approach to an overworked text, an eccentric twist or a makeshift inference, a slight change in inflection—few scholars would deny. Fewer, if any, however, would deprive Pope Gregory VII of his central place in this history.[53]

[53] Walter Ullmann has argued that the earliest collections of papal correspondence yield evidence of a remorseless papal pursuit of world domination, but he also concedes that

The editor of Gregory's register and one of this century's most sure-footed explorers of papal history, Erich Caspar, has alluded to Gregory's distinctiveness, coming to terms at the same time with his awkwardness (*in der Beweisführung unbeholfen*) and flawed logic (*und gibt sich auf Schritt und Tritt logische Blossen*). Subsequent popes and their apologists improved on Gregory's reasoning when critics drew them into the realms of law and philosophy. But Gregory expressed himself with "grand simplicity" and enormous force, speaking often to friends and enemies alike in prayers and petitions to God and St. Peter. He consecrated the imperial papacy with the Petrine commission, binding and loosing on earth as well as in heaven, and he fastened Rome's claims to universal rule to his incontestably sincere dedication to the church's liberty and reform. Gregory VII's pontificate was the apotheosis of the redeeming politics of the medieval church.[54]

Gregory's pontificate, in some respects, was the culmination of previous developments. See Ullmann's *The Growth of Papal Government in the Middle Ages: A Study in the Ideological Relations of Clerical to Lay Power*, 2nd ed. (London, 1962), particularly pp. 448–51; but also consult Friedrich Kemp's rejoinder, "Die päpstiliche Gewalt in der mittelalterlichen Welt," *Miscellanea historia pontificae* 21 (1959): 135–39.

[54] Caspar, "Gregor VII," pp. 25–26.

Chapter Six

JOHN CALVIN'S GENEVA

THEOLOGIANS have said that justification is a journey, a single continuous journey commencing in this life and completed in the next. Roman Catholic theorists, particularly the proponents of papal sociolatry, assumed the church should have some significant say at every stage of the trip. The earliest Protestants objected. One was saved, they said, in an instant—the instant one accepted that Christ died to reconcile sinners with their God. Live with faith in God's atonement, God's promises, and God's mercy, and one need not worry about the sudden swerves and turns of fortune that usually disrupt life and raise doubts about redemption. Accordingly, one need worry little about the political order, save as the current regime might try to interfere with worship. The second generation of Protestant reformers, however, revived some Catholic and clerocratic ways of thinking about redemption that presented public life as the arena in which the community's salvation was measured. For Protestants, the road to redemption no longer passed through the old church and its sacraments. They denied that popes had either the right or the responsibility to review political decisions. But how then could God's revelations be made part of the political order? Who would measure and monitor the community's sanctification and salvation? The answer occurred to John Calvin as he evolved a political theory from his biblical theology and translated theory into practice in the city of Geneva.

Reams of paper are regularly devoted to Calvin studies, but one of the best accounts of Calvin's theory and practice is still André Bieler's analysis of the reformer's social and economic thought. Bieler probed Calvin's works with sympathy as well as scholarly interest. He abhorred the fragmentation of moral and political order in the twentieth century, as he thought Calvin had abhorred it in the sixteenth. For recent problems, Bieler blamed the notion then current in western Europe that "rationality" and "modernity" were incompatible with a comprehensive moral theology. John Calvin, he said, would have scoffed at the prejudice, and Calvin was celebrated in some quarters as the first modern man. Bieler argued that, at the very least, John Calvin was the first of the reformers to have appreciated the functional interdependence of economic development, political development, and morality.

After Calvin, according to Bieler, public morality deteriorated. The competing imperatives of family life, social caste, marketplace, and nation created chaos. Citizens yearned for a way to organize their lives, and their nostalgia for a morally purposeful commonwealth made them easy prey to purveyors of dangerous ideologies who hawked their totalitarian systems to catastrophic effect. Haunted by the memory of Hitler's Germany, Bieler reminisced about Calvin's Geneva. He commended Calvin for having fortified Geneva against both moral disorder and surrogate idealism, for having turned the Bible into a splendid textbook for government and social order. In Bieler's grand tribute, Geneva was a theocracy that worked because Calvin was an agile and thoroughly committed theorist, thoroughly committed, that is, to redeeming politics.[1]

Bieler had no difficulty classifying Calvin's government as theocratic. Scholarly solemnities invariably attach themselves like barnacles to the word *theocracy*, which intermittently sinks from sight and resurfaces in discussions of religion and government. Yet the word can still be useful. It tells us that a stock of religious images has been deployed to sanction a particular regime, and in this sense, Calvin's Geneva was theocratic. By now, however, a general affirmation of that kind should only whet our appetites for further inquiry. Did John Calvin insist that his community's salvation depended upon the distribution of power and the maintenance of a particular political order in the city? Did he allege that God's plan for the city's salvation was mediated by specific councils or courts? And were Calvin and his clergy the chief pursers of those public institutions and the most influential assessors of public morality as well as personal righteousness? If the answer is yes, John Calvin was a progenitor of Protestant sociolatry and Geneva may have cause to claim a place in religious and political history as Protestantism's first clerocracy.

· · ·

Catholic Geneva, like other prince-bishoprics, was a clerocracy long before John Calvin was asked to reform its churches. Early in the fourteenth century, citizens agreed to undertake nothing that would jeopardize the political authority of their bishops, who were ordinarily members of the Duke of Savoy's family or household.[2] Magistrates in Geneva acknowledged the dukes as their ultimate sovereigns, but on most matters they submitted to episcopal government.[3]

During the second decade of the sixteenth century, several crises nearly

---

[1] See Bieler's *La pensée économique et sociale de Calvin* (Geneva, 1959), especially pp. 515–20.

[2] Michel Roset, *des chroniques de Genève*, ed. Henri Fazy (Geneva, 1894), pp. 28–30 (1.18).

[3] Paul E. Martin, "La communauté de Genève et la maison de Savoie de 1449 à 1455," *Société d'histoire et d'archéologie de Genève, Bulletin* 12 (1963): 265–67.

resulted in armed conflict. In 1513, the cathedral chapter in Geneva did not bother to consult the Savoyards and elected a local candidate as bishop. The duke appealed to Pope Leo X to set aside the election and confirm his own nephew's appointment. Michel Roset, who chronicled the controversy, observed that citizens did not resist the substitution out of respect for Rome, but he also divulged that the duke's nominee, as absentee bishop, received little local cooperation.[4] Evidently, the people of Geneva were displeased with their duke and his ecclesiastical deputies. Commerce with other Swiss and South German cities made them less and less dependent upon their Savoyard lords and more openly resentful of their authority. In 1519, the bishop had no choice but armed intervention. He and hundreds of troops entered Geneva, punished dissidents, dismissed the city's principal elected representatives (its four syndics), and named their replacements. The incident dramatized the fact that Savoyard, Catholic clerocracy in Geneva had more years to run.

Geneva was the largest city in Savoy. Its ecclesiastical province was Savoy's largest diocese. The bishop owed it to his ducal patron to maintain the order and loyalty of such an important territory. Before leaving with his soldiers, he issued an edict that prohibited the city's syndics from taking office without episcopal consent, yet he soon learned it was hard to enforce such measures and to exercise any oversight at all from a distance. In 1527, a new bishop gave up the distractions of the Savoyard court and settled in Geneva. Apparently he decided that residence was the only alternative to rebellion; but he was too late, and he proved no match for forces then arrayed against Savoy and its agents. The bishop fled and left Geneva's newly independent magistrates with the task of finding formidable allies and thus dissuading the Savoyards from reprisal and reconquest. Catholic Freiburg made the mistake of carrying on negotiations with Geneva's exiled bishop, so Genevans turned instead to Freiburg's principal competitor, Protestant Bern, and eventually to Protestantism as well.[5] William Farel was asked to journey from Neuchâtel, where he had steered religious reform around that city's political obstacles, and to introduce Protestantism to Geneva. But the magistrates in the city's three assemblies were reluctant to surrender some of the prerogatives seized from their bishop only a short while before.[6]

John Calvin was passing through Geneva, probably on his way from France to Ferrara, when Farel prevailed upon him to stay and assist with the local reformation.[7] Several years earlier, Calvin had left the Catholic

[4] Roset, *Chroniques*, pp. 67–68 (1.69).

[5] Roset, *Chroniques*, pp. 179–81 (3.19–3.21).

[6] See Marc Chenevière, *La pensée politique de Calvin* (1937; rpt. Geneva, 1970), pp. 253–57.

[7] Roset, *Chroniques*, p. 238 (4.2).

church in Picardy and agreed to help French Protestants make their case for religious toleration. He had undertaken no duties, however, that prevented him from accepting Farel's invitation in 1536. He and Farel labored for two years, until the city elections in 1538 brought unsympathetic magistrates to power; whereupon the two reformers were banished. Farel returned to Neuchâtel, and Calvin moved to Strasbourg, where Martin Bucer appeared to have orchestrated Protestant reform much more successfully. Calvin applied himself to his studies and temporarily left Protestant politics to others.[8]

Meanwhile, magistrates in Geneva turned to Bernese reformers for guidance. They were not drawn back to Catholicism, but Cardinal Jacopo Sadoleto, bishop of Carpentras in southern France, was persuaded that prospects for reconversion were excellent with Farel and Calvin out of the way. In March 1539, he forwarded an indictment of Protestant innovations to one of Geneva's government councils. Sadoleto lectured the magistrates on the basic cause of the schism: behind all the specific grievances and the many gestures of municipal defiance, Satan schemed to divide the church and to throw all Christendom into confusion. The cardinal, for his part, schemed to persuade Genevans that reunion with Rome would doom the devil's work.[9]

Sadoleto was probably surprised when Calvin himself responded. Genevan officials, after consultation with reformers in Bern, admitted that their exiled pastor was the best man to answer the cardinal's charges. Calvin let it be known that his ostracism and exile diminished neither his pride in nor his sense of responsibility for the reforms in Geneva. "I can no more throw off (*abiicere*) that responsibility than throw off my own soul."[10]

Calvin first scolded Sadoleto for preferring peace to piety. Divisions, he said, were Christ's way of shaking sense into Christianity. The reformer went on to accuse the cardinal of silencing complaints in the name of peace and charity to protect the reputations of those who had presided over the deterioration of church discipline for generations.

Magistrates in Geneva were happy with Calvin's vindication of their reformation. Perhaps they were even warming to the possibility of his return when, in 1540, they authorized the publication and distribution of the response composed by their former reformer. The next year, Calvin's banishment was rescinded, and he promptly returned.[11]

Calvin moved quickly to resolve critical questions about church government. His *Ordinances* of 1541 set standards for clerical conduct and

---

[8] For difficulties during Calvin's "first term," see Walther Köhler, *Zürcher Ehegericht und Genfer Konsistorium*, vol. 2 (Leipzig, 1942), 512–17.

[9] CR 33: 382.

[10] CR 33: 387.

[11] Roset, *Chroniques*, p.286 (4.48).

stipulated procedures for the investigation of crimes and misdemeanors.[12] At the time, other citizens were reevaluating civil procedures, but the city's magistrates were anxious about their slow progress. Calvin, therefore, was entrusted with that task as well. He was relieved of his pastoral duties, save for sabbath sermons, until he could complete correcting and copying his drafts of the magistrates' new *Edicts*.[13] As he was conferring with and counseling Geneva's councilors, Calvin also took time to prepare a third edition of his compendious theological textbook, known today as *The Institutes of the Christian Religion*. He originally composed a sketch of his Protestant doctrines in 1536, shortly before coming to Geneva. He expanded the text in Strasbourg, after he had been banished. A third edition, several times the size of the first, was released in 1543, soon after he started working for the government once again. The *Institutes* then contained, and despite his further revisions still contains, Calvin's most comprehensive remarks on the relationship between political power and ecclesiastical authority.

To open the *Institutes* is to pass from the history of Calvin's Geneva into the twisting corridors of the reformer's political theory, yet the detour is necessary if we wish to understand Calvin's redeeming politics. He thought he was obliged first to redeem politics from the popes and their theorists, so the *Institutes* deliberately tried to torpedo Roman Catholic clerocracy and Rome's apostolic ideology. Calvin argued that the popes' estimation of St. Peter derived from a calculated misreading of Scripture. Undeniably, St. Peter died in Rome, but would St. Paul's letter to the Roman church have been silent about Peter, Calvin inquired, if Peter had been at all influential among the Christians in Rome? Calvin accused the papacy of having inflated St. Peter's importance in order to license its unapostolic desires for power within the church and for powers over the world's political leaders. Rome, according to Calvin, tricked princes into relinquishing their authority over territorial churches. Popes, in other words, had consistently taken unfair advantage of lay officials' generosity and piety. Papal clerocrats smuggled secular powers into the Petrine commission. They forged documents and invented precedents to overawe secular sovereigns. When all else failed, popes had been prepared to join battle, shed blood, and plot the ruin of armies and entire kingdoms in order to increase their own power. Calvin recalled how the last few centuries had been filled with impudent little men (*homunciones*), who paraded as St. Peter's heirs and successors but left only political devastation in their wake.[14]

---

[12] See Harro Höpfl, *The Christian Polity of John Calvin* (Cambridge, 1982), pp. 99–102.

[13] Chenevière, *Pensée*, pp. 205–21.

[14] The polemic sprawls across several sections of the *Institutes'* fourth book, but see particularly *JCOS* 5: 96 (*ICR* 4.6.8), 101 (*ICR* 4.6.13), 122–23 (*ICR* 4.7.19), 205 (*ICR* 4.11.9), 209 (*ICR* 4.11.14).

Dominion over worldly goods and great estates had been withheld from and forbidden to the apostles. Bernard of Clairvaux confirmed the prohibition in the twelfth century (*apostolis interdicitur dominatus*), and Calvin echoed Bernard in the sixteenth. He turned the celebrated Cistercian's observation into a pivotal proposition for his own efforts to rebuild the relationship between ecclesiastical and secular powers.[15]

A less likely foundation for Protestant clerocracy seems beyond the powers of imagination, especially since Calvin's *Institutes* seasoned Bernard's remark with several distinctions devised to increase the force of the prohibition. Calvin carefully contrasted the church's authority to persuade with the government's responsibility to coerce. Faith, he said, was the aim of the first approach; order was the goal of the second. This distinction alone would seem to interdict clerical ambitions to rule, but clerocratic principles are subtly reinstated as the author confronts the pressing problems of Genevan political life. Calvin's opposition to Catholic clerocracy was uncompromising. He scrapped papal petrinology because he thought it scripturally and historically indefensible. He insisted that Rome's apostolic ideology was a hideous distortion of the apostles' views on authority. Calvin, then, had to justify clerical political influence without returning to influential Catholic theorists. In fact, he discovered that he need only adapt other reformers' concepts of ministry in his discussions of civic morality and trade on the new Protestant soteriology to make civic order a matter of theological and clerical concern.

Soteriology is that part or branch of theology that explains propositions about justification, sanctification, and salvation. Protestants ardently maintained that believers had done nothing to effect their justification. In essence, nothing could be done to cover sin or propitiate God. Justification was a free gift from God. Righteousness was imparted to, but not earned by Christians, who lived righteously because they had been made righteous by God through faith in Christ, which was also a gift rather than an achievement or reward. Yet Calvin pronounced, perhaps most trenchantly in his sermons on Deuteronomy, that once divine favor, faith, and grace had been extended to Christians, the recipients were obliged to seize every opportunity to use God's gifts to demonstrate their election to the world.[16]

The particulars of election would remain a mystery. Why had God chosen some and not others? If not to reward prevenient works of righteousness, was it some perverse playfulness on God's part that led to Jane's justification and salvation and to John's damnation? Calvin knew it was not easy to silence such speculation. He also knew that irreverent probing

---

[15] *JCOS* 5: 207 (*ICR* 4.11.11).
[16] *CR*, e.g., 56: 591.

would persist as long as the elect exhibited manners that made their election appear unjust and even preposterous. But he wanted to make sense of Protestant soteriology and deprive doubters of every reason to suspect that God was unwise to have deposited divine truths with the Christians of Geneva.

Calvin wanted to assure others that making sense did not mean scratching for solutions to unsolvable problems. He conceded that the finite mind reached an impasse, a mystery that defied unraveling, when the time came to sift reasons for redemption. Making sense must mean something else. The most intelligent appreciation for God's gifts, including election, must be less like an answer to a question than a response to a summons. Calvin concluded that Christians were not first to comprehend God's justice and mercy but rather to vindicate them. The elect must make sure that the world knew their election had not been a mistake.[17]

Catholic Christendom did not appear to Calvin to have understood the full implications of election. Theologians of the old church had not assimilated the good news of the gospel, the news that election was also liberation. The church retained restrictions, dietary laws, and ceremonial obligations reminiscent of Hebrew piety. It had not weaned Christians from the laws and standards from which Christ's atoning death delivered the elect.[18]

On one flank, then, Catholics continued to use obsolete regulations and restrictions to articulate and enforce Christian piety. That was what Calvin perceived when he looked to his right. On the other flank, to his left, he caught sight of radicals and Protestant sectarians, of whom we shall hear much more, who seemed to Calvin to have taken their deliverance and their new Christian liberty as an opportunity to create societies of libertines. Calvin scolded them for having made a farce of their election. They completely misunderstood the nature of their deliverance from sin and they demonstrated to the world that the evil in human nature was ineradicable. The fact that the reformation's first generation had produced such absurdity convinced Calvin that someone must preside over, monitor, and manage Christian liberty if election were not to be mocked.[19]

This need for surveillance and supervision probably accounts for the importance John Calvin gave to the parish ministry. He saw to it that candidates were diligently prepared for ordination and pastoral service. But it was not simply a successful settled ministry that made Calvin's Geneva in Harro Höpfl's words, "unusually supervisable." The city in the

---

[17] *JCOS* 4: 237–38 (*ICR* 3.14.19).

[18] *CR* 55: 206.

[19] See Benjamin Wirt Farley's "Editor's Introduction," in *John Calvin: Treatises against the Anabaptists and against the Libertines* (Grand Rapids, 1982), pp. 161–86.

sixteenth century enclosed only thirteen thousand inhabitants within its walls. The lakefront to the south of the Rhone estuary, where the walled territory more than doubled that portion of the city across the Pont-Bati, extended only a thousand yards. No more than half the distance separated the shore from the city's gates. One might say that political life was equally compact, and it was further pruned by the edicts that Calvin himself had composed by 1543. No more than one administrative unit or committee came between a citizen and the twenty-five member Petit Conseil. All this meant that indiscretions of individuals and factions were seldom secrets to those responsible for their detection.[20]

Calvin frequently railed against citizens' "crimes," particularly against those carefully concealed behind kind gestures. He taught clerical colleagues by example to direct their sermons against misers' evil dispositions, which the most scrupulous deacons might easily overlook when outward acts of charity seemed to conform to what was expected of well-intentioned Christians.[21] Beware of what outwardly seems virtuous, he preached; apparent virtues might well be soaked in sin.[22] In fact, Calvin so emphasized this theme that his sermons have been taken as tokens of his despair in the face of utter human depravity. Richard Stauffer has argued persuasively that such an inference is one-sided and misleading, yet Calvin obviously feared the social and theological consequences of citizens' irrepressible and sinful urges, which threatened to disrupt discipline and disfigure his community's witness to its election.[23]

Time did not still Calvin's anxieties. His partisans were elected to the city councils and, as we shall soon see, his opponents exiled from Geneva; nonetheless, he kept glancing over his shoulder. Rebellious Israelites populated his sermons on Deuteronomy, in which the pentateuchal record of their infamy and their mistrust of authority figured as a mirror from which the undeclared malice of Genevans glared back at them. At least this was how Calvin contrived to express his misgivings.[24] In 1556, he spoke of his troubling anticipation that citizens' defiance and disreputable behavior would increase after his death. He feared his work would come

---

[20] See Josef Bohatec, *Calvins Lehre von Staat und Kirche mit besonderer Berücksichtigung des Organismusgedankens* (Breslau, 1937), pp. 482–91; Erik Wolf, "Theologie und Sozialordnung bei Calvin," *Archiv für Reformationsgeschichte* 42 (1951): 17–21; Höpfl, *Polity*, p. 57; and E. WIlliam Monter, *Calvin's Geneva* (New York, 1967), p. 116.

[21] CR 55: 331–33.

[22] CR 55: 210.

[23] Richard Stauffer, "Un Calvin reconnu: Le prédicateur de Genéve," *Bulletin: Société de l'histoire de Protestantisme français* 123 (1977): 199–200. Also see William J. Bouwsma, "John Calvin's Anxiety," *Proceedings of the American Philosophical Society* 128 (1984): 252–56; and Bouwsma's *John Calvin: A Sixteenth-Century Portrait* (Oxford, 1988), pp. 142–43.

[24] CR 56: 485.

to nothing. Those contemptible and rebellious Israelites lived on: the new Protestants gave them fresh life by disregarding obligations associated with their election. Calvin warned that the fate of the rebels, old and new, was the same. Innumerable afflictions would assail Genevans if they did not mend their ways. Wrongdoers would be tormented by their consciences and hounded by the courts, which, in Calvin's estimation, had a special ministry to perform with respect to the property of innocents and the improprieties of the city's most sinister citizens.[25]

Calvin tried to encourage justices and law officers (*gens de justice*) in a sermon preached on a homicide investigation in Deuteronomy's twenty-first chapter. He exhorted constables to be more aggressive. It was true, he said, that to make inquiries only after complaints had been received and registered was tantamount to indifference. Pious and exceptionally vigilant officials must take greater initiative. They should search for the seeds of disorder and antisocial behavior before offenses were committed. Only then could the moral contours of God's community be preserved, and only then would divine election be vindicated.[26] From the pulpit and the lectern, Calvin pressed his own war on crime, answering the charges leveled against government by the reformation's radicals and sectarians. The dissidents realized that law enforcement involved coercion, and they believed that only the devil would practice coercion to achieve conformity, no matter how valuable conformity might be to the maintenance of public order. The earliest editions of the *Institutes*, composed before Calvin had a Christian commonwealth to protect, show how far he was willing to go in order to reprimand the radicals and to inspire and defend government officials.

Calvin conceded that the radicals were correctly concerned by the litigiousness and contention that seemed to plague reformed communities, but he disagreed with those who blamed courts and magistrates for having provoked Christians to contend for their property and for their civil rights. He thought lawsuits a permissible way to preserve civil order as long as litigants were not ruthless. To the extent that courts had become breeding grounds for envy and enmity, they must be reformed rather than dissolved. They must be transformed into forums in which disputes could be composed honorably, in which God's peace could be maintained by arbitration. Yet Calvin also confided that the route to court reform passed directly through the dispositions of citizens who used the courts, citizens who were reluctant to find amicable settlements, citizens who seemed obsessed with display and debate. Those same citizens, he said, must be taught to avoid acrimony and to use the courts and court officials as God

[25] CR 56: 654–55.
[26] CR 55: 642–43.

intended them to be used. The courts were there, according to Calvin, to encourage dialogue, to address Genevans' legitimate complaints about their neighbors, and to restrain impetuous and unregenerate persons. As for madmen (*fanatici*), who recklessly condemned government, magistrates, and courts, Calvin had no patience with their insubordination, which was, in his judgment, politically as well as soteriologically hazardous.[27]

The political hazard was obvious. When radicals opposed civil order they gave the reformation's enemies an easy target. Critics had predicted that reform would inevitably lead to revolution, so Calvin himself was compelled to allay the concerns of monarchs and magistrates alike about Protestantism's apparent incompatibility with existing institutions. The radicals' insolence seemed to belie Calvin's assurances and to confirm his critics' allegations. Unless someone convincingly disassociated Protestantism from the radicals' positions, the reformation was unlikely to spread and reformed communities would slip quickly into anarchy.[28]

The soteriological hazard was equally clear. The radicals, rebels and reluctantly governed alike, could not be counted among the elect. They suffered badly from the sin of pride. They thought themselves too perfect for the courts, too good to be governed. The *Institutes* sealed its censure of such audacity with a message for political authorities that was also meant to quiet the sectarians' complaints about compromises required of Christians who wished to participate in public life and assume positions of leadership, compromises that purportedly killed their Christianity. Calvin would have none of this; he both cautioned and encouraged officials: "Consider what you do, for you judge not for man but for the Lord; He is with you in giving judgment."[29]

From Calvin's perspective, Luther and other reformers of the so-called first generation were partly to blame for the second generation's difficulties with the radicals. The early reformers had underscored the centrality of Christ's atonement and the liberty granted Christians who truly believed that Christ died to liberate them. Luther and his associates, however, left no directions for the management of communities filled with liberated Christians. Calvin insinuated that the first reformers left the reform of government to chance and circumstance. He believed that government must be carefully monitored, although he was aware that deductions of this kind could hardly be verified from the evidence in the New Testament, where the few magistrates mentioned were hostile to the gospel. His efforts to redeem politics and his generalizations about redeem-

[27] *JCOS* 5: 490 (*ICR* 4.20.18).
[28] *JCOS* 5: 472–73 (*ICR* 4.2.2).
[29] *JCOS* 5: 476 (*ICR* 4.2.6), citing 2 Chron. 19:6.

ing politics could be illustrated best with anecdotes from the Hebrew scriptures. Calvin was a tireless and prolific student of the Old Testament, where collaboration between magistrates and ministers appeared to be a critical part of God's providential direction of history. Calvin concluded that God had appointed two ministries to assist the elect in shaping and policing a civil order that reflected the importance and influence of their election.[30]

Lessons for rulers were conveniently stored in the Old Testament; the good news about the second election and about redemption was presented in the New. God furnished the church and its preachers so that magistrates and citizens might not wander aimlessly through their biblical texts as if they were casual tourists. Everything had been arranged so wonderfully that Calvin could not but wonder why radicals were straying so far from the truth. Of course, his own deference to political authorities was somewhat expedient. After all, he served at the government's discretion, so that at least for a time he thought it more prudent to feed than to fight the Minotaur. To underscore Calvin's prudence, however, is not necessarily to forget his theology and soteriology. Unlike the Minotaur, the government was no beast. Constables, courts, and town councils were indispensable for public order, and Calvin once suggested that unless public order were preserved and mutual affection officially enshrined in law, election might well be forfeit and eternal life beyond reach.[31]

Hired, fired, and rehired, Calvin learned that magistrates could be quite capricious. He labored under no illusions. Originally an ally, the duchess of Ferrara proved irresolute, and her apostasy deeply affected the Genevan reformer, who confided to his friend Farel that he no longer trusted public officials to remain constant in the cause of reform.[32] Nonetheless, Calvin never ceased to petition princes for their aid. He told Europe's politicians that they could and should be full partners in the reformation from start to finish. The popes, he said, relegated secular governments to inferior and humiliating roles. Rome's apostolic ideology coasted from one absurdity to another until public administrators all but abdicated their responsibilities to supervise the church's reforms. Calvin thought he was exposing the frauds that once convinced those administrators they were no better than their pontiffs' pawns. His supplications to the princes of his day offered them partnerships, opportunities to purge their

---

[30] *JCOS* 5: 477 (*ICR* 4.2.7). Also see Sheldon S. Wolin, *Politics and Vision: Continuity and Innovation in Western Political Thought* (Boston, 1960), pp. 179–83; Jürgen Baur, *Gott, Recht, und weltliches Regiment im Werke Calvins* (Bonn, 1965), pp. 25–39; and Höpfl, *Polity*, pp. 45–55, 188–92.

[31] CR 79: 190–91 ("potiri nos vita aeterna aliter non posse quam si inter nos vivamus unanimes in hoc mundo").

[32] CR 43: 298.

churches of unscriptural practices and to serve the new evangelical order in meaningful ways.[33] But Calvin made it perfectly clear that the senior partner in any arrangement, in partnerships with princes and in compacts with municipal councils, was the reformed church. Before magistrates had been converted to Christianity, the church's jurisdiction over all believers had been confirmed by Scripture and tradition. The conversions of emperors changed nothing in this regard. Emperors joined their subjects as *ecclesiae filii*, sons of the church. Truly pious emperors, princes, and magistrates should not wish to stand apart from fellow Christians, all of whom subjected themselves to the church's counsel and rule. Lay rulers must not haggle with their pastors over immunities and exemptions. "The emperor is within and not above the church." Calvin borrowed those words from St. Ambrose, the very words that once braced the most dramatic claims of the imperial papacy. The message was self-evident and the same; only the church has changed.[34]

That message made its debut in one of the later editions of the *Institutes*, though the foundations for Protestant clerocracy in Geneva were laid in the very first, when Calvin offered some editorial comments on the economics of court life. Taxes and most other revenues, he said, were public funds that might be diverted, within limits, to cover costs associated with the private wants and tastes of magistrates and princes. Calvin learned that David and other holy kings maintained large households and vast estates at public expense, but he knew that European princes and government authorities in his own time frequently got too greedy. They overtaxed their subjects to fill their vaults, which they then emptied to gratify their illicit and unholy desires. Calvin insisted that they must be taught limits (*docendi sunt quantum sibi liceat*) and shielded from divine retribution. The best instructors, of course, were those who understood how to read Scripture and how to interpret God's will.[35] This meant that the magistrates' ministry was subject to review by pastors trained and inspired to brew political theology and to pour pronouncements on the conduct of war and collection of revenues from their casks of specially treated and blended biblical quotations.

The critical question was whether magistrates who failed to listen and obey were subject to dismissal or deposition. By the twelfth century, partisans of the imperial papacy, we now know, would not have hesitated to answer in the affirmative. Calvin was more ambivalent. At one point, the *Institutes* strictly prohibited sedition. Princes and magistrates, however worthless they might be, were not to be unseated. But Calvin also echoed

---

[33] CR 34: 523, 530, for the original supplication to the princes; CR 44: 731–34, for its recirculation.

[34] *JCOS* 5: 200 (*ICR* 4.11.4).

[35] *JCOS* 5: 486 (*ICR* 4.20.3).

another directive found throughout the Christian traditions when he declared that disobedience was not just an alternative; it was every Christian's duty to defy authorities who formulated policy that patently endangered God's plans for the elect.[36]

It could be argued that Calvin sent prospective insurgents mixed signals, unquestionably the result of his efforts to write both to encourage evangelical reformers and to appease authorities who opposed them. He hoped to win over each regime's most intractable conservatives, yet in the interim, the preachers he trained and inspired were engaged in risky business. Calvin acknowledged that resistance to rulers would exact a tremendous price from resisters. Their evangelical campaigns, in instances, might turn against political regimes, a turn that could well be both reasonable and conscionable even though unlawful. And if resisters and reformers were compelled to break the law, they must be ready to accept the consequences.

Calvin ostensibly preferred to instruct rather than to disobey and depose sovereigns and public administrators. If committed Christians could teach and tame their rulers, they would have no occasion to defy them. The catch was to find some way in which religious reformers could govern their governors. By no means was Calvin disillusioned with the power of the pulpit, yet he did not depend exclusively on his sermons or on those of his colleagues for evangelical teaching (and taming). He allowed that a mixed group of ministers and laymen, assembled as a court or consistory, should oversee the magistrates' performance and piety to assure the Christian conduct of all citizens. The earliest churches, he noted, had been served by such overseers or *gubernatores* as well as by prophets and apostles. In his judgment, the need for a senate of this type and its steady censorship was as great in the sixteenth century as it has been in the first.[37]

Catholicism had its own consistories. According to Calvin, they were all aberrations. He claimed that the earliest gubernatores were laymen, whereas the medieval church packed its consistorial courts with highly placed prelates. The change could be dated at least to the fourth century, when Ambrose lamented that the consistories had been infiltrated. Calvin volunteered that the sage and sainted bishop of Milan would have been horrified by the subsequent history of the church's courts: Ambrose's worst fears, as Calvin imagined them, had been realized, for by delegating powers to their colleagues and friends, medieval bishops had wholly corrupted their consistories.[38] The *Institutes*, on this count, paused only to welcome Ambrose into the argument, for invective or lengthy historical

---

[36] Cf. *JCOS* 5: 489–90 (*ICR* 4.20.17) with *JCOS* 5: 501 (*ICR* 4.20.32).
[37] *JCOS* 5: 50 (*ICR* 4.3.8).
[38] *JCOS* 5: 201–2 (*ICR* 4.11.6).

analysis seemed pointless. Calvin thought it within his power to redistribute the functions of the Christian ministry and to restore what centuries of Roman Catholicism were said to have effaced. The restoration was quite simple: the ministry of the word was entrusted to pastors and teachers; deacons supervised the community's charitable work; and a new consistory received the authority formerly awarded the gubernatores. The consistory in Calvin's narrative received the right to govern the conduct, public and private, of Geneva's governors and governed alike.[39]

So much for the *Institutes'* narrative reconstruction of early church order! We shall see that it was one thing for Calvin to conjure up the past and quite another thing altogether to shape the present and plan the future. And it was one thing to codify the relationship between the government and the consistory's gubernatores in successive editions of a text and quite another to get one's program enacted. Probably from the time Calvin returned to Geneva from Strasbourg, he counted on the consistory to regulate "the outer life" of the church and community, though this may not as yet have implied the consistory's contribution to government policy.[40] In his *Ecclesiastical Ordinances* of 1541, Calvin set the ground rules. The consistory was to include all the town's ministers along with twelve laymen appointed by the Petit Conseil after deliberation with the clergy. It was to enforce discipline; yet its disciplinary jurisdiction was somewhat ill defined, so the town's magistrates insisted that Calvin add a codicil to safeguard their authority.[41] Apparently the magistrates were not as confident as some recent scholars of Genevan political history that Calvin desired only to collaborate with the government and not to dominate or supplant it.[42] We will leave the question of Calvin's intent for others to ponder. The magistrates' foreboding, however, is of special interest inasmuch as the *Ordinances* stipulated that the consistory should subject every citizen's life to scrutiny, and this stipulation placed the new gubernatores in the position of umpiring the convictions and conduct of persons who themselves were magistrates.[43]

From Walther Köhler's survey of the consistory's proceedings, we learn that the court was preoccupied with misdemeanors that seemed to indicate the citizens' enduring attachment to Catholic practices. The consistory summoned and admonished persons who had been heard invoking the saints or who had been caught fasting. A number of culprits were charged with having kept and concealed crucifixes. Others were accused of and disciplined for blasphemy, for criticism of the reformation and the

---

[39] *JCOS* 5: 57–58 (*ICR* 4.4.1).
[40] Köhler, *Zürcher Ehegericht*, pp. 569–71.
[41] *JCOS* 2: 361, lines 3–6.
[42] E.g., Chenevière, *Pensée*, p. 251.
[43] *JCOS* 2: 339.

consistory amounted to criticism of God's election.[44] The insolent were easy to identify, but no one escaped surveillance and supervision. By 1551, members of the consistory were making annual house-to-house searches to check for irregularities in behavior and belief.[45]

The town's magistrates demanded that the consistory's verdicts be reviewed in one of Geneva's other councils because excommunication had grave social, economic, and political consequences. The penalty deprived offenders of the sacraments. It shamed them, but since neighbors, clients, and colleagues usually shunned excommunicated citizens, it could also bankrupt them. When magistrates refused to sanction the excommunication of a prominent politician, Philibert Berthelier, whose troubles began when he declined to attend worship, the consistory—particularly its clerical members—battled in earnest for consistorial independence.

The battle lasted from 1553 to 1555. Geneva's ministers appealed to reformers in Zurich, Basel, and Bern, as if they hoped to fashion a Swiss clerical alliance against town governments. Those other reformers, however, gave Calvin and his consistory little encouragement; they had no wish to give their magistrates cause for alarm by supporting the Genevan initiatives. Although Calvin could not rally these reluctant friends, he did win in Geneva when the councils capitulated after a heavy barrage of scriptural passages supporting exclusive clerical control over sacraments and spiritual sanctions.[46] In January 1555, Geneva's Council of Sixty yielded to members of the consistory ultimate authority to excommunicate. In February, Calvin's candidates were elected syndics. Michel Roset, barely twenty years old at the time, remembered all this as a turning point in the city's history, a deliverance from servitude comparable to Israel's Old Testament exodus.[47]

A slightly different picture develops from Calvin's correspondence, which never really pulses with the same excitement that animates Roset's chronicles. In fact, Calvin's announcements of the triumphs, in some respects, seem downright demoralizing. He told Heinrich Bullinger in Zurich that the consistory's conquest was unstable, that Berthelier and his influential friends, Ami Perrin chief among them, were intractable. They had controlled the Petit Conseil from 1549 to the election of 1555. Calvin reasoned that they had become too accustomed to their mastery of public administration to accept their electoral setback graciously and to permit Geneva to edge closer to consistorial clerocracy. On May 15, Calvin wrote to Farel that Perrin's party was relentlessly slandering him and that

[44] Köhler, *Zürcher Ehegericht*, pp. 580–83.

[45] Roset, *Chroniques*, pp. 332–33 (5.27); Köhler, *Zürcher Ehegericht*, p. 590; and Bouwsma, *Calvin*, pp. 218–19.

[46] Amadée Roget, *Histoire du peuple de Genève*, vol. 4 (1877), 142–54, 188–90.

[47] Roset, *Chroniques*, pp. 363–65 (5.60–61).

Perrinist bellowing could be heard around the city. "Satan spreads gloom everywhere. Things here are in such complete disorder. The city is inflamed against us and fresh charges are added daily to increase the heat." Calvin warned Farel to expect the worst. It was as if a sense of panic had overtaken him, as if the consistory's success with the councils meant only that Perrin and his supporters could make the consistory a more attractive target. The report to Farel was drenched in pessimism, yet Calvin also expressed his commitment to hold the ground taken and the advantages gained during the early months of 1555. He was tested (or, at least, he thought that the test had come) the following night. Perrin and his cronies dashed from their taverns and clamored against French emigrés, on whom Calvin had long relied for sympathy and support. Calvin charged, to devastating effect, that the rioters' real purpose was to bring down the consistory and the new government as well. Although evidence for this reading of the riot of May 16 is inconclusive, rioters were treated as rebels: some were apprehended and put in prison, while the more fortunate fled to Bern.[48]

From Bern, Perrin fumed as his comrades caught in Geneva were executed. He insisted Calvin had engineered a reign of terror provoked only by some spontaneous street brawling. Calvin replied that the refugee's version was a transparent lie, yet he lavished considerable energy on exculpating himself and reincriminating the consistory's enemies.[49] Perrin's charges and other rumors circulating throughout Switzerland may have had damaging effects on Calvin's reputation, but in and around Geneva, he all at once appeared to be master of the situation. Officials in Bern tried to intercede for Perrin. They made clemency in Geneva a condition for the renewal of several treaties due for reconsideration. When that failed, they negotiated for a temporary amnesty that would permit prominent outlaws to return and see to their affairs. But Geneva would not budge. Citizens who had only gradually—and grudgingly—accepted the consistory's supervision were suddenly united against the consistory's alleged assailants.[50]

In a late September sermon, Calvin reflected on the year's developments. He recalled that the consistory had been under attack for seven or eight years. The Perrinist mutiny, he said, was the culmination of treach-

---

[48] For the correspondence, see CR 43: 617–18 (to Farel), 449 (to Bullinger). For the uprising, Roset, Chroniques, pp. 372–76 (5.69–70), but also review Calvin's account, CR 43: 676–85.

[49] CR, e.g., 43: 830–32.

[50] See Roget, Histoire 4: 245–67; 5 (1879): 34–35, 92–95. Also see E. William Monter, Studies in Genevan Government (1536–1605) (Geneva, 1964), pp. 105–6, which suggestively brands Perrin's disturbances as the last expression in Geneva of "the uncouth democracy of the medieval commune."

ery that had long tried the patience and faith of the elect. Counterforces prevailed in 1555 because the order they defended and the mutineers were eager to overthrow was not simply a municipal political arrangement. Calvin asserted that the consistory was part of God's order. God's vengeance preserved it and scattered its enemies, just as God had retaliated against Dathan and Abiram in the Old Testament (Numbers 16). Calvin suggested that divine chastisement in Scripture and divine chastisement in Geneva were blessings and lessons from which the elect should learn how steadfastly God stood by his true ministers and gubernatores. Naturally, Calvin also concluded that God would reward those laymen loyal to their pastors and that God would wreck the fortunes of those, like Perrin and Berthelier, who conspired against them.[51]

After the Perrinist mutiny, the consistory moved with greater dispatch. In 1555, twice as many offenders were excommunicated as in the previous year, during which the consistory's critics had still held some control over the city's councils. Opposition continued to disintegrate, and the number of excommunications doubled again in 1557, when nearly two hundred men and women were ostracized.[52] From his pulpit, Calvin sparred verbally with citizens who had not yet learned the lesson of Perrin's fate and still contested the consistory's claims. But Calvin left enforcement to the court itself. Members heard more cases, assigned more penances, and determined more punishments. Of course, Calvin sat and voted with the other judges, but his unique position in Geneva furnished him with the opportunity to perform a different kind of service as well. He was the city's preeminent theologian and political theorist. He composed stirring sermons to create and sustain an environment in which consistorial clerocracy was unlikely again to receive a serious challenge. Those sermons are surely the best expression of John Calvin's Protestant sociolatry. They alerted citizens to the soteriological stakes or implications of their political commitments. They put Geneva on its guard against religious and political subversion. Possibly it came to the point, as some have charged, where neighbors regularly turned informers, for Calvin warned the people of his city that they need not look only to Bern, where Perrin continued to protest his conviction, or to Rome to find their most treacherous enemies and the enemies of the gospel. Geneva still lodged menacing and stubborn sinners. The wicked might still seduce and corrupt the righteous and elect, so Calvin advocated clerical supremacy

---

[51] CR 55: 88–93, 96.

[52] E. William Monter, "The Consistory of Geneva, 1559–1569," in *Renaissance, Reformation, Resurgence: Papers and Responses Presented at the Colloquium on Calvin and Calvin Studies*, ed. Peter de Klerk (Grand Rapids, 1976), p. 70. Monter also provides some interesting attendance figures (pp. 65–66). Calvin was there each year for over half of the consistory's meetings and, in one term (1561–62), he attended nearly all of them.

and made the church and its consistory agencies of social and political control.[53]

I do not mean to suggest that Calvin created a police state. Geneva's constables did not wear clerical collars. Calvin, however, was able to redefine the roles of ministry and magistracy to assure that his consistory could defend its rights to discipline his Christian commonwealth. Up until this page, we have been able to quarry sizable blocks from Calvin's *Institutes*, and we have reset them here in order to restore the theological foundations for consistorial clerocracy in Geneva. Reexamination of two themes from Calvin's September sermon in 1555, which was something of a state-of-the-canton address, should enable us to conclude and to see how well the reformer built. We will see, first, that he persistently identified the city's political order with God's purpose and, second, that he demanded that Genevans accept clerical leadership in public life as part of their ministers' management of (and responsibility for) the community's corporate redemption.

In Calvin's work, the identification of local political order with God's design or God's reign never, to my knowledge, amounted to an explicit, festive, boastful proclamation that Geneva was a sacred city. Chauvinism and self-congratulation of that kind were not John Calvin's style. Nonetheless, I would not be the first to point out that the scrupulous and systematic cultivation of civic morality was an indication that municipal officials and many citizens were persuaded that Geneva was a saintly community in the making, a new *res publica Christiana*, which must be sifted regularly and monitored closely to remove impurities. As for Calvin, even before the Perrinist conflict, he hinted that "immense difficulties" could be offset or overcome and that God's purpose might be realized on earth and in his own time.[54] Writing to Bullinger, Calvin rehearsed the story of his earliest problems with Genevan officials and then he confided to his friend that he would have left the city at the first signs of trouble had he not been convinced that "the reign of Christ" would eventually develop in Geneva and, from there, spread elsewhere.[55]

The measures taken to neutralize opposition and to establish consistorial jurisdiction and autonomy certainly licensed some triumphalist sentiment. The reign of Christ, it seemed, could be levered into place now that Calvin had an invaluable instrument for the supervision of public morality. If bathing practices appeared conducive to lewd conduct, the gubernatores could intervene and reform them. When gravediggers thoughtlessly chattered as they collected corpses for burial, the consistory

[53] CR 55: 93.
[54] CR 43: 429.
[55] CR 41: 268.

could reprimand them. All citizens pledged obedience to God's holy laws. The government required oaths; the consistory enforced them.[56] One might say that, by common consent, Geneva was a city set apart. Other Swiss and South German cities translated prescriptions for holiness into oaths, starched prohibitions, and statutory rules, but Geneva's leading citizens seem to have been more deeply committed to making their reform work. The ill-fated experiment that closed taverns and replaced them with salons for pious conversation shows that the stubborn defense of simple pleasures might occasionally frustrate otherwise formidable crusades for corporate righteousness. On the whole, however, citizens had to accommodate Calvin's requirements for civic holiness as those requirements were mediated and enforced by his consistory.[57]

Though it is hard to imagine that the consistory did not give ground on some smaller matters, Calvin appears to have been unyielding. And on issues of considerable consequence, it is equally hard to imagine that Calvin, after 1555, did not call all the shots. He was loath to compromise. Compromise was the course that led away from the reign of Christ. He berated Philip Melanchthon, Martin Luther's lieutenant, who seemed ready to barter some of Protestantism's new practices for peace, if not for reunion, with Roman Catholics. He told Melanchthon that "by ceding the most trifling point (paululum), you provoke greater anxiety than would the wholesale apostasy of a hundred lesser men."[58]

Irenic and more flexible reformers might periodically adjust and temper demands a Christian polity made upon citizens. Calvin would not allow that to occur in Geneva. In his mind, the reign of Christ was proclaimed when the elect assembled and distributed obligations, powers, and privileges according to a pattern cut from the scriptural records of the earliest communities. God's will preserved Geneva from the Perrinists' outrage and, with the consistory's cooperation, God would keep the community safe and morally sound.

Calvin's second theme, the provision that citizens accept clerical leadership in public life, is best reconsidered in connection with a discernible tension in his thought. There—and arguably in Geneva as well—skepticism about citizens' willingness to conform to exacting moral standards conditioned and often wholly obscured the opinion that the reign of Christ had already started. Calvin rarely papered over the moral and political problems that plagued his Christian commonwealth. He was not the reformer to equivocate about sin. Still, he insisted God had delivered Geneva from the Perrinists and continued to shape Geneva's reformation.

---

[56] Köhler, Zürcher Ehegericht, pp. 587, 589; CR 40: 334–35.
[57] Roset, Chroniques, pp. 315–16 (5.5).
[58] CR 41: 595.

Citizens, according to Calvin, were remarkably fortunate to have been provided with magistrates who so enthusiastically cooperated with their church's reformers. They were God's magistrates and, in a way, God's ministers; to impeach them was out of the question. Prospects for the future, however, were somewhat ambiguous. Would the elect persist in electing honorable, devout, and cooperative syndics or would their choices at the polls disgrace their election and imperil their redemption? Calvin simply could not be sure of the answers; therefore, he could not be an exuberant democrat. He understood that divine election had not completely erased evil. Conceivably the electorate could turn on the consistory, cripple church discipline, and destroy civic order and public peace by selecting treacherous magistrates. There was a need, then, for electoral supervision, and that need created something of a clerical aristocracy. What we might consider civil liberties and religious freedoms, to some extent, were subjected in Geneva to consistorial review and clerical control.[59]

If magistrates were to formulate policy that corresponded to God's laws, pastors must instruct them. If citizens were to nominate and support able, pious magistrates, pastors must counsel and direct them. To say this is not to quarrel with the observation that "massive lay participation" characterized religious reform in Geneva.[60] But it must also be said that the clergy never relinquished their roles as the chief monitors and guarantors of God's new order and that lay gubernatores in the consistory, in Calvin's judgment, were part of the ministry of the church—part of its scriptural and properly reformed administration.

The consistory saw to it that citizens and their elected officials were instructed by their pastors. In many instances, they also saw to it that the instructions were followed. From the start, Calvin made the consistory a distinctive feature of the city's public life. His *Ordinances* gave gubernatores authority to groom the whole community, not simply the faithful members of reformed congregations.[61] Progressively, the consistory became a part of Genevan government, and one might even say the city became a church. The special doctrinal arrangement between election and civic order determined the character of Calvin's redeeming politics, particularly after Calvin and his partisans had chased their enemies from the city.

It is not altogether whimsical to play with possessives and write about "Calvin's consistory" or indeed about "Calvin's Geneva." The reformer,

---

[59] See David Little, *Religion, Order and Law: A Study in Pre-Revolutionary England* (Oxford, 1970), pp. 71–80.

[60] Robert Kingdon, "The Control of Morals by the Earliest Calvinists," in de Klerk, *Renaissance, Reformation, Resurgence*, pp. 95–106.

[61] Köhler, *Zürcher Ehegericht*, pp. 513–14.

after all, brought Protestant sociolatry to blossom; he made Geneva Protestantism's first clerocracy. Calvin himself, however, typically understated his achievement. When one petitioner alleged that the consistory's procedures were unapostolic and that, despite the growing number of disciplinary actions, the gubernatores were not emulating the apostles' rigor, Calvin replied rather temperately and modestly. He recalled how close the consistory had come to extinction during the Perrinist rebellion, and he noted how delicate its job still was. If not optimal and authentically apostolic, the results of reform in his city, he said, were nonetheless agreeable and undeniably redemptive.[62]

[62] Roget, *Histoire* 5: 169–70.

PART THREE

Crisis

My kingship is not of this world; if my kingship were
of this world, my servants would fight that I might not
be handed over to the Jews; but my kingship is not
from this world.
—John 18:36

JESUS' INTERVIEW with Pilate, executor of justice in "this world," was an influential exchange. Confrontations between later martyrs and public authorities bore striking resemblances to it. From Jesus, then, Christians seem to have learned to distinguish redemption from earthly rule. "You say that I am king," Jesus replied to Pilate, who was merely repeating what had been reported to him. Jesus' disclaimer set him straight: "For this I was born and for this I have come into the world, to bear witness to the truth" (John 18:37). The implication is that *the* truth was different from and, for that matter, opposed to politically advantageous truths and libels.

During the second and third centuries, however, Christian apologists occasionally deemphasized the differences. They suggested that Christ's kingship did not imperil arrangements made by emperors and their executors to rule the Mediterranean world. *The* truth, few Christians denied, had forbidden the worship of emperors as gods. Some refused to pay homage to emperors' effigies and suffered for their stubbornness. They showed that their citizenship, like Christ's kingship, was not of this world, and, in some instances, martyrdom hastened their arrival in the next. Martyrs were honored for their steadfast devotion, but among and on behalf of those left behind in this world, apologists continued to assure rulers that Christianity posed no grave threat to their rule, even while alleging that pagan political theologies were profoundly flawed.

Tertullian was a prolific apologist and moralist who lived in the late second and early third centuries. He disputatiously questioned claims made for the pagans' and government's gods. Had prayers for the safety of emperors averted their diseases and deaths? Had prayers for the safety of cities averted their destruction? Imperial Rome's conquests were undeniably impressive, but those conquests, Tertullian recalled, were accompanied by slaughter and sacrilege. And the horror of war, the unending cycle of crime and vengeance, spread impiety throughout the expanding empire. Tertullian thought it crazy to associate all that with religion, any religion.[1] If authorities listened to him at all, they probably dismissed him as a crank. To the end of the second century and through much of the third, deaths, plagues, and political crises were generally offset by conquests that kept Rome and her satellites in power. The government's gods appeared to be performing admirably. It was only later that crises undermined faith in the government's religion, but by that time, the government's religion was Christianity.

Rome was sacked a century after the conversion of Constantine. To prevent a resurgence of paganism in the wake of the humiliation, Augustine, bishop of Hippo Regius in North Africa, echoed Tertullian's argu-

[1] *CSEL* 69: 83–87.

ments. He had to admit the Christians' God was not protecting the empire from its enemies, but he reminded readers of his *City of God* that Rome's old deities had not always protected worshipers from defeats, droughts, famines, and plagues. Those old gods, he said, were unreal, pasteboard deities. The Christians' God was real and sovereign, but reality and sovereignty did not guarantee worshipers would be delivered from every misfortune. In fact, personal and political crises and setbacks were God's ways to instruct the faithful, shake them from complacency, and test their faith. Eusebean triumphalism was ready-made for conquest and the euphoria that followed; crisis called for another recipe. It compelled Augustine to adjust rather than abandon redeeming politics.

Other adjustments punctuate the history of the Christian traditions. Of particular interest are those changes made by the radical reformers of the early sixteenth century, whom until now we have seen only through John Calvin's eyes. The radicals in Switzerland and southern Germany asserted that when Protestants' entered into partnerships with political authorities they retarded the progress of religious reform. What some apologists celebrated as Christianity's great successes, the church's alliance with Constantine and subsequent churches' alliances with the town councils of Zurich, Strasbourg, and Geneva, radical or sectarian Protestants decried as Christianity's great crises. "Friendship with the world is enmity with God" (James 4:4). Dissidents decided to remain unfriendly. Yet those fortunate to escape reprisals in this world actually created new worlds in which the requirements of rule and redemption were consolidated. Hence, they only seemed to forswear redeeming politics. Critics like Augustine and secessionists like Conrad Grebel and Michael Sattler still lived in Constantine's shadow.

Chapter Seven

AUGUSTINE'S CITIES OF GOD

IF WE WANT TO LEARN how the decomposition and recomposition of Christian sociolatry were related to political crisis, the place to start is the monumental *City of God*, which is still Christianity's most influential treatment of piety and politics. Sourcebooks for political theory compress it for student use as if Augustine's tale of two cities (one "at home" on earth and the other on pilgrimage to God) were easier to abridge than Dickens's. The bishop, of course, did not write his *City* for college surveys. It was composed as a sprawling response to the great crisis of the Christian empire, the invasion of Italy and sack of Rome in 410, so Augustine and his text show us quite clearly what happened when defeat and disenchantment left the claims of Christian sociolatry dangerously exposed.

Some of my colleagues have said the *City of God* does away with sociolatry. They contend that Augustine devalued political life and political culture, and there is ample support for their contention.[1] Before the so-called barbarians humiliated Roman soldiers in the very precincts of Rome, most Christians accustomed to Eusebius's triumphalism lived comfortably in Constantine's shadow. The events of 410 shocked them. The tragedy seemed to many to herald the world's end.[2] Nearly inexpressible dismay and disappointment attended the social dislocations occasioned by invaders' raids throughout Italy and the empire's other European territories. Augustine wrote to remind fugitives who crossed to North Africa as well as those Christians who remained behind that their true empire was heaven's everlasting "city," not earth's perishable provinces.[3] Unquestionably, the bishop's reminder set limits to Eusebean triumphalism, but I will argue that it hardly marked the end of Christian sociolatry in late antiquity. We will see that Augustine tried to bend rather than break the enthusiasms generated by Constantine's conversion. The

---

[1] Consult Robert A. Markus, *Saeculum: History and Society in the Age of Saint Augustine*, 2nd ed. (Cambridge, 1988), particularly pp. 43–46, 69–70; Franz Weissengruber, "Zu Augustins Definition des Staates," *Römische historische Mitteilungen* 22 (1980): 31–35; and Charles Norris Cochrane, *Christianity and Classical Culture* (1940; rpt. Oxford, 1980), pp. 509–10.

[2] Otto Zwierlein, "Der Fall Roms im Spiegel der Kirchenväter," *Zeitschrift für Papyrologie und Epigraphik* 32 (1978): 45–49.

[3] CCSL 47: 64–65 (DCD 2.29).

City of God reoriented the redeeming politics of Latin Christendom; it is sociolatry in a new key, adaptable to crisis as well as conquest.

To the extent that Eusebius had conditioned Christians to think of Constantine's conversion as the signal that God intended a consummate and lasting regeneration of political culture, there existed a crisis of confidence in the new but badly bruised Christian empire. Augustine tried to assure that disillusionment would not lead to disaffection, but his task was complicated by the pagan response to the empire's misfortunes. Pagans blamed worshipers of Rome's new Christian God for the city's sack and the empire's losses, and their recriminations blended well with the widespread nostalgia for Rome's old gods that political and military reversals had triggered. Not all pagans flocked to Christianity with Constantine and his heirs. Many remained outside the official religion and seized every opportunity to clamor against the church. Christians were accused when the rains came too often and when they failed to come at all. Learned pagan critics might not have indulged in the polemics of deluge and drought, but early fifth-century defeats could surely be used, Augustine feared, to shake the faith of the faithful. Moreover, by retailing preposterous stories about Christianity's limitless culpability for the latest developments, critics were also likely to incite mobs to violence.[4] Not long before Italy was infested with "barbarians," an unauthorized pagan festival in a village known to Augustine led to the stoning of the local church, the flight of its bishop, and the death of one believer.[5]

The threat of further violence as well as the possibility of disaffection and defections prompted Augustine to answer the pagans' accusations, even as he wrote to console his coreligionists for their losses. The principal battle was against nostalgia. The *City of God* insisted that it was both impossible and undesirable to turn back the clock. The pagans' retelling of Rome's pre-Christian history needed to be demythologized; the critics of the church had fallen prey to their own campaign of misinformation and devoted themselves to the recovery of a past that had never existed. Soon after news of Rome's troubles reached North Africa with the first wave of fugitives, Augustine started his *City* as he would have started a history lesson. In the next seven years, and in ten tendentious volumes, he labored to set the record straight. Polytheism, he argued, had never proved to be a route to peace. Neither republican nor imperial Rome had enjoyed peace while the pagans' gods ruled at the city's altars. Pagans were wrong when they said that wars were shorter and more easily won when their old gods were custodians of Rome's prosperity. All Augustine had to do was recount the long wars and the military catastrophes that

---

[4] *CCSL* 47: 36 (*DCD* 2.3).
[5] *CSEL* 34: 432–33.

predated the conversion of Constantine.[6] Still, the bishop probably despaired of convincing the ruffians (*ineruditorum turbae*) chiefly responsible for the violence against Christians; he planned the initial ten books of his *City* to persuade ringleaders who might yet listen to reason. Perhaps he hoped that learned critics would come to accept the ahistoricity of their idealization of Rome's past and then renounce their intense prejudices against Christianity. Perhaps his unremitting assault on nostalgia had other objectives as well. Whatever the case, the author's strategy reinforces the impression that the *City* was also an assault on Christian sociolatry because the *City* deflated myths about Rome's pre-Christian political culture in a way that suggested the debasement of all political culture.

The best evidence for the bishop's alleged debasement of political leadership and public service may well be his remarks on Sallust's assessment of political morality. Sallust, the first governor of Africa Nova, had declared that fear was the source of public virtue. Citizens and their governments, he said, behaved commendably only when confronted by an external enemy or when they realized that injustices, resulting grievances, and lingering antagonisms weakened their cities' defenses. This made complete sense to Augustine.[7] He admitted that from time to time Rome had been blessed with bold and resourceful leaders; no history lesson, however iconoclastic its intent, dared omit the triumphs of inspirational soldiers and Caesars. Nonetheless, he carefully distinguished between the desire for fame, which spurred pagan warriors and politicians to defend their territories and to annex those of their neighbors, and the admirable passion for immortality that animated Christian martyrs and saints. The bishop staged the comparison to make the desire for reputation appear crude and ignoble, and at one point he held that the difference between eminent politicians and petty criminals was one of scale or degree. A Caesar's vast navy made him no less a pirate than the blackguard who wrought havoc on the high seas with a single boat.[8]

Censorious statements of this kind are the ingredients for a substantial case against sociolatry, and tales of political treachery are scattered through the *City of God*'s first ten books. Furthermore, the remaining twelve books develop the distinction between the corruptible terrestrial city and the glorious city of God in terms selected specifically to discountenance Eusebius. Augustine dramatized the distinction by splitting humanity into two societies at the very beginning of the fifteenth book. The

---

[6] CCSL 47: 158–59 (DCD 5.22).

[7] CCSL 47: 48–50 (DCD 2.18).

[8] CCSL 47: 101–2 (DCD 4.4). For a discussion of the *City*'s brief against pagan passions and arrogance, see Klaus Thraede, "Das antike Rom in Augustins De civitate Dei," *Jahrbuch für Antike und Christentum* 20 (1977): 119–20, 139–45.

first was fathered by Cain, who, according to Genesis, established a city. Augustine admitted that to speak of either of his two societies as a city was to speak metaphorically, yet he boasted scriptural warrant for the application of political imagery to Cain's kind.[9] Abel, Cain's brother and victim, built no city. Abel was a prototypical pilgrim, whose part in history was to suffer rather than rule. Early in Genesis, then, the politician squared off against the pilgrim, who was bested in the conflict. Cain's terrestrial city grew and prospered, and the righteous were tempted to join it. Floods of superstitions washed over the next generations of pilgrims, and many were carried into the terrestrial city. The city of God on earth, however, was never wholly depopulated. Faith in God's promise of an everlasting kingdom sustained pilgrims who resisted the currents that dragged others from one compromise to the next along the route to worldly power and success.[10]

Augustine's pilgrim city intrigues scholars, although scholarly discussion usually adjourns before any consensus has been reached. Whether or not, and in what ways the pilgrim city prefigures the church are questions of long-standing importance in the history of the Christian traditions. Attempts to answer them still spark controversy. Yet, whatever Abel is said to represent, no controversy surrounds Cain; most readers consider him the progenitor of political culture.[11] Cain, after all, founded a city, and Augustine's *City of God* caged timid citizens and grand Caesars into that society of the selfish and the damned, from which few escaped in this life and none in the next. Was this terrestrial city assembled deliberately to libel political culture? Some would say so, but I think otherwise.

If we read the *City of God* closely, we find most of what was written about Cain's kind applies equally well to the vast majority of humankind, governors and governed. Augustine charged that citizens of the earthly city were preoccupied with goods that gave immediate gratification. When we claim that politicians alone are Cain's heirs, we blame the pursuit of political authority for sins that, according to Augustine, most persons of his time were busy committing most of their time.

Circumstantial evidence allows only a provisional coupling of Cain's city with the political cultures of late antiquity. Recall, for instance, that political crisis impelled Augustine to compose his text, that pagans had accused Christians of failing the empire. It was said that Christians deprived Rome's trustworthy gods of citizens' adoration. Christian church

[9] CCSL 48: 453–54 (DCD 15.1).

[10] CCSL 48: 494 (DCD 15.26), 521–13 (DCD 16.10).

[11] For controversies over the identity of the pilgrim city, see Yves Congar, "Civitas Dei et Ecclesia chez saint Augustin," Revue des études Augustiniennes 3 (1957): 1–14. Also consult Jean-Claude Guy, Unité et structure logique de la "Cité de Dieu" de saint Augustin (Paris, 1961), particularly pp. 89–93, 112, 116–20.

officials were suspected of beguiling Rome's trusted leaders, who fool-
ishly permitted hostile tribes to settle within Rome's frontiers. Generals
steadily gave ground to intruders. Hadrian all but withdrew from the
East, much to the Persians' advantage and delight. Augustine accepted
parts of this description of decline, explaining, however, that his God had
arranged the setbacks for a purpose. In a sermon preached just after the
capital's humiliation, he went on to argue that the calamities had been
divinely ordained and orchestrated to show how unstable the world's successes and pleasures actually were. Augustine decreed, moreover, that
God had planned the empire's most recent political crisis as a test. Prosperity made Christians complacent; adversity put faith under fire. The fall
of Rome was a furnace in which gold and dross were separated. Patient
Christians, for whom tribulation was training (*exercitatio*), proved themselves pious pilgrims by relinquishing their political ambitions and by
clinging tenaciously to God's promises of eternal rewards.[12]

Augustine's lecture on God's smelting met both his apologetic objectives. First, he explained to pagans why God's assent to and complicity in
Rome's misfortunes did not justify their accusations against God's vigilance. The Christian God was the watchful caretaker of Christians' souls,
but the Christian God had never promised to guard cities besieged by
enemies. Pagan nostalgia was based on a calculated misreading of history
and on the naive belief of some poets in an empire without end (*imperium
sine fine*).[13] The second objective was equally important to Augustine. He
repeatedly reassured refugees that their truest sovereign placed their
properties and persons in peril in order to redeem their souls. God's
smelting, as Augustine depicted it, made sense of their suffering.[14]

But the *City* is not simply Christian apology. It is an extended sermon
exposing preoccupations that kept Cain's heirs from becoming pilgrims.
The crisis of contemporary political culture provided Augustine a splendid contrast when he juxtaposed perishable political cultures with the
eternal kingdom that awaited citizens who placed their mourning in the
context of their faith, as pilgrims should. Their faith, in a sense, booked
them passage to a realm unrivaled by any found on earth, yet the faith of
many seemed rivaled by their concerns for the kingdoms, dioceses, estates, and freedoms the barbarians had taken from them. The bishop's
real target in the *City*'s later books was insatiable and uncontrollable lust
for mastery and glory. Augustine unambiguously associated that lust with
political culture and with the political life of late antiquity. Nevertheless,
he far more frequently and unequivocally identified it as the defect that

[12] CCSL 46: 260–62.
[13] PL 38: 622–23.
[14] Zwierlein, "Fall Roms," pp. 56–65.

fettered most citizens to their worst instincts and enslaved them to their grief for losses that were, on the whole, quite inconsequential.[15]

The *City of God* is not a direct and deliberate attack on Christian sociolatry. Political history galvanized Augustine's lessons about sin and salvation that made the history of recent mishaps meaningful sub specie aeternitatis. It was sin and salvation that most concerned the bishop. He held that faithful citizens of the pilgrim city could still know themselves as a "holy city of God." Their response to tragedy, their perseverance and unflinching desire for eternal life, were unmistakable signs of God's grace, compassion, and purpose.[16] God kept the pilgrim city on course. As long as pilgrims were alive, subject to grief and temptation, their will to subordinate sorrow and self-love to their love for and trust in God was the surest indication of God's will to save their souls. Augustine acknowledged pilgrims would still experience sorrow and fear, but those jolting feelings should only increase their diligence against sin. Citizens of that other city, however, were so shaken by their sufferings that they lived feverishly, with confusion, and without peace.[17]

Augustine suggested, almost as an afterthought, that some of the unrighteous exercised greater self-control than others. He found that these exceptional citizens of Cain's city were indifferent to everything around them, but the bishop held no brief for this kind of equanimity. The battle between self-love and the love of God was not one that could be avoided or contemplated away in some philosophically induced narcosis, any more than history could be dissolved by dreams of eternity. God staged political crisis, according to Augustine, to fortify and refocus human will, to recall it to obedience during its pilgrimage in time.

Augustine's afterthought and much of what he wrote in the second half of the *City* suggest that he wanted to forge a weapon in the battle for the human will. Though his cities originated with biblical figures, Augustine maintained that those cities were regularly reconstituted in the postbiblical age by human choice. Some elected to live according to the standards of the flesh. Others chose to live by the standard of the spirit.[18] Even when it had been identified, the correct choice could not be made easily, Augustine explained, because Adam's sin crippled human will. That primordial crime resulted in the phenomenon of the divided self, an emotional conflict that continued to plague would-be pilgrims. Hence he urged readers to accept God's grace and God's governance and to stay within the pil-

---

[15] *CCSL* 48: 460–61 (*DCD* 15.7).

[16] *CCSL* 48: 426 (*DCD* 14.9). Cf. Reinhart Maurer, "Thesen zur politischen Theologie: Augustinische Tradition and heutige Probleme," *Zeitschrift für Theologie und Kirche* 79 (1982): 349–51.

[17] *CCSL* 48: 429–30 (*DCD* 14.9).

[18] *CCSL* 48: 414 (*DCD* 14.1).

grim city: to love God and neighbor, to endure disappointment patiently and with undiminished faith in divine sovereignty and benevolence, and to yearn for the consolations of faith, which restored the will to obedience.[19]

The *City* is a collection of stories and scriptural passages accumulated principally to repair Christian confidence and to teach Christians what they should expect (and should not expect) of God's sovereignty over history. The choices those Christians had to make would reconstitute Augustine's cities of God, so the *City* was composed to dramatize their options and, as it happened, to reify the two fields of force that shaped Christians' longings and influenced their decisions. Augustine vividly depicted the tension between those two fields, yet he nowhere seems to have encouraged readers to run from the tension, to closet themselves and collect dust as if the end of Christian triumphalism were an excuse for inaction. Peter Brown is quite right: "The *City of God*, far from being a book about flight from the world . . . is a book about being otherworldly in the world."[20]

What does this appraisal mean for the evaluation of political culture? As we noted, Augustine conscientiously exposed the frauds that braced classical political teleology and pagans' hopes for an empire without end. Such disclosures were part of his polemic against his church's critics and their ways of rewriting history. It was another thing altogether—and it certainly would have been a trickier assignment—to repeal and permanently proscribe political optimism and to alter radically Christians' understanding of God's interventions in the empire's history. Eusebius's Constantine could not be purged from the church's self-presentation, or even demoted, without considerable consequence. Had Augustine wanted to unleash a frontal assault on Christian sociolatry, he would have had to edit the current stories of Constantine's piety and prosperity. Instead, he repeated what other apologists had said about the first Christian emperor. Albeit quickly and without much fanfare, he inventoried evidence usually cited to attest God's approval of Constantine's government. He singled out the emperor's designs for a new capital city, where pagan worship was purportedly forbidden. He seemed to agree with previous eulogists that the new regime and the new city signaled that history had been given a fresh start, yet he was more restrained than Eusebius.[21] Restraint, after all, was reasonable, inasmuch as the intervening century had failed to supply Christian sociolatry with material from which a record of uninterrupted good fortune could be narratively constructed. Au-

[19] See, e.g., *CCSL* 48: 421–23 (*DCD* 14.6–7).

[20] Peter Brown, *Augustine of Hippo* (Berkeley, 1967), pp. 319, 323.

[21] *CCSL* 47: 160–61 (*DCD* 5.25).

gustine, however, did *not* hold that the failure necessitated a root-and-branch reassessment of Constantine's mission and achievement.[22]

Augustine readily, almost eagerly, conceded that developments during the fourth century made it impossible to sustain the triumphalists' unconditional optimism for the new Christian empire. Eusebius's more ecstatic pronouncements must have sounded as hollow as the pronouncements of pagan poets who thought that the *pax Romana* would forever crown Aeneas's victories. Neither Eusebius nor Virgil, however, could be utterly dismissed. They exerted too formidable an influence on Augustine's perspective, and several passages in the *City of God* show that their enthusiasms occasionally got the better of the bishop's restraint. At the end of the eighteenth book, for example, Augustine mocked the pagan prophets who had predicted Christianity's disappearance. Oracles had decreed that the new official religion would not survive beyond the year 365. But Augustine boasted that in that very year the emperor's deputies purged Carthage of pagan worship. No doubt, the parallel with Constantine and his new capital came to mind, yet Augustine was too wrapped in the irony and in his defiance of pagan prophecy to linger for another history lesson. The worship of Christ, he noted, had increased from 365 to the time of his writing. And more could be expected. The psalmist was a much more reliable prophet than the pagans' oracles when he assured Christian exegetes that Christ would "have dominion from sea to sea . . . to the ends of the earth."[23]

For a moment, then, Augustine was just as optimistic and cheerful as the Christian triumphalists had been. But, unlike them, he had to explain hardships, betrayals, and wicked officials—all the stresses and strains of the Christian empire. He tried a novel approach. He argued that the sincerity of politicians would be suspect if every Christian emperor had been rewarded as was Constantine, or every apostasy promptly punished. Magistrates would than have been tempted to convert to Christianity or to uphold the church's liberties for the wrong reasons. The *City* is a book about expectations: both those that impart a false sense of security and those that hold inner peace and eternal reward as the genuine objectives of the Christian life. Only the latter could make the magistrate or, for that matter, any citizen a pilgrim. Augustine's point was simple: uncertainties authenticated God's control over history, for they guaranteed that conversions would not be based on prudence, greed, or ambition.[24]

That the disjunction between personal piety and political success strikes at some of sociolatry's claims cannot be denied, although that

[22] See Johannes Straub, "Augustins Sorge um die *regeneratio imperii*: Das *Imperium Romanum* als *civitas terrena*," *Historisches Jahrbuch* 73 (1954): 53–57.

[23] CCSL 48: 571–72 (DCD 17.8), 653–56 (DCD 18.54).

[24] CCSL 47: 160 (DCD 5.24).

seems not to have been Augustine's purpose. The bishop was faced with a dilemma; having accused others of falsifying history, he was unlikely to get away with conspicuous omissions. Readers would remember that Emperor Julian reinstated Rome's old gods and that Emperor Theodosius's record was far from immaculate. More to the point, perhaps, Augustine composed his *City* during the empire's most profound crisis. He could not honorably ascribe permanence to the *pax Romana*, to the Christian empire, or to any particular political culture, no matter how pious the politicians. Yet, as far as Augustine could tell, Constantine placed one change beyond the possibility of reversal. The Christian empire survived the first waves of invasions in the fifth century; strictly speaking, Rome did not fall—it did not even fall into the hands of the empire's enemies in 410. The barbarians came but they soon moved on. Earlier misfortunes, particularly Julian's brief pagan revival, could still be taken as interruptions. Christianity endured and quickly recaptured Rome. For Augustine, the change that was beyond change was the conversion of political culture. Magistrates might not yet be steadfastly loyal to the church. Measures for the eradication of idolatry and heresy might not yet be enforced with appropriate vigor, but God, according to Augustine, had given clear indications that the time had arrived for the persecutors of Christianity to become persecutors *for* Christianity.[25]

To understand why Augustine valued certain remnants of Eusebean sociolatry, we must reconsider problems peculiar to the North African church. From 312, dissidents, subsequently known as Donatists, had organized churches in nearly every community. They claimed that established churches had been defiled because authorities permitted sinful members to mingle with the sinless, yet the Donatists' original grievance, which carried weight to the end of the fourth century, was that church authorities themselves could be numbered among the sinful. During the long period of persecution that preceded Constantine's conversion and conquests, some bishops frequently handed over the Christians' sacred texts to hostile imperial officials. And those same bishops retained authority after peace was restored. Some of their equally culpable fellow conspirators were named to succeed them. If innocent Christians continued to mix with these soiled bishops and with bishops and priests whom they consecrated, the contagion would spread. To guard against contamination, Donatists insisted that the unsoiled separate themselves.[26]

One suspects that disagreements about the source and perpetuation of pollution could have been composed, or at least contained, without involving government powers, but one schism led to another. The record of

[25] CCSL 47: 104 (*DCD* 4.7), 162 (*DCD* 5.26); 48: 648 (*DCD* 18.50).
[26] E.g., *CSEL* 53: 66–67.

confusion in North Africa, even the account of quarrels among Donatists in Numidia, would run to many thousands of pages. Augustine, however, was less interested in description than reconciliation, and he pinned his hopes for peace on the authority of Christian emperors and their deputies. Augustine's confidence in the government increased during the second decade of the fifth century, just at the time he was contemplating and then composing the *City of God*.

In North Africa, only the civil government remained to pull things together. Augustine's colleagues and allies were powerless to prevent further disintegration, and the Donatists could not keep their ranks in order. Augustine predictably turned Donatist disunity to his advantage. He pointed out that the Donatists were condemning one another in his time much as their ancestors had condemned Caecilian, bishop of Carthage, at the start of the schism. The charges against Caecilian, he said, were manifestly unfair, and his accusers were wrong to discount rulings that vindicated the accused. Augustine then related the origins of Donatist dissent to the internecine disputes that divided Donatism many decades later, whereby the accusers' heirs experienced the same kind of injustice from their Christian brothers as Caecilian endured from his. Yet the danger of disunity was not confined to Donatism. One schism had turned into several, and the disharmony threatened to tear to shreds the whole fabric of North African Christianity.[27]

Donatist extremists were most responsible for the growing problem. They had taken to intimidating rival bishops and their patrons. Several of Augustine's close associates had been victimized by malcontents and vagabonds who occasionally attached themselves to the Donatist cause, if not the Donatist church.[28] Augustine chronicled the violence and presumably exaggerated it to embarrass Donatist moderates who were still willing to debate him. But the debates yielded few converts, and although the instances of intimidation and savagery helped Augustine make his case against Donatist intemperance, he increasingly feared for the safety of his church. He also suspected that leading Donatist officials either encouraged or sanctioned the extremists' tactics. Augustine's apparent inability to persuade his opponents with eloquence and argument as well as the

[27] *CCSL* 38: 367. For Augustine's other references to the Maximianist schism, see A. C. de Veer, "L'exploitation du schisme maximianiste par S. Augustin dans sa lutte contre le Donatisme," *Recherches augustiniennes* 3 (1965): 219–37.

[28] For Augustine's catalogue of the crimes of the Circumcellions and for the general contention that "l'Afrique fut le théâtre d'une agitation sociale relativement organisée" between 380 and 400, see Jean-Paul Brisson, *Autonisme et christianisme dans l'Afrique romaine* (Paris, 1958), particularly pp. 331–41; but also note W.H.C. Frend, *The Donatist Church*, 3rd ed. (Oxford, 1985), pp. 171–77; and Emin Tengstrom, *Donatisten und Katholiken: Soziale, wirtschaftliche und politische Aspekte einer nordafrikanischen Kirchenspaltung* (Göteborg, 1964), pp. 43–52, 71–78.

persistence of violence induced him to endorse, reluctantly, his colleagues' petitions for imperial assistance and for coercive measures
against their rivals.

Admonitions that Augustine first offered from the pulpit were easily
adapted to justify government intervention in religious disputes. Government officials, at the very least, should be dutiful Christians, and dutiful
Christians were obliged to bring errant clergy and laymen—lost shep-
herds and lost sheep—back to Catholic Christianity. If Christian politicians were silent, they would seem to approve the schism. If they approved the schism, they incurred God's wrath.[29]

In their successive councils of Carthage, Augustine's colleagues could
appeal to such logic as well as to the tradition of imperial concern for the
realm's religious unity. For some time, government officials had been the
church's champions. Periodically they passed laws against the Donatists,
who were spared only because political conditions occasionally made enforcement difficult.[30] From 401, North African bishops petitioned for
new, more stringent prohibitions against their rivals' worship. They also
asked that old restrictions be enforced more scrupulously. After some
hesitation, Augustine consented to join the campaign and then to lead it.
He had once argued that religious conviction could not be coerced, and
moderate Donatists, surprised by the apparent change, scolded him for
trampling upon his own convictions as well as for summoning the government to legislate against theirs. As often and as contemptuously as
Augustine had called to mind the offenses of violent extremists, some
Donatists could not believe that rare incidents of that kind could have
swayed their opponent so suddenly. Vincent of Cartenna wrote Augustine in 408 requesting an explanation.

Augustine's reply opens with a staggering claim. He admitted that his
allies' appeals to the government once seemed ill-advised to him. At the
time, he did not think that divine compassion could work through coercion. But Augustine now declared that his assumptions about God's work
in the world had been mistaken. Donatist apostates who rejoined his colleagues' churches expressed their gratitude effusively. Their thanks for
the political pressures used to pry them from their puritanical sect persuaded Augustine that God had no compunctions about using the force
of law and the threat of punishment to prevent Christians from falling
further into sin.[31]

---

[29] PL 38: 278–80.

[30] See Ernst Ludwig Grasmück, *Coercitio: Staat und Kirche im Donatistenstreit* (Bonn,
1964), pp. 195–97.

[31] CSEL 34: 445–46. Augustine also claimed that Vincent had no right to fuss. The Donatists, he said, were the first to appeal to political authorities. They developed their aversion
to imperial intervention only after Constantine and his heirs refused to credit Donatist ar-

Augustine built a theology of persecution with inferences drawn from the apostates' gratitude. Cruelty, he agreed, had no place in official policy or religious conversion, but if authorities had been moved by mercy or pity, moved *ex caritate*, to rescue errant Christians from their errors, Augustine now saw God's hand in the matter. Donatists, of course, perceived things differently. They made a virtue of their outcast status. From their perspective, Christianity had no room for ruling elites; authentic Christians always suffered for their faith—blessed were the persecuted. Augustine, however, would not allow the identification of suffering with righteousness to stand unchallenged. He argued that the persecuted were not always servants of God and that persecutors were not uniformly God's enemies. With consummate skill, he deployed relevant biblical verses to make and illustrate his point. To the objection that it was wrong and wicked to coerce free will, he responded that free will was chimerical. To Donatists who either blamed Catholic bishops and government officials for coercing those appreciative apostates or ridiculed them for believing that a sincere and lasting faith could actually be coerced into existence, Augustine replied that persecution and coercion were not the direct and intrusive causes of conversion. Persecution and coercion merely prompted former Donatists to contemplate their leaders' crimes and their own misconceptions. Such contemplation then led to genuine repentance and a spontaneous profession of faith. Augustine claimed that the government acted responsibly. Measures taken to restore property confiscated by Donatists were evenhanded, and measures to outlaw the worship of schismatics were pious political efforts to restore order, unity, and charity to the churches of North Africa.[32]

Some Donatists acknowledged that their party had asked for government intervention during the early stages of the quarrel with Caecilian. They denied, however, that Constantine or his deputies had issued a final verdict.[33] Augustine effectively challenged their misreading of the documentary evidence, yet he was more interested in emphasizing Donatist resistance to the idea of a Christian empire. Notwithstanding their first appeals for government arbitration, Donatists refused to recognize Constantine's conversion as a divine ruling on the legitimacy and usefulness

---

guments and started to legislate in favor of their rivals. Augustine often reiterated his claims and made it impossible for his adversaries to tiptoe around documentary evidence of early Donatist petitions in the dossier compiled by Optatus, former bishop of Milevis. See, for instance, *CSEL* 26: 25–27 for Optatus's narrative report; Hubert Cancik, "Augustin als constantinischer Theologe," in *Der Fürst dieser Welt*, ed Jacob Taubes (Munich, 1983), pp. 142–43, 148; Thraede, "Antike Rom," pp. 137–38; Maurer, "Thesen," pp. 355–57; and Grasmück, *Coercitio*, pp. 202–22.

[32] *CSEL* 34: 493–94.
[33] *CSEL* 53: 89–90.

of imperial political culture. They refused to obey the laws passed by emperors and circulated by their deputies, refused to accept that diligent public officials were God's ensigns and champions of the church. Could such refusals, Augustine wondered, amount to anything other than sedition?[34]

Had Augustine sought a compelling illustration for his argument, he could not have found one better than the Donatists furnished during the last decade of the fourth century. At that time, some leading Donatists openly supported enemies of the Roman empire in North Africa, and the Donatist bishop of Thamugadi was eventually executed as a rebel. Augustine labored in his letters to present the Donatists as a violent and dangerous faction. At hand he had evidence that would surely impress Emperor Honorius, relatively fresh evidence of Donatist subversion and treachery. He pressed Honorius to renew the partnership between the government and the church—the Catholic church—to rid North Africa of secessionists, both political and religious.[35]

There should be no secession from the kingdom that God had given the Christians; nor could there be much doubt that the Roman empire was that kingdom. To be sure, the empire was not the heavenly city walled off, so to speak, from history. But it answered to the psalmist's prophecy that Christ would have dominion "from sea to sea . . . to the ends of the earth." Augustine repeated the psalmist's assurances in his *City of God*, perhaps because they had assumed such a prominent role in his anti-Donatist polemic. The Donatists said that the New Testament yielded no examples of Christian rulers. Augustine countered that Scripture predicted and promised a new dispensation in which emperors would collaborate with their bishops to spread the true religion to every corner of the known world. What else could the psalmist have meant? Notwithstanding their foothold in North Africa and popularity in Numidia, the Donatists were fools to presume that their church was the sole descendant of the first church in Jerusalem, while Christians elsewhere languished in sin. Christianity started with a small assembly of committed believers, Augustine admitted, but it had spread, as promised, throughout the Mediterranean world and beyond. He scoffed at the idea that Christianity must remain small and politically disadvantaged because it started that way. God had seen to the church's growth. The universal empire had abetted Christianity's progress even before Constantine's conversion. Now that the Catholic church prospered, now that emperors and their officials, as its champions, belonged to the church, to mistrust the psalmist's forecast was inexcusable.[36]

[34] See Brisson, *Autonisme*, pp. 268–69, 288.
[35] Cf. Frend, *The Donatist Church*, pp. 224–26 and Tengstrom, *Donatisten*, pp. 84–86.
[36] E.g., *CSEL* 34: 516–20; 52: 585–86.

To dispel doubts and defend the degree of universality achieved by the Catholic church against provincial and sectarian Donatists, Augustine fitfully pushed his arguments to the frontiers of Eusebean triumphalism. Hence, even as he composed the first books of his *City*, he was checking the ties between political culture and providence, pleading with authorities in North Africa to make plain and incontestable the emperor's will. For his part, he would continue to explain God's will and to demonstrate that the two wills were one.

The shock of—and aftershocks from—Rome's collapse in 410 did not tempt Augustine to dissolve the partnership between church and government, probably because imperial officials in North Africa had not been immobilized by developments on the Italian peninsula; they still used their authority to assist Augustine and his colleagues against the Donatists. Moreover, Augustine's friend Marcellinus had been sent from the imperial chancery to convene and preside over a much-heralded council in Carthage. Six hundred North African bishops descended on the city for the three sessions in June 411. The Donatists' involvement in the insurrections suppressed years before led to some deterioration in their position, but they still held a slight numerical edge at the conference. Their numbers, however, did not count for much. Marcellinus made critical procedural decisions during the third session that prepared the way for a final judgment favoring Augustine and his party. The Donatists insisted that their rivals, as accusers, either substantiate or drop their charges against Donatus and his heirs. But Marcellinus resolved that the Donatists' charges against Caecilian were at issue. They had to prove their century-old case or else stand justly accused of having originated and perpetuated the accursed schism.[37]

Augustine had won. Catholic cooperation with the authorities turned out to be highly advantageous. Emperor Honorius repealed a previous edict of toleration, perhaps to lure Donatists to the negotiations by giving them a greater stake in the results. (Honorius's preemptive action made them outlaws again; they could only improve their standing.) Marcellinus circulated the emperor's call for the council and added incentives of his own. He promised that Donatist bishops who attended would be allowed to hold their positions until the council's debates were adjourned. All this occurred after Rome is said to have fallen. And from the time Emperor Honorius acceded to Augustine's request for the council to the moment Marcellinus delivered his verdict, the outcome was certain.

The council's effect on Augustine can hardly be overstressed. He so admired Marcellinus that he dedicated the *City of God* to him, and Mar-

---

[37] For a slice of the Donatists' strategy, see *Actes de la conférence de Carthage en 411*, ed. Serge Lancel, vol. 3 (Paris, 1975), 1138–40. Also note Alberto Pincherle, *Vita di Sant'Agostino* (Rome, 1980), pp. 313–16, 360–64, and Cancik, "Augustin," pp. 146–50.

cellinus's honorable and shrewd management of the affair was featured prominently in the bishop's several accounts of the deliberations. If Augustine had been disillusioned by the apparent ease with which Rome capitulated in 410, he was reassured by the empire's effectiveness in bringing the Donatists to heel in 411. Of course, Augustine still produced illustrations of the empire's vulnerability in the *City*, illustrations quite compatible with the book's aim. Disappointments and defects associated with the finest political cultures were symptomatic of the impermanence of all worldly gain and glory. The disappointments and defects were drawn from fact and overdrawn for effect, because Augustine was persuaded that ambitions for gain and glory deflected Christians from the whole-hearted worship of their God. The crisis of 410, the grand empire's political and military disgrace, was an excellent example of how the mighty might fall. Nonetheless, given the course of the Donatist controversy, we can see why the crisis did not place at risk Augustine's trust in the premises that had steadied Christian sociolatry for generations. The crisis simply compelled the bishop of Hippo to make adjustments that would keep the premises sturdy.[38]

It is reasonable to assume that Augustine influenced his amanuensis Orosius, who found it possible to sustain both the optimism and the triumphalism of earliest Christian sociolatry. Orosius probably heard Augustine reiterate the psalmist's prophecy, and he heard from others that intruders in Italy were converting to Christianity. He came to believe that Rome's religion would ultimately conquer the conquerors of Rome, that the empire would rebound from its recent setbacks, and that the Christian kingdom, "from sea to sea," would soon exercise greater authority than ever before. But Orosius's expectations outdistanced those of Augustine, who dared not hope for a deliverance of that amplitude.[39]

Despite his triumphs over the Donatists at the Council of Carthage and thereafter, Augustine was no triumphalist. We shall see that the *City of God*, making its adjustments, actually took the triumphalism out of Christian sociolatry. But this does not mean that the Christian empire was an inconsequential part of Augustine's political vision. All that we have found thus far suggests the contrary. But Giovanni Garilli many years ago proposed that Augustine was partial to polyarchy and that the *City of God* reflected his fondness for the peaceable kingdoms that circled the Mediterranean before Rome obliterated their boundaries and suppressed regional autonomy.[40] As Garilli pointed out, the *City* speaks well of the

---

[38] See Grasmück's conclusion in *Coercitio*, p. 249.

[39] Consult, in this connection, Theodor F. Mommsen, *Medieval and Renaissance Studies*, ed. Eugene F. Rice, Jr. (Ithaca, 1959), pp. 265–98, 325–48.

[40] Giovanni Garilli, *Aspetti della filosofia giuridica politica e sociale di S. Agostino* (Milan, 1957), pp. 174–76.

way things were before imperial expansion, but it also notes that the failure of many kingdoms to keep the peace gave Rome the chance to expand. Augustine harbored no regrets; he told the Donatists that the universal empire made possible universal religion. It enabled Christianity to fulfill the psalmist's promises, promises incompatible with polyarchy. Had Augustus and his heirs not tamed the disruptive, cannibalizing tendencies that characterized tribal political life, Christianity could not have spread as quickly and efficiently as it did. On the issues of polyarchy and political pluralism, then, Augustine agreed with Eusebius, and his remarks prefigured Dante's more detailed analysis of the problems that beset a world without world monarchy. Augustine did not begrudge Rome's expansion, yet he was not mortified by its more recent contraction. In his estimation of the political problems and religious prospects of his time, continued expansion and contraction were not mutually exclusive.[41]

The place of this paradox in Augustine's program for the rehabilitation of Christian confidence is an important one. It helped Augustine accommodate the traditional themes of Christian sociolatry to historical crisis. If we eavesdrop on him as he consoles his colleague Hesychius, a bishop in Dalmatia, we hear how cleverly he works.

Hesychius had written to tell Augustine that Europe's side of the Mediterranean was in turmoil. The empire's distress was so great that the psalmist's prophecy afforded him no encouragement. He even speculated that the promise to extend Christ's dominion "from sea to sea" referred only to the apostles' preaching during the first century, not to some future condition; for Hesychius believed that the empire's military disasters doomed Christianity's chances for global influence.

Augustine first tried to avoid the implications of Rome's disasters. He informed Hesychius that the empire's authority in North Africa was expanding even while it was contracting in Europe. In North Africa, he said, Rome's soldiers were annexing new territories and new tribes. Peoples who had never heard of Christ were adopting Christianity. But fresh conquests were not enough to calm Hesychius, who predicted the end of all civilization, so Augustine introduced observations that would have seemed paradoxical to apologists like Orosius, addicted to the intoxicating political prognoses of previous Christian sociolatry. Augustine alleged that Christianity might expand even if the empire contracted. He suggested that the beleaguered empire was not God's only instrument for the spread of Christ's kingdom. Recent crises indicated that history had turned against Rome, yet history would never turn against Christianity. Augustine told Hesychius that peoples beyond the empire's frontiers had joined the new religion in the past and, he advised, others would join as

---

[41] CCSL 47: 111 (DCD 4.15); 48: 643–44 (DCD 18.46).

the frontiers receded. Even if the empire's new North African acquisitions failed to compensate for European losses and were themselves lost, Christians would be foolish to lose hope.[42]

Triumphalists once considered Rome's Christian empire the culmination of history, but that would no longer do. True, Romans had been agents of divine retribution. They flattened the temple in Jerusalem and razed the Jewish kingdom soon after the Jews scorned Jesus. After the conversion of Constantine, emperors shielded the church from its enemies. Honorius and Marcellinus came to Augustine's aid and put the Donatists in their place. The memories of Rome's many services need not be effaced, yet after 410, triumphalism and self-congratulation seemed untimely and excessive. Recent misadventures and misfortune made older expressions of Christian sociolatry obsolete and historically naive.

History reminded Augustine that political culture was a human phenomenon. Because humans and human societies were invariably torn by conflicting desires, justice could only be administered imperfectly. The best motives, the most prudently codified laws, often produced unwanted consequences. Enmity, dread, and anxiety were inextinguishable, despite apologists' energetic efforts to paper over political culture's inadequacies with triumphalist pronouncements.[43] Augustine did not dodge the implications of his darker view of political life (which was an extension of his understanding of the human condition after Adam's fall and without God's grace). Having formulated the darker view, however, he also offered a personalist platform for the renewal of political culture. The Christian empire was not God's only instrument and it was not a perfect instrument, but the empire had been serviceable. And, from Augustine's perspective, there were still services to be performed—recalcitrant Donatists, for instance, to be retrieved.

Augustine's personalist platform was built on admonitions, injunctions, and exhortations, the immediate objective of which was to mend and maintain the coalition between leading prelates and politicians. The ultimate objective was to rehabilitate the redeeming politics of the Christian empire so that the government might continue to help Christianity win its battles for the human will.

The *City of God* grants that the government must order citizens' lives if the church is successfully to reorder their passions and expectations. Inconstant and uncooperative public officials stymied the church's work, so Augustine urged them to reform and to oblige their bishops.[44] He also suggested that persons of proven piety be appointed to important govern-

---

[42] *CSEL* 57: 277–78, 284–85.
[43] *CCSL* 47: 55 (*DCD* 2.21); 48: 578 (*DCD* 17.13), 684 (*DCD* 19.17).
[44] *CCSL* 47: 64 (*DCD* 2.29); 48: 680–81 (*DCD* 19.14).

ment posts. He trusted their piety would prevent them from taking pride in their talents and promotions and that they would constitute a spectacular demonstration of the power of Christian virtue to withstand ambition and avarice.[45] While the Donatists harped on those blessings that God promised to the persecuted, Augustine blessed the government's peacemakers (*beati pacifici*), who were committed to preserving the religious character of political culture, saving the church from squalls generated by local rivalries, and protecting the church in North Africa from Vandal invaders.[46]

Augustine's pastoral concern was beyond compromise and thus, in a sense, beyond politics. As Gerhart Ladner remarked, he wanted to include "ever larger areas of human terrestrial life in the idea and reality of reform."[47] This goal prompted Augustine to pitch Christian sociolatry in a new key. Oughts and exhortations replaced triumphalists' inflated claims, lyrical descriptions, and sunny forecasts. We might say that Augustine's sociolatry was deliberately studded with subjunctives, for the bishop used the rhetoric of personal reform to address the political and religious crises of his time. He wanted to create "a spiritual earthly city" somewhere between Cain's kind and the perfected city of God. He not only encouraged politicians to greater displays of piety; he also tried to shape a political culture for that spiritual earthly city that would produce the most auspicious environment for Christians to make the choices he would have them make.[48]

Christians' political choices were limited. Augustine prohibited civil disobedience, and he counted on government, even tyrannical government, to keep the peace until the pilgrims remaining on earth could be redeemed at the end of time. The *City of God* seems to end on this note, so Peter Brown was quite right to point out that the final books betoken Augustine's pessimism. He was also right to compare the *City* with a prize fight, "all movement, ducking, and weaving," but Brown does not extend the analogy to one plausible conclusion.[49] The mammoth text bears witness to Augustine's stamina, yet the author appears weary in the later rounds. He tries neither to redeem the standing (yet unsteady) political culture of the Christian empire with a flurry of rhetoric nor to sever the

---

[45] *CCSL* 47: 156 (*DCD* 5.19).

[46] *CSEL* 57: 497.

[47] See Ladner's *The Idea of Reform* (New York, 1967), pp. 184–85. Also see F. Edward Cranz, "The Development of Augustine's Ideas on Society before the Donatist Controversy," *Harvard Theological Review* 47 (1954): 308–11, and Garilli, *Aspetti*, pp. 185–86.

[48] See Paolo Brezzi, "Una *civitas terrena spiritualis* come ideale storico-politico di Sant'Agostino," *Augustinus Magister* 2 (1954): 921.

[49] Peter Brown, "Saint Augustine," in *Trends in Medieval Political Thought*, ed. Beryl Smalley (Oxford, 1965), pp. 1–21.

government from the unregenerate world with one final and decisive blow. What Augustine fails to do in the final books, however, hardly tells against what he had done in the earlier rounds. There, without idealizing the Christian empire, he argued that it was absurd to stress the incompatibility between Christianity and successful government. Only "success" needed redefinition. The empire was successful, in Augustine's terms, if, as part of God's providential order, it protected the church from idolators and heretics, exchanged the lust for glory for the love of God, and preserved peace so that those "larger areas of terrestrial life" might be reclaimed by God—person by person and choice by choice. The pilgrim city lived in hope, and its hope was not for terrestrial expanse or some terrestrial kingdom. Yet, for Augustine, Constantine had given the empire its redeeming politics and the psalmist had given Christians the promise of dominion "from sea to sea." Recent crises taught Christians that ultimately they had to trust God's promise of a celestial city. Biblical texts, imperial edicts, and faithful government officials like Marcellinus, however, persuaded Augustine that the present political culture was part of God's saving work in the world.

Chapter Eight

SECTARIAN DUALISM AND SOCIOLATRY

AUGUSTINE ruled out triumphalism after Rome's "fall," but crisis killed neither the ideals of Christian empire nor the Christian empire itself. The influential North African bishop set about conceptually to repair and, one might say, to temper Christian sociolatry. His critics, notably the leaders of Donatist churches in Numidia, were more mistrustful of the Christian empire. They suspected political culture was irredeemable. The very concept of a Christian empire seemed preposterous to them. More than a millennium later, their objections to Augustine and to Christian sociolatry were revived by sectarian Protestant critics of redeeming politics in Europe, both Catholic and Protestant.

The story of sixteenth-century crisis and reform begins with protests against Roman Catholicism. Where, dissidents demanded, were the scriptural warrants for the Catholic church's sacraments, laws, customs, and courts? Scripture appeared to them to illustrate a much simpler form of religion than the one that had developed in Europe under papal auspices. Catholic authorities maintained that Scripture permitted what it did not outright forbid or condemn, but neither this argument nor the argument from precedent (if the precedent were unscriptural) convinced evangelical preachers and reformers. They charged Catholicism with elevating tradition and precedent to keep Christianity chained to extrabiblical practices that just happened to profit Roman pontiffs and their accomplices.

Naturally, dissidents dreaded ecclesiastical reprisals; to guard against them, some of the more outspoken preachers sought the support of local magistrates and barons. Martin Luther found the Elector Frederick of Saxony an accommodating patron and effective shield. Frederick found his patronage was a convenient way to assert his independence from the Holy Roman Emperor; he refused to comply directly and energetically with imperial and papal orders to have Luther silenced. There are good reasons to suspect that Luther's prince and protector was not suddenly converted by the content of reform preaching. Frederick continued to acquire new specimens for his imposing collection of saints' relics years after the reformers had ridiculed that popular enterprise. The elector was also slow to give up the Catholic mass. Along with other princes and public authorities, however, Frederick was eager to reduce Roman influence in German politics and over German churches. On this count alone, one might argue that the reformations of the sixteenth century fused religious and political aspirations. Luther and other reformers obtained political support and protection, whereas the German princes and magistrates retained and, in most cases, increased their control over the political and economic affairs of their territories' churches. Strive as they might for the independence of the pastoral ministry, the reformations' standardbearers—for their safety—ultimately traded appreciable shares in the administration of their churches' reformations to regional and municipal authorities. And those trades generated some distinctly sociolatrous sentiments.[1]

Beginning in 1523, the town councils of Strasbourg intervened to protect evangelical preachers from their bishop, and Martin Bucer gratefully acknowledged the importance of their intervention. Bucer's *Instruction on Christian Love* stipulated that his government's political assistance and public service were consummate expressions of Christian charity and neighborly love. He allowed that the Christian magistracy, although it had no business censoring reformed preachers, played a highly significant role in stabilizing the Christian commonwealth. Magistrates led and legislated their constituents away from evil, toward the good that God willed for them all. Bucer averred that Strasbourg's politicians were his partners in the reform of ecclesiastical institutions, worship, and public morality, partners with considerable authority over the spiritual and secular contours of civic life.[2]

Public officials apparently took Bucer quite seriously, and they continued to protect him from his critics. Officials agreed to outlaw assemblies of those citizens angered by Bucer's endorsements of government interference. Complaints originated with several more radical reformers who imagined that Bucer's partnership with the government in Strasbourg did not simply revive "Constantinian" Christianity—that would have been bad enough—but actually laid the ground work for a hideous and unscriptural Protestant empire. The radicals considered government influence a serious obstacle to thorough evangelical reform and Protestant sociolatry a profound betrayal of the Protestant cause.[3]

Augustine had acknowledged that the empire's misfortunes created a profound crisis for Christian sociolatry early in the fifth century. Eleven hundred years later, radical reformers in Strasbourg, in Saxony, and as we shall soon see, in Zurich, agreed that Christian sociolatry was itself

[1] See Ingetraut Ludolphy, "Luther und sein Landesherr Friedrich der Weise," *Luther* 54 (1983): 118–23, and Gottfried Maron, "Luther und die Germanisierung des Christentums," *Zeitschrift für Kirchengeschichte* 94 (1983): 327–31.

[2] *Martin Bucers deutsche Schriften*, ed. Robert Stupperich, vol. 1 (Gütersloh, 1960), 55–59.

[3] See Marc Lienhard, "Les autorités civiles et les Anabaptistes: Attitudes du magistrat de Strasbourg (1526–1532)," in *The Origins and Characteristics of Anabaptism / Les débuts et les characteristiques de l'anabaptisme*, ed. Lienhard (The Hague, 1977), pp. 200–201.

the crisis that signaled the collapse of evangelical reform. Political authorities seemed ready to swallow up the churches they had helped liberate from papal imperialists. Leading Protestant reformers—Luther, Bucer, and Ulrich Zwingli—seemed ready to assist.

The radicals saw their liberation from Rome as an opportunity to restore apostolic and thus authentic Christianity. They yearned nostalgically for Christianity's best centuries, when the way of Christ was clearly distinguished from the ways of the world. At that time, there were no Christian emperors, no papal clerocrats. The radicals were perplexed and then angry when colleagues, after liberating Christianity from pope and emperor, sold their reformations and churches to new masters, to local barons, princes, and municipal officials. But what could be done to liberate Christians from their liberators and from their liberators' allies, protectors, and clients?

To place that question and the radicals' answers in some context, we can examine efforts to reform the church in Zurich. There, during summer 1522, Ulrich Zwingli and several of his associates disrupted sermons delivered by some monastic and conservative preachers. In those episodes, discourtesy was also civil disobedience, for the town councils had proscribed disorderly conduct at sermons. Yet the councils had also decreed that preaching be scriptural. Zwingli violated the first order, hoping to compel magistrates to enforce the second. He contended that the sermon he interrupted was unscriptural, and he demanded that Catholic preachers either produce scriptural warrants for the veneration of saints, which their sermons defended, or cease preaching such idolatry.

Zwingli believed that allusions to hermits, virgins, and miracles, which crowded the offensive sermons, leashed guileless citizens to superstitions already distracting them from the direct worship of God. Months before the summer disturbances, one of Zwingli's critics, Konrad Hofmann, warned him to be more respectful of the church's legends. He feared that Zwingli's assaults against the church's favorite stories of local saints and against those who preached about them would turn into assaults against Catholic tradition and the holy church itself.[4] And the summer campaign for scriptural preaching proved Hofmann a prophet. The disruptions mobilized dissent, provoking the town councils to take sides. After interrupting Franz Lambert, who had traveled from Avignon to defend the church's saints, Zwingli insisted his disagreement with the visiting preacher be debated before the Zurich magistrates. The government's response was encouraging, Lambert capitulated, and additional hearings on the reform of religion were convened.

All such proceedings troubled the bishop of Constance, who sent his

---

[4] *Aktensammlung zur Geschichte der zürcher Reformation*, ed. Emil Egli (Zurich, 1879), pp. 63–64.

chief deputy, Johann Faber, to remind Zwingli and his allies in government that reform was an ecclesiastical prerogative. Faber promised a future council in Nuremberg would judge grievances and investigate the
case for reform. Zwingli replied that the church's councils had only confused issues in the past and that any conclave of pious and disciplined
Christians could ponder the prospects for reform more objectively than
Faber's bishops and scholars. "Here in this room," Zwingli said, referring
to Zurich's magistrates, "we have infallible and impartial judges."[5]

Some of Zwingli's more radical friends probably remained sceptical.
They had disrupted Catholic sermons in summer 1522 and before
Zwingli challenged Lambert, but now their disruptions seem to have been
more aggressive. They exhibited contempt for the preachers they interrupted as well as irritation with irenic Zurich magistrates.[6] Zwingli's in-
dignant friends must have been thrilled when he told Faber that the only
government the church needed was the order that naturally developed
when serious believers (recht Christglöbigen) assembled to consult Scripture.[7] They must have been puzzled, however, when Zwingli virtually
transformed the city council into a church council. If the radicals did not
shudder, they were not listening.[8]

It can be argued that Zwingli was simply playing the cards dealt him.
His radical friends wanted immediate and encompassing reform. He was
cautious because sudden and drastic changes engineered without government sanction were likely to scandalize citizens and jeopardize the effectiveness of any reform.[9] Citizens in Switzerland had learned to rely on
their governments for many decisions about church life and church order.
Radicals discovered as much when they solicited peasants' support for the
reform of worship. Claus Hottinger, for example, intercepted a miller on
his way to the tavern and badgered him about idolatry. Hottinger wanted
the thirsty miller's help in destroying the saints' images in nearby

---

[5] CR 88: 495–98 ("Hie in diser stuben ist ein christliche versamlung. . . . Wir haben hie
unfäliche unnd unparthysch richter"). For impressions of the summer disturbances, see Heinold Fast, "Reformation durch Provokation: Predigtstörungen in den ersten Jahren der Reformation in der Schweiz," in Umstrittenes Täufertum, ed. Hans-Jürgen Goertz (Göttingen,
1975), pp. 85–89, and Gottfried W. Locher, Die zwinglische Reformation im Rahmen der
europäischen Kirchengeschichte (Göttingen, 1979), pp. 100–102. For the bishop's earlier
troubles with the Zurich council, see Hans Morf, "Obrigkeit und Kirche in Zürich bis zu
Beginn der Reformation," Zwingliana 13 (1970): 170–77, 198–202.

[6] Egli, Aktensammlung, p. 94, and J. F. Gerhard Goeters, "Die Vorgeschichte des Täufertums in Zürich," in Studien zur Geschichte und Theologie der Reformation, ed. Luise
Abramowski and Goeters (Neukirchen, 1969), pp. 254–58, 273–74.

[7] CR 88: 536–37, 561.

[8] The alternative, of course, is that they were not yet radicals, but this explanation will be
discounted as we proceed.

[9] CR 88: 119.

churches. He was told that good but unlearned Christians would tolerate no error, although they would wait—as the miller was waiting—for local magistrates to determine what was wrong and to teach simple and pious citizens how to make it right.[10]

We know very little about Hottinger. In March 1522 he and several others broke the Lenten fast, a violation that some scholars commemorate as the beginning of reformation in Zurich (although Zwingli had been petitioning his bishop for reforms soon after his arrival in 1518). Hottinger was certainly not in competition with Zwingli; after the broken fast, he planned a festive celebration to demonstrate the strength of Zwingli's support. Hottinger was one of the radicals accused of orchestrating the summer disturbances of 1522, and a year later he was banished from Zurich for destroying a large crucifix. Early in 1524, he was executed in Lucerne for publicly advocating the elimination of the Catholic mass. Hottinger learned from millers, magistrates, and an executioner the lesson that Zwingli had grasped earlier and enthusiastically: governments were parts, obviously honored parts, of late medieval religious life.

We know much more about one of Hottinger's close collaborators, Conrad Grebel, and Grebel's story allows us to plot the course of the radical reformation in Zurich and its environs from 1522 to 1527. Moreover, it was Grebel, as Martin Haas has alleged, who gave radical dissent in Zurich its sectarian character or identity.[11]

When we first encounter Grebel, however, his own identity is a problem. Borrowing the idiom of a later age, we might say Grebel had difficulties finding himself. He spent six years studying in Paris, Vienna, and Basel before returning to his father's house in Zurich in 1520. Thereafter he was restless, yet he complained to his friend Vadian of St. Gall that he lacked energy to alter his drab existence. Grebel's father used his appreciable political influence to obtain a stipend that would have enabled Conrad to continue his studies in Pisa. But the younger Grebel was uncooperative. He wrote to Vadian that he had developed an aversion to Italy and would not accept the papal pension his father had landed for him. His letter was soaked in self-pity. "I linger on here," he churlishly confided; "I only pretend to study." Grebel ceaselessly announced his misery and hatched plans for his escape.[12]

For the better part of 1521 Grebel thrashed about for some purpose. After several false starts, in the summer he fled to Basel to join his mis-

[10] Egli, *Aktensammlung*, pp. 163–65.

[11] Martin Haas, "Der Weg der Täufer in die Absonderung," in Goertz, *Umstrittenes Täufertum*, p. 66.

[12] *Die vadianische Briefsammlung der Stadtbibliothek St. Gallen*, ed. Emil Arbenz, vol. 2 (St. Gall, 1894), 329, 337.

tress, whom he had sent ahead. But a few months later, he sheepishly obeyed his father's summons and returned to Zurich. In November, he informed Vadian that he was finished traveling about irresponsibly, that for better or worse, he and his mistress would settle in his hometown as husband and wife.[13]

Having resettled in Zurich, Grebel sought ways to continue his literary studies. He associated himself with a group of men who met regularly with Ulrich Zwingli to discuss the literature of classical antiquity. Zwingli's paramount interest, however, was ecclesiastical reform; he read the classics to find models for the Zurich reformation. He tantalized colleagues with the prospect of installing a simple, scriptural, yet urbane Christianity in Zurich once the city had been cleared of superstitions and cleared as well of the prelates who propagated them.

Grebel was captivated by his new mentor. He, Claus Hottinger, and several others showed initiative, if not great ingenuity, and conspired to hasten the changes. We know that they called attention to their cause, which they identified as the cause of the gospel, by interrupting Catholic preachers during summer 1522. Zurich politicians, offended by what they considered excessive zeal, had no choice but to discipline the radicals. In early July, before Zwingli had committed himself to the policy of disruption, Grebel was reprimanded and instructed not to harass Catholic preachers again. Unrepentant, he accused his judges of doing the devil's work, of standing in the gospel's way. The magistrates overlooked his sedition and sent him home. For his part, Grebel had ostensibly found a fresh purpose for his life, complete with obstacles and enemies.[14]

For a while, Grebel remained on good terms with Zwingli, though unwilling to conceal his displeasure when magistrates seemed to interfere with the progress of religious reform. Zwingli conceded that reformers could not countenance policies that thwarted the evangelical cause, but he was prepared to pursue greater government cooperation and altogether unprepared to organize or sanction preemptive measures. When several priests stopped performing the mass, authorities in the city bristled. At first, Zwingli tried to negotiate a compromise, but eventually he pressed the priests to reconsider their position and obey Zurich officials who insisted on gradual rather than abrupt changes in worship.[15] Grebel charted a different course. When the Zurich council refused to act swiftly to abolish tithes, he wrote to Vadian that local politicians were no better than "Turks and tyrants." He could not pardon Zwingli's forbearance,

---

[13] Arbenz, *Briefsammlung* 2: 398–99; *The Sources of Swiss Anabaptism: The Grebel Letters and Related Documents*, ed. Leland Harder (Scottdale, Pa., 1985), pp. 155–56.

[14] Egli, *Aktensammlung*, p. 94.

[15] John Howard Yoder, *Täufertum und Reformation in der Schweiz* (Karlsruhe, 1962), pp. 25–28.

and by the end of 1523, he had denounced Zwingli as a spokesman for postponement and an apostate from reform.[16]

Apostasy in Zurich has kept historians busy for centuries, yet it is still uncertain who had forsaken whom. To some—and to Grebel—Zwingli appeared to have lost his courage and compromised his ideals and friendships to obtain official license for limited reform. Other scholars argue that Zwingli consistently lobbied the magistrates for support and that those who thought otherwise at the time either misunderstood their man or deliberately shut their eyes to the politic or prudential character of his policies. From this second perspective, Grebel was the apostate. Zwingli did not lose courage; Grebel lost patience. His resentment mounted as Zwingli's restraint made religious reform dependent on the government's patronage. Then, when Grebel realized how measured the Zwinglian movement had become, he bolted from his friend's stable.[17]

The two rival views of Zurich's reformation have been argued convincingly, although representatives of each have misfiled remarks and reactions emphasized by the other (and the omissions sometimes suggest cunning more than carelessness). But the point beyond dispute is that Zwingli's partnership with local magistrates struck some radicals as the great crisis and crime of the reformation. Late in 1523, though apparently too late, Zwingli tried to appease his critics. Months before, he had proposed several changes in the mass yet stopped short of pressing for the elimination of clerical vestments and prescribed liturgical prayers. Thereby, he seemed to Grebel to have condoned and commended vestiges of the Catholic ceremony that Grebel and his associates wanted completely removed from worship in their reformed churches. By October, Zwingli was admitting he had blundered. The radicals, he said, had a good case against vestments. Such attire disposed citizens to believe that the mass was still a priestly sacrifice rather than a commemoration of Christ's sacrifice. On the matter of prescribed prayers, however, Zwingli would not budge, and his intransigence made the radicals suspect their former friend was still picking his way through the reform of worship with one eye on Christians' inveterate Catholic habits, the other on the council's conservative prejudices.[18]

The radicals refused to hold reform hostage to the town's politicians, who seemed to them more concerned with public order than with the

---

[16] Arbenz, *Briefsammlung* 3 (1897): 26, and Goeters, "Vorgeschichte," pp. 267–69.

[17] Compare Yoder, *Täufertum*, p. 162 ("Zwingli selbst verlar aber den Mut und wagte nicht mehr sein Programm durchzuführen") and Robert Walton's remarks on Zwingli's "policy of patience," *Zwingli's Theocracy* (Toronto, 1967), pp. 143–45. Also consult the debate between Walton and Yoder in *Mennonite Quarterly Review* 32 (1958): 128–40; 42 (1968): 45–56.

[18] CR 89: 620–21; Harder, *Swiss Anabaptism*, pp. 227–28.

gospel's truths. But the best that Grebel and his comrades could hope for was a meager crop of concessions. Either they lost Zwingli or left him behind; it was time to hunt for other allies.

In Saxony, Thomas Müntzer was just then grumbling about the halting progress of Martin Luther's reformation. Grebel was particularly taken with Müntzer's *Protestation*, which registered several complaints about Luther's moderation. Here was a chance to make common cause with someone already sparring with cautious and conservative reformers. Grebel wrote to Müntzer assailing the "false forbearance" of leading evangelical preachers, and he let the Saxon radical know how excited likeminded Protestants in Zurich were to find another student of Scripture who dared to correct the likes of Luther.[19] Grebel acknowledged that Luther and Zwingli had reintroduced Christians to their Bible. For that, they deserved and acquired great influence. Grebel protested, however, that leading Protestants were disinclined to use their influence to speed evangelical reform. Their partnerships with princes and magistrates—among the first signs of Protestant sociolatry—according to Grebel, were the last dreadful chapters of the story of failed reform. What was worse, Luther and Zwingli used their influence to silence critics who spoke of the failure. Grebel suggested that magistrates, princes, and their principal Protestants conspired to create problems for Europe's most earnest and thoroughgoing reformers. Hence, "Christ must suffer still more in his members."[20]

When Zwingli turned politicians into arbiters of church worship and then urged obedience as a Christian duty, a dark cloud descended on Grebel's reformation. For the radicals, there was no silver lining; the letter to Müntzer is marked by a spirit of resignation. Grebel confided that barely twenty had joined him in opposition. A referendum would only confirm that Zwingli had captured and now held nearly all of Zurich. Scholars debate whether the radicals ever entertained the prospect of converting the "Turks and tyrants" on the town's councils, but one thing is certain: by the end of 1524, the radicals were persuaded that their destiny was to persevere rather than prevail.

The letter to Müntzer tells us that the radicals in Zurich considered themselves a persecuted minority, a remnant of the evangelical reformation that had advanced only a short way before coming to terms with magistrates and thus becoming something other than evangelical. The radicals were faced with a difficult choice. They could rebel against leading reformers and former friends or accept their fate and remain shackled to their oars. Grebel resigned the political order to those misguided colleagues prepared to accommodate their preaching to the conservatism of

---

[19] *QGTS* 1: 14 ("faltsh schonen"); Harder, *Swiss Anabaptism*, p. 286.
[20] *QGTS* 1: 20; Harder, *Swiss Anabaptism*, p. 293.

politicians. Notwithstanding his earlier spiteful remarks about the Zurich council, in 1524 he was not yet disposed to insist on the incompatibility between political office and Christian piety. Another year passed before some tentative suggestions to that effect appeared and several years more before the clearest statements about such incompatibility were circulated. But Grebel's letter to Müntzer permits us to watch the seeds of sectarian dualism germinate. In Zurich, the radicals abjured conquest and learned to accept the unpleasant consequences of their crisis and the crisis of early Protestant sociolatry.[21]

The historian Clarence Bauman found a helpful way to dramatize the radicals' resignation. He classed the Protestant reformations as Pauline, the radical reformations as Johannine. Bauman referred explicitly to 1 John 5:19: "We know that we are of God, and the whole world is in the power of the evil one." For Pauline reformers, "the whole world" was a more ambiguous place, a place to be reclaimed for God. For Johannine reformers, the world could not receive the spirit of truth (John 14:17), and the bearers of truth, as Grebel put it, "must suffer still more . . . until the end." Grebel's task was to keep the guiltless outcasts together, defiant, persistent.[22]

Grebel intensified the radicals' sense of their righteousness, and he used protests and proposals for sacramental reform to establish their sectarian identity. He declared infant baptism unscriptural and urged followers to accept rebaptism and to rebaptize others. In part, he promoted rebaptism to distinguish radical reform and the righteous from magisterial reform and those unrighteous reformers who conflated Christianity and political culture. The radicals' rebaptism was a ritual response to Protestantism's redeeming politics. Because they believed that the world, as then conceived and ruled, could not receive the spirit of truth, the radicals reasoned that it was senseless to baptize children before they matured and distinguished themselves from the world by taking on a new life (*ein neu leben an sich nehmend*). After all, the very first apostles baptized adults to signal that a fresh and vital movement had entered history and to show that mature believers must be ready to make discriminations and join.[23]

Zwingli's accounts of his discussions with the radicals on this matter were somewhat self-serving. He took great pains to assure reformers in other cities and realms that his cocksure opponents in Zurich were driven by malice to turn scriptural stories, which were vague about baptism among the earliest Christians, into seditious protests against current practices.[24] Zwingli stressed the radicals' scurrility, and he leaves the impres-

---

[21] Haas, "Weg der Täufer," p. 71; Yoder, *Täufertum*, pp. 31–33.
[22] See Bauman's *Gewaltlosigkeit im Täufertum* (Leiden, 1968), pp. 289–93.
[23] CR 90: 369–71.
[24] CR 95: 274–75.

sion that Grebel used the controversy over baptism to segregate his few followers from citizens who obeyed church officials and magistrates. On that point, Zwingli's observations confirm mine. By 1525, Grebel was giving theological and ritual expression to sectarian dualism in order to assure sectarian solidarity and ostensibly to harmonize religious practice with Scripture.[25]

In January 1525, Zwingli's preaching was interrupted, whereupon he decided to take the question of infant baptism before the council. From January to June, the magistrates listened to several debates. During the same period peasant armies in Swabia were circulating grievances and taking to the field to put serfdom to the sword, so this was not a time to treat dissent lightly. The Zurich council decided to silence Grebel and Felix Mantz, who had been airing their complaints in the villages surrounding the city as well as before the council. Magistrates told the two that they could not continue their war of words with Zwingli. Should they have questions about the sacraments, they could inquire for information. But they could no longer volunteer information.[26]

Grebel anticipated the verdict. While traveling through the canton in January and February, he had been particularly acerbic. Witnesses said he had so soured on the justice available in Zwingli's city that he encouraged others to disobey the council. He claimed he had beaten Zwingli in debate. He charged that Zwingli nonetheless had made sure the council heard nothing but praise for the government's willingness to nurse its fledgling reformation. From a not-so-safe distance, Grebel virtually dared the authorities to arrest him. He announced that he would subscribe to no law, that, if necessary, he would carry on his campaign from prison.[27]

Grebel protested and lectured to whoever would listen. He is reported to have had some success in attracting laymen to his cause in Zollikon, Schaffhausen, St. Gall, and Grüningen. Legends later traveled farther than Grebel himself: the radicals, it was rumored, possessed a secret tonic that compelled sympathy for, or at least dissolved opposition to, radical ideas. But Grebel's successes were not attributable to potions. His denunciations largely accounted for his popularity, such as it was; they stirred simmering resentments against the clergy, reformed as well as Catholic. He promised a simplified and tax-free religion, responsive to scriptural instructions and resistant to clerical control. He aired his suspicions about corruption, and he ridiculed the notion that corrupt clerics and corrupt politicians could somehow create a Christian political culture worthy of redemption. He was sociolatry's incorrigible enemy. In St. Gall, Grebel counseled radicals against commerce with neighbors who

[25] CR 90: 374–12.

[26] Egli, Aktensammlung, p. 278.

[27] QGTS 1: 89–90; Harder, Swiss Anabaptism, pp. 421–22. Also see Yoder, Täufertum, pp. 70–71.

had not yet acknowledged the need to break with the world. In Zollikon, after Grebel's mission, public worship was disrupted and the congregation was advised to shun the false prophets who presided over it. Grebel and his friends incited citizens in Schaffhausen to stage a debate about the propriety of infant baptism. Although the Schaffhausen council later denied that it ever contemplated acquiescence, the vehemence of the denial suggests that the radicals may have gained a sympathetic hearing in the city.[28]

Unfortunately, no extensive record of Grebel's stay in Schaffhausen survives. What little we know fits neatly in a modest paragraph, but outrageous inferences have been drawn from that slight stuff. At issue is the character of the radicals' objectives before the radicals themselves were outlawed, so a close look at Schaffhausen sheds light on important and complicated questions. Were the radicals interested in political coups? Did they hope to win Schaffhausen and then carry the Zurich reformation beyond Zwinglian limits? Or were they opposed to any partnerships with political authorities in Schaffhausen as well as in Zurich? Were they inconsistent or bewildered? Or were they committed and more or less content to operate on the fringes of political culture?

The outrageous inferences can be collected and rendered by a single contention: in Schaffhausen (and, by implication, elsewhere), Grebel and his associates searched for a new territorial and political base for their radical reformation. Zurich was in Zwingli's net, and Zwingli belonged to the town's councils. According to this view or contention, Grebel was indisposed to repudiate Protestant sociolatry. He simply wanted to hitch his reformation to a more tractable town council. I consider this conclusion unwarranted because the best pieces of evidence for it are the Schaffhausen denial and a few notations that Grebel was in conversation with Sebastien Hofmeister, the city's most influential preacher. Hofmeister may have been tempted to reconsider the scriptural precedents for infant baptism. The council, despite its denial, may even have planned a disputation. But Grebel's alleged hunt for a more accommodating government and for a new partnership between religious reformers and political authorities is more fiction than fact. Its sturdiest foundation is the conviction that the radicals' separatism surfaced only after repressive measures had been passed against them, that they were treacherous opportunists— a conviction that undervalues Grebel's early appeal to certain primitivist notions that a righteous, defiant, persecuted minority would carry God's will forward "until the end."[29]

---

[28] Egli, *Aktensammlung*, p. 286. For St. Gall and Zollikon, see Haas, "Weg der Täufer," pp. 72–76.

[29] Cf. Haas, "Weg der Täufer," pp. 57–60; James M. Stayer, "The Swiss Brethren: An Exercise in Historical Definition," *Church History* 47 (1978): 182–86; and Hans-Jürgen Goertz, *Die Täufer: Geschichte und Deutung* (Munich, 1980), pp. 19–20, 53–54, 96–97.

Contrary inferences from the Schaffhausen depositions can as easily be collected and rendered by a single contention, one that our analysis of the 1522 disturbances has already adumbrated. Grebel and his friends perceived that the government in Zurich promised religious reform but also compromised it. Experience in Zurich from 1522 to the end of 1524 taught them that it was useless to press their suit before the council. In Zollikon, the radicals went from house to house to lobby for the freedom to preach.[30] In places, their preaching was so well received that the righteous minority became a righteous majority, yet Grebel and others from Zurich seem not to have courted political interference other than the decrees passed against them by the Zurich council.

To say Grebel courted political interference in that peculiar way is merely to say that he pushed Zwingli and the council too far. Indifferent to their bad showing in most public disputations and forgetful of magistrates' warnings, the radicals persisted in proselytizing. Another hearing on infant baptism was held in winter 1525, but unlike previous inquiries, this one was followed by a trial that landed Grebel in prison. Hofmeister from Schaffhausen gave the most damaging testimony. Grebel, he said, had told him that the climate in courts and councils was unsuitable for the survival of Christian piety. Here surely was the snap of sedition! Purportedly Grebel had insinuated that magistrates were ungodly, that no good Christian could become a politician and remain a good Christian.[31]

Were the radicals framed? Grebel said that the charges of sedition were stem to stern falsifications, but if we recall Grebel's deliriously reckless demonization of the Zurich council in summer 1522, we can understand why no one seems to have taken the radicals' denials too seriously. Grebel and Felix Mantz were sentenced to life imprisonment. The Zurich government promptly dispatched a report to outlying areas where the radicals had preached. Zwingli and his patrons wanted to assure citizens that the scriptural foundations for infant baptism had never been more solidly confirmed.[32] Continued agitation against the practice and reformers who upheld it could only be injurious to public order and orderly reform. For his part, Grebel remained consistent. Resignation meant suffering in the world rather than isolation from the world. Several months after his first trial and soon after the case was retried to the same effect, Grebel and Mantz escaped from prison. Grebel was contemplating other missions— at least once he considered coming to America to convert "the red indians"—when he died of the plague five months later.[33]

[30] Egli, *Aktensammlung*, p. 285.

[31] *QGTS* 1: 123.

[32] *QGTS* 1: 132–33.

[33] For the escape, Harder, *Swiss Anabaptism*, pp. 450–52; for Grüningen interest in the Zurich proceedings, *QGTS* 1: 138–53.

Others were indicted with Grebel and Mantz during the trial in November 1525. Margaret Hottinger was given a choice between penance and prison. Ulrich Teck was told to leave the canton or join his friends in jail. Martin Lingg and Michael Sattler were exiled. Lingg, also known as Weninger, took to the circuit after his dismissal and advocated the radical cause in a number of public disputations. Ten years later, he returned home to Schaffhausen and composed a "vindication" that summarized the views of the Grebel circle. The reformed church, he said, was still a worldly church. It was filled with sinners, and priests responsible for discipline were themselves undisciplined. The true Christian's only recourse was to steer clear of such congregations.[34] Weninger also rejected the idea that Christians might assume political office and redeem politics. Persons who proposed nonsense of this sort, he said, had obviously forgotten the apostles' directives, which he reformulated in his injunction against the magistracy.[35] But Weninger, at his most persuasive, was less compelling than his fellow fugitive in Zurich, Michael Sattler, former prior of a Benedictine monastery, who drafted ultimata and defined sectarian dualism during and immediately after his conversation with reformers in Strasbourg.

Sattler arrived in Strasbourg in 1526. The leading reformers there, Martin Bucer and Wolfgang Capito, at first were willing to discuss the case for radical reform. They insisted, however, that God had ordained municipal government to keep the peace and bridle passions that, if unrestrained, could jeopardize religious worship as well as public order. Sattler thought their justifications were rationalizations. Christ's "order," he declared, could not be suspended while preachers and reformers pursued proximate aims. And Christ's order was neither identical nor compatible with Strasbourg's political order. Politics cobbled discipline to compromise and maintained civic harmony (or conformity) by coercion; Christ required unconditional clemency and compassion. Politics was forever outside the perfection of Christ and was an eternal disappointment to God.[36]

Before statements of this sort utterly alienated the leading Strasbourg reformers, Sattler drew up a document for their perusal. Bucer and Capito said that the exercise of political authority was not per se impious (*oberkeyt nit wider got*).[37] Sattler replied with a list of scriptural slogans, the

---

[34] *QGTS* 2: 111.

[35] *QGTS* 2: 113.

[36] See *The Legacy of Michael Sattler*, ed. John Howard Yoder (Scottdale, Pa., 1973), and Arnold Snyder, "The Schleitheim Articles in Light of the Revolution of the Common Man: Continuation or Departure?" *Sixteenth Century Journal* 16 (1985): 429–30, especially n. 32.

[37] For example, *QGTE* 26: 299; 27: 29, 201.

cumulative effect of which was to set the world's kingdoms against Christ's kingdom. Christians who belonged to the latter obeyed the law of love. As citizens of heaven, they resigned their citizenship in the world's cities, therefore the world hated them. The devil, however, was this world's prince; he ruled only "the children of darkness."[38]

Conditions were unfavorable for the reception of Sattler's stark expression of sectarian dualism. Scarcely a year had passed since the so-called peasants' wars in Alsace. Bucer and Capito were courting political authorities in order to place their reform of worship on a more secure footing. They despaired that Strasbourg had become home for a host of competing Protestant sects, a hothouse of sectarian activity that greatly complicated their efforts to legislate religious conformity. Sattler was soon shown the exit.[39]

But it is hard to imagine political conditions favorable for the reception of Sattler's message since Sattler considered Satan the master of all political culture. His evangelical dualism seems to have been tailored for small communities of exiles and outcasts, whose sole political activity was prayer. And we cannot be certain whether sectarians prayed for an end to intolerance in this world or for the advent of the next, that is, for an end to the suffering to which Grebel alluded ("until *the* end").

After leaving Strasbourg, Sattler tried to consolidate the radicals' scattered communities. At Schleitheim, near Schaffhausen, he and his associates composed a document now considered the first sectarian Protestant confession. The articles plainly renounced ambitions to redeem politics. Sattler reminded those assembled that Christ fled when it appeared he might be made a king. He assumed that God enjoined authentic Christians to do likewise rather than accept political office. The confession predicted the collapse of all earthly government and warned it was time "to forsake Babylon" and abandon public worship that had been only partially reformed. The Schleitheim articles are the clearest expression of sectarian dualism, which, as I have suggested, Conrad Grebel had advocated several years before as an antidote to Protestant sociolatry. Sattler was present in Zurich in November 1525 when the magistrates there wrecked the movement for radical religious reform and imprisoned Grebel and Mantz. He failed in Strasbourg when he attempted to generate interest and support among that city's leading reformers. The political situation seemed hopelessly repressive. Sattler's Schleitheim articles, therefore, understandably prohibited all partnerships with public officials. Yet they also pointed the way to a new, sectarian form of sociolatry consonant

---

[38] *QGTE* 26: 68–69.

[39] Klaus Deppermann, "Die strassburger Reformatoren und die Krise der deutschen Täufertums in Jahre 1527, *Mennonitische Geschichtsblätter* 30 (1973): 24–41.

with contempt for this world, a contempt as old as Donatism and Christian monasticism.[40]

Capito was struck by the similarity between the reformations' radicals and some Catholic conservatives. He called Sattler and his friends "new monks," and he implied that if they had their way, the reformation in Strasbourg would take several steps backward, possibly reinstituting the Catholic conventions and conventicles that he and Bucer had labored to dismantle.[41] In 1527, the magistrates proscribed sectarian assemblies; the government was beginning to address fears that the radicals' unrelenting struggles against Bucer and Capito threatened the progress of reform and the preservation of public order.[42] But apparently both citizens and councilors were slow to enforce their new edict, because six months later the council had to remind members of their duty to report radicals' activities so dissidents could be punished.[43] Neither apathy nor indolence induced the radicals to alter their estimates of political opponents and politics in general. The enduring element in sectarian polemic was its uncompromising distinction between this world and the genuine church, which had been "called out," that is, selected from the world to bear witness to God's will and Christ's suffering.[44]

At first glance, Pilgram Marpeck seems the exception. He arrived in Strasbourg in 1528, nearly two years after Sattler left, and he made no reference to the Schleitheim articles. For a time, Marpeck and Martin Bucer discussed prospects for a more radical reform of the sacraments. Marpeck appreciated Strasbourg's reluctance to employ capital punishment against dissidents, but he grieved that Bucer, forgetting the "rule" of Christ, made a beeline to the Old Testament to justify the partnership in Strasbourg between leading reformers and the government.[45] Relations remained cordial, even when Marpeck and his coworker Leupold Scharnschlager were ordered to leave the city. Scharnschlager's final plea for toleration sharply divided the world of politics from the word of Christ, yet the petition was polite, even politic.[46]

That changed; rejection and persecution turned the temper of the most moderate radical. Scharnschlager had already reminded magistrates in Strasbourg of the fate of Ulrich Zwingli, who had chased radicals from

[40] *Der linke Flügel der Reformation*, ed. Heinold Fast (Bremen, 1962), pp. 64–70.

[41] *QGTE* 26: 82.

[42] *QGTE* 26: 22–23.

[43] *QGTE* 26: 148.

[44] See Heinold Fast, "Variationen des Kirchenbegriffs bei den Täufern," *Mennonitische Geschichtsblätter* 27 (1970): 5–18.

[45] Goertz, *Die Täufer*, pp. 108–9, and William Klassen, "The Limits of Political Authority as Seen by Pilgram Marpeck," *Mennonite Quarterly Review* 56 (1982), notably 350–52.

[46] Fast, *Linke Flügel*, p. 127.

Zurich. Zwingli had been killed on a battlefield three years earlier, a violent death that Scharnschlager regarded as divine retribution.[47] After his petition failed to win over Strasbourg officials, he was disgruntled, more critical, more intent upon consigning political culture to the devil's portion of the created (and unregenerate) order. Scharnschlager demanded that Christians separate themselves from their neighbors and disavow all activity that would bring them into contact with government officials. His *Admonition* and "war cry" (*Fechtgeschrei*) urged followers to stay away from the marketplace. The purchase of a house, in Scharnschlager's estimation, was as sinful as adultery.[48]

Scharnschlager's final report on "the true faith" worked the sectarian dualists' polarities into nearly every proposition. He was as confident as radicals who had preceded him that "Christ's members" were guided by the spirit and instructed exclusively by scriptural sources to manage their affairs and resolve life's problems. But this world resolved problems differently, with less faith, and, in terms of personal and corporate regeneration, with less success.[49]

This world, as the radicals understood it and condemned it, daily edged closer to the completion of the great compromise that would ruin the reformation. From Grebel and Müntzer, some radicals learned contempt for magistrates and reformers whose caution weighed down their better instincts. Grebel, Sattler, and Scharnschlager concluded that the real problem was the office itself, not the officeholder. Political society was steadied by caution. It demanded caution of its servants and sovereigns. This was why dualists averred that no Christian could accept political office and remain a Christian.[50] But caution was not the only crime. Of greater consequence was the magistrates' frequent recourse to coercion, particularly when force was used to compel religious conformity. The radicals insisted Christ had forbidden it. His Sermon on the Mount, they said, unequivocally repudiated evangelical preachers' efforts to justify coercion and collaborate with governments founded on and perpetuated by force. The centuries had not diminished the power or changed the meaning of Christ's injunctions, and neither his kingdom nor his church was of this world. Martin Bucer was quick to respond that the church was nonetheless *in* this world. He concluded that Christians must therefore submit to governments capable of preserving peace and guarding the reformation against its enemies.[51] To radicals, increasingly numbered

---

[47] Fast, *Linke Flügel*, p. 124.

[48] *Kunstbuch: Ältester Täuferhandschriftensammelband*, pp. 226–27. (The reference is to the typescript at the Mennonite Historical Library, Goshen, Ind.)

[49] *Kunstbuch*, pp. 294–304.

[50] *Kunstbuch*, pp. 285–86.

[51] QGTE 26: 424.

among those enemies, Bucer had contracted an unholy alliance. Martin Luther had erred when he addressed belligerent feudal rulers as a "Christian nobility." Ulrich Zwingli, touting the Zurich council as a Christian court of appeals, had shamelessly pandered to unregenerate magistrates. True Christians were fugitives from the Babylons of Europe.

For a short spell, some of those true Christians declared Münster a new Jerusalem. The year Scharnschlager left the Babylon of Strasbourg, several hundred miles north of that city friction between the Münster town council and the craft guilds led to the radicals' seizure of the government. The guilds supported Bernhard Rothmann, a reformer increasingly influenced by radical preachers. While Münster's neighbors and many leading citizens were looking to Luther and Wittenberg theologians for doctrine, Rothmann endorsed ideas that originated in Zurich. He sided with Zwingli against Luther on the Lord's Supper, disavowing a literal understanding of Christ's presence in the sacrament. His position on infant and believers' baptism resembled that of Grebel, a position he derived, however, from the disciples of itinerant evangelist Melchior Hoffman and then defended in a public disputation before the town council in August 1533. The more opposition he experienced from that quarter, the more he endeared himself to members of the guilds and the closer he came, step by step, to the course plotted by the Zurich radicals. When the council condemned to death one of Rothmann's outspoken partisans, the *Gesamtgilde* or union of guilds sprang to his defense, compelling Rothmann's enemies to withdraw, first from government and then from Münster. Alderman Heinrich Redecker, gaining prominence during the protest, charged hostile members of the council with complicity in a conspiracy hatched by Catholics and Lutherans outside the city, a conspiracy to rid Münster of Rothmann and its radical reformers.[52]

How many of those radicals were associated with the existing separatist community in Münster? Did the separatists eagerly listen, as Rothmann did, to the Melchiorites? Answers are hard to tease from the accounts left chiefly by the radicals' enemies; hardly anything survives of records kept by friends. Still, it stands to reason that the role of the separatists in developments to this point was rather small. Their uncompromising opposition to usury presumably distanced them from public life and antagonized citizens responsible for civic prosperity and order. In late

---

[52] For Rothmann's disputation, see *Die Schriften Bernhard Rothmanns*, ed. Robert Stupperich (Münster, 1970), pp. 95–119, but also note in the same volume his "Bekenntnis von beiden Sakramenten," pp. 186–91, and "Restitution rechter und gesunder christlicher Lehre," particularly pp. 238, 256. Consult, as well, Taira Kuratsuka, "Gesamtgilde und Täufer: Der Radikalisierungsprozeß in der Reformation Münsters: Von der reformatorischen Bewegung zum Täuferreich, 1533/34," *Archiv für Reformationsgeschichte* 76 (1985): 246 ("Schritt für Schritt"), 257–58 (Redecker).

January 1534, however, forces gathered outside the city, demanding re-
nunciation of radical reforms. This striking and menacing confirmation
of some of Redecker's suspicions prompted the council to encourage municipal cooperation. It issued an edict of toleration, instructing evangeli-
cals and separatists to live in harmony, *freundlich und friedlich*.[53] Apparently the citizens' solidarity disheartened the outsiders, for the siege was
lifted in early February. Word of Münster's deliverance rapidly reached
radicals in northwest Germany and the Netherlands; their preachers and
prophets did not hesitate to embellish the Münster miracle. As Catholics
and Lutherans hurried to leave the city, inspired immigrants rushed to it.
Among them, two newcomers, baker and Melchiorite prophet Jan Matthys and his disciple Jan Bockelszoon of Leiden, were welcomed as if they
were God's special envoys. Their authority almost immediately eclipsed
that of Rothmann and Redecker.[54]

Within weeks of the February miracle, Matthys was declaring that Jerusalem delivered should be purged of remaining "papists and Lutherans." He insisted direct revelations from God commanded him to make
and enforce "Christian laws," but he was content to allow the council,
now dominated by radicals, to legislate reforms.[55] Guided by Matthys's
revelations, the government required baptism of all adults, ordered citizens to deposit their wealth for redistribution, and awaited the imminent
end of history predicted by the new Münster prophets.[56] The separatists'
condemnation of usury speedily evolved into an official rejection of the
old economic order, but slightly more than a month after Matthys had
instigated such tremendous social and economic changes, he was killed
outside the city, battling to break another siege. Undaunted by his death
and by history's refusal to end as promised, a newly constituted council
of elders invested Jan of Leiden with prophetic and regal authority in their
"new state of Israel."[57]

Geneva under Calvin became a church; the city of Münster under Matthys and Leiden became a sect. Commerce with this world was restricted
not only by besieging armies but by municipal prohibitions. New provisions for the new Jerusalem distinguished that company of God's elect
from Christians elsewhere. Matthys tried communism. Leiden, with the
daring of Daedalus, violated what passed in Europe as natural and divine

[53] *Das Täuferreich zu Münster, 1534–1535: Dokumente*, ed. Richard van Dülmen (Munich, 1974), pp. 48–49.

[54] Van Dülmen, *Täuferreich*, pp. 58–59.

[55] Van Dülmen, *Täuferreich*, p. 71.

[56] Van Dülmen, *Täuferreich*, pp. 97–98.

[57] Van Dülmen, *Täuferreich*, p. 117. Formally, the office of prophet was held by Johannes
Dusentschur, who proclaimed Jan, "der Mann Gottes und heilige Prophet," as "über den
ganzen Erdkreis König" (p. 148).

law when he promoted polygamy. Exigencies of the siege must have contributed to the development of both policies. Nonetheless, they show that when this world proved unsympathetic and inhospitable, radicals' redeeming politics might fashion an alternative.[58]

Sectarian sociolatry, then, started on a critical note. Spokesmen or prophets of sects denounced laws or customs regulating and purportedly stifling religious life. Sometimes they also deplored the absence of better and biblical standards. Both kinds of criticism assumed reform had not gone far enough. When radicals reached their principal objectives, even when the only articulated aim was separation, they frequently devised new prohibitions, rules, and rituals, introducing a lifestyle and language different from those of this world. Occasionally, apocalyptic expectations and restorationist rhetoric were fed into the mix. Matthys forecast the end of history and the apotheosis of Münster. Leiden and Rothmann asserted that polygamy in the new kingdom of Israel recapitulated the way God's chosen lived in the old. Transcending time was possible for radical reformers. And whether they drew inspiration from images of an approaching apocalypse or from ideas about patriarchal and apostolic piety, worship, and social organization, radicals generally did not bother to distinguish between religious and political realms or redemptions. Matthys and Leiden ranted as prophets and ruled as kings. Other sects, expecting the Holy Spirit to discipline and direct the faithful, evinced no concentrations of pastoral authority and political power. Ostensibly, consensus regulated the community; consensus was the Spirit's voice.

It is hard to make headway toward generalizations about early Protestant sectarianism. The number of sectarians in the sixteenth century is not staggering, but the number and variety of sects overwhelm scholars eager to spare readers endless qualifications. Moreover, the evidence rarely yields adequate information on the origins and fate of the radicals' plans. Perhaps all we can say with certainty is that radicals like Grebel believed themselves called to withdraw from unreformed and partially reformed churches and to make a fresh start. Fresh starts often involved new baptisms; hence radicals were known as rebaptizers or Anabaptists. Much was left behind, but radicals seldom relinquished their highly charged

---

[58] Hermann Kerssenbach's unfriendly yet vivid account makes Jan seem a lecherous wolf among sheep. The passage from his *Anabaptistici furoris . . . narratio* is reprinted in Van Dülmen, *Täuferreich*, pp. 143–44. For the practical purposes of communism and polygamy, see respectively James M. Stayer, "Christianity in One City: Anabaptist Münster, 1534–1535," in *Radical Tendencies in the Reformation: Divergent Perspectives*, ed. Hans J. Hillerbrand (St. Louis, 1988), pp. 129–34, and R. Po-Chia Hsia, "Münster and the Anabaptists," in *The German People and the Reformation*, ed. Hsia (Ithaca, 1988), pp. 57–60. For a discussion of Rothmann's rationalizations, Otthein Rammstedt, *Sekte und soziale Bewegung: Soziologische Analyse der Täufer in Münster (1534/35)* (Cologne, 1966), pp. 87–100.

propositions about the Babylon of this world and the "false forbearance" of its political authorities and religious reformers. Ten years after Grebel's death, dissidents around Zurich and Schaffhausen openly defamed Christians who accepted political office.[59]

Fresh starts also required a readiness to govern what was started, but at this point, conjecture must help uphold conclusions and generalizations. To be sure, ordinances were passed episodically to assure that sectarians' dispositions conformed with those of their respective sects. Sattler suggested guidelines at Schleitheim in 1527. More than a decade later, Scharnschlager composed articles to address the need for discipline, leadership, and punitive policies in the dispersed communities. For Sattler and Scharnschlager, each congregation as a whole possessed powers to deprive individuals of membership, that is, to disenfranchise persons incompletely purged of this world's nasty habits. Such political or demographic decisions had profound soteriological implications, for heavenly rewards awaited only the elect, purified, and suffering "members of Christ," not offenders banned and shunned by them. The congregation, in effect, possessed the keys to Christ's kingdom; recalcitrant Christians were sent back into this world's kingdoms of perpetual and irreversible perishing.[60] Controversies over decisions of this significance invariably erupted; Jan of Leiden's word in Münster did not go unchallenged. Months before the city was betrayed, its gates opened to enemies, some citizens seceded and set up a separate spiritual kingdom. Dutch radicals experienced tremendous difficulties stemming confusion about policy and punishment. Other sectarians, we may presume, learned, as did consistories and councils in cities they had left, how complicated it was simultaneously to countenance change and keep order.[61]

Yet complications were probably kept under some control because sects were small. Several radicals in Grebel's day drew considerable crowds; as the century wore on, however, the Anabaptism dreaded by Calvin, Bullinger, and other reformers amounted to a collection of communities, seldom comprising more than a preacher, a dozen earnest recruits, and their families. Their modest size allowed communities to develop congregational forms of government. An assembly of all adult members, perhaps a delegation of elders, ordered the political, economic,

[59] QGTS 2: 94–96.

[60] See, in this connection, Bryan Wilson's discussion of "sect allegience" in his *Religion in Sociological Perspective* (Oxford, 1982), pp. 118–20.

[61] Eike Wolgast, "Herrschaftsorganisation und Herrschaftskrisen im Täuferreich von Münster," *Archiv für Reformationsgeschichte* 67 (1976): 193–95; George Huntston Williams, *The Radical Reformation* (Philadelphia, 1962), pp. 493–99 ("The Withdrawal of the Waterlanders").

and religious life of each group.[62] Thus the sects strike some scholars as miniature democracies. Despite sectarian dualism, biblical literalism, apocalyptic fervor, and restorationist rhetoric—all of which compares unfavorably with modern secularism and rationalism—Anabaptism has found a place "on the way to modernity," in the history of political liberty and religious pluralism. But radical reformers, establishing their new orders, often identified political and religious conformity with redemption. That identification, in turn, prompted sweeping and manifestly sociolatrous restructuring of social life. To the extent conformity was required and redeeming politics compelled sectarians to exercise what George Huntston Williams called "neoapostolic authoritarianism," sectarian Protestantism could hardly have led directly, if at all, to liberties enshrined in bills of rights and many constitutions.[63]

Were they to rise from their graves, the radical reformers would be unlikely to contest or regret this minimization of their influence on modernity and political culture. They accepted their parts as pariahs, usually with passion, resolving to live as outcasts "until the end." What is most relevant here is that living until the end meant distributing authority within fugitive communities, and as far as we can tell, the radicals justified provisional political arrangements in religious terms, joining rule and redemption. Dualism and diaspora made most radical reformers wary of the universalist pretensions that flavored much of Christian sociolatry. After conquest, optimism knew few bounds and there could be little question which political culture to redeem. Crisis, exile, and ongoing persecution obliged sectarian Protestants to reconceive as well as redeem politics.

[62] See Claus-Peter Clasen, *Anabaptism: A Social History, 1525–1618* (Ithaca, 1972), pp. 49–76, 425–28.

[63] Williams, *Radical Reformation*, p. 236; Hans-Jürgen Goertz, "Das Täufertum—ein Weg in die Moderne?" in *Zwingli und Europa*, ed. Peter Blickle, Andreas Lindt, and Alfred Schindler (Zurich, 1985), pp. 179–80.

CONCLUSION

THE LAST chapter's account of Zwingli and the sectarians brought two forms of Christian sociolatry into the same narrative. There was no serious dissension among reformers in Zurich at first. Zwingli was the undisputed leader of the group whose agitation against episcopal government and clerical conservatism brought Johann Faber to the city. On behalf of the bishop, Faber urged patience and advised reformers and magistrates alike that the church had plans to review grievances. If submitted to the council soon to be convened in Nuremberg, complaints and alternative policies would be carefully considered by highly placed prelates and their clerical colleagues from the universities. Zwingli asserted that previous councils had poor records on the issue of reform; they gave him and his accomplices in Zurich no cause for confidence in the next council. Zwingli also insisted that any assembly of serious Christians, who disciplined themselves to receive God's word in Scripture, should be able to determine the course of church reform and church government.[1]

The proposition Zwingli used to outflank Faber was soon used against him by his more radical associates. They were dismayed because Zwingli announced that Zurich's political officials, as serious and disciplined Christians, were competent enough to assess alternative interpretations of church law and liturgy. Zwingli seemed to them to have made peace with a conservative and corruptible government. He tried to persuade the radicals that God empowered government to legislate order as well as change, and he warned them that they risked divine vengeance as well as public prosecution should they disobey the city's councils and attempt to sabotage his partnership with public authorities. For their part, the radicals seized upon Zwingli's rejoinder to Faber to justify their opposition to Zwingli's reformation; they gathered passages from Scripture for polemics against all compromises with cautious political officials. Thereafter, the radicals generated standards, rules, liturgies, and governments for their separatist communities or sects. Although they contemptuously turned away from Zwingli and other leading reformers, they agreed with them that redemption ultimately depended on obedience and conformity. Hence, two related yet distinct forms of Christian sociolatry developed during the third decade of the sixteenth century, the second as a protest against the first.

This brief summary reintroduces the two perspectives presented in all

[1] CR 88: 536–37.

our case studies. From the first, each apology for government seems unique. Constantine's Christians appear to have as much in common with Cromwell's as the plains of Anatolia with the marshes of East Anglia. *Redeeming Politics* tries to put the apologies in their historical contexts, and I hope that I have written fairly about the clients—and the confusions—of the apologists. But the case studies also suggest a second perspective. The book's chapters are episodes in the life of a grand gesture. When we watch political theologies colonize Christian soteriology in a variety of settings, what we actually see is a single apologetic strategy, a tradition in the history of the Christian traditions, which registers its claims rhetorically to real worlds of political power.

Everywhere in redeeming politics, idealizations of political order and political leadership stipulate conditions for the salvation of citizens' souls. To my knowledge, apologists never regarded those conditions as sufficient for salvation. They never presumed that their idealizations described God's redeeming presence in the world exhaustively. They did not lavish or squander all their faith on God's promises or on a promising political candidate. Most apologists would have acknowledged that God saved souls principally through the church's liturgies and related pastoralia and/ or that God choreographed individuals' private struggles for saving faith. The difference between redeeming conversations in the confessional and redeeming struggles with temptation and doubt, on the one hand, and redeeming politics, on the other, is that the first set of strategies reclaimed souls one by one, while politics reclaimed entire armies, cities, sects, churches, territories, and empires. The extravagant rhetoric of political reclamation often seems to preclude personal reclamation; in effect, it did not.

To sift all known narratives that either commemorate or predict God's redeeming politics and large-scale divine reclamation would require several lifetimes liberally seasoned with insomnia. By crowding ideal imperial pastors, papal monarchs, Protestant consistories, and Puritan preachers into a small volume, I afford only a glimpse of that self-perpetuating discourse that determined, in part, how each successive idealization of political order and authority realized its apologetic possibilities. To be sure, we have had to range from one century and text to another before readers could take a very close look at publicists, patrons, and political circumstances. Regrettably, much detail stayed in the cutting room; some comments on contested issues were relegated to the bibliographical remarks that follow. Readers may justifiably complain that they have viewed developments from too great a distance, from the cheap seats. Perhaps there are too many incidents and instances of Christian sociolatry here, perhaps too few. But this conclusion's conceit is that there is enough in *Redeeming Politics* to suggest that Christian sociolatry imparted meaning and dignity to history and political authority by associating them with some prescribed order of salvation. Ideally, that will be enough to prompt readers to reconsider the problematic relationship between religious and political commitments in the history of the Christian traditions.

Undeniably, there is enough here to annoy colleagues committed to the ferociously materialistic orientation characterizing many contemporary studies of ideology. I have intimated that the search for soteriological sanctions sustained a discourse relatively autonomous with respect to its various social and political contexts. For materialists and many social historians, however, those contexts determine everything. Idealizations and ideologies are fully explained by patterns of conduct they idealize, that is, by their social and material foundations and by their social and political functions.[2]

I agree with much that has been said about the social functions of apologetic strategies. The strategies of redeeming politics were not stages somewhere offshore and unrelated to the worlds of power and wealth to which they laid claim. Narrative and ritual efforts to relate redemption to rule were always parts of larger processes of socialization. Idealizations of political order had a particularly palliative effect because they raised the stakes of political nonconformity. If dissidents were convinced that they risked their souls' eternal rest and reward when they repudiated prevailing political settlements and social conventions, seditious sentiments would seldom surface unaccompanied by tremendous personal stress— by dread, guilt, and shame. Social psychologists maintain that such stress is a barrier between the self and anomic states, between the self and both social and intrapsychic disorder. Specialists who research and write history from the bottom up usually censure the political and ideological manipulation of that barrier. Their assessments, if not their indignation, are very much to the point here: Christian sociolatry structured political expectations by emphasizing the conditions of election, the conditions for salvation, and the threat of divine vengeance. Citizens eager for redemption, though not always as eager for rule, were told that their imperial or pontifical rulers were God's deputies and that their institutions, armies, and churches were God's sacred instruments. Dogmatic statements about the elect and the elites that governed them may strike some readers as primitive, but social historians, social psychologists, and other students

---

[2] In this connection, consult alternative counterstatements: Reinhard Bendix, "Sociology and Ideology," in *The Phenomenon of Society*, ed. Edward A. Tiryakian (New York, 1971), pp. 173–87; Robert Wuthnow, "The Critical Theory of Jürgen Habermas," in *Cultural Analysis*, ed. Wuthnow, James Davison Hunter, Albert Bergesen, and Edith Kurzweil (London, 1984), particularly pp. 206–9; and Gertrude Himmelfarb, *The New History and the Old* (Cambridge, Mass., 1987), pp. 1–12.

of popular sentiment attest that they once were and, in places, continue to be persuasive.[3]

Studies of the social role of political idealizations should be more widely known. Studies of the social foundations of idealizations and apologetic strategies, to the extent that they reduce apologies to the status of epiphenomena, should be more widely disputed. The history of the human imagination is not only the history of the material conditions of human existence; to argue otherwise is to undervalue the dialectical relationship between mind and environment. But this last assertion will not seem much of a disincentive to those who insist that the dialectic is an obsolete fantasy, a humanist's last line of defense against the deconstructive impulses of poststructuralism. And *Redeeming Politics* may have played right into those sceptics' hands by admitting that real worlds of political power dictated the trajectory of Christian apology.

For that reason, I resubmit *Redeeming Politics*' second perspective—the single apologetic strategy—for your consideration, along with a final question. From that perspective, it seems that Christian sociolatry, in order to transform politics into redeeming politics, annexed real worlds of power to apologists' dreams of religious renewal. The outcome was a remarkable series of imaginings that blended rule and redemption, reality and romance, political theory and Christian soteriology. How can we appreciate, in their various contexts, the individual idealizations that made up that series unless we also understand that the series itself was a cultural context, a discourse or tradition, of both cogency and consequence?

[3] For example, see Fred Weinstein and Gerald M. Platt, *Psychoanalytic Sociology: An Essay on the Interpretation of Historical Data and the Phenomena of Collective Behavior* (Baltimore, 1973), pp. 91–95, 118–19.

BIBLIOGRAPHICAL REMARKS

These remarks suggest background reading, identify more comprehensive treatments of each case studied, record some general debts and disagreements unmentioned in the footnotes, and introduce scholarly controversies associated with particular instances of redeeming politics.

CHAPTER ONE
CONSTANTINE

Norman H. Baynes, *Constantine the Great and the Christian Church* (London, 1929) and A.H.M. Jones, *Constantine the Great and the Conversion of Europe* (London, 1949) are short, basic studies of the emperor and imperial policy. I rely on the recent work of Timothy D. Barnes, particularly his *Constantine and Eusebius* (Cambridge, Mass., 1981) but also *The New Empire of Diocletian and Constantine* (Cambridge, Mass., 1982). Averil Cameron, "Constantinus Christianus," *Journal of Roman Studies* 73 (1983) is a useful discussion of Barnes's contributions.

To place Constantine in the context of early church history, consult E. R. Dodds, *Pagan and Christian in an Age of Anxiety: Some Aspects of Religious Experience from Marcus Aurelius to Constantine* (Cambridge, 1965), Francis Dvornik, *Early Christian and Byzantine Political Philosophy*, 2 vols. (Washington, 1966), W.H.C. Frend, *The Rise of Christianity* (London, 1984), Ramsay MacMullen, *Christianizing the Roman Empire* (New Haven, 1984), and Robin Lane Fox, *Pagans and Christians* (New York, 1986). Relevant material on Roman ritual, religion, and politics can be mined from *Le culte des souverains dans l'empire Romaine*, ed. Willen den Boer (Geneva, 1973), *Römischer Kaiserkult*, ed. Antonie Wlosok (Darmstadt, 1978), especially the essays by Joannis Karayannopulos and Leo Koep, and Sabine MacCormack, *Art and Ceremony in Late Antiquity* (Berkeley, 1981).

Surprisingly, studies of Eusebius in English are hard to find. The introductory sections of H. A. Drake's *In Praise of Constantine* (Berkeley, 1976) are valuable, and the short, seminal piece by Norman Baynes, "Eusebius and the Christian Empire," in his *Byzantine Studies and Other Essays* (London, 1960), originally published in 1934, should not be overlooked. Robert M. Grant, *Eusebius as a Church Historian* (Oxford, 1980) offers suggestive readings of the *Ecclesiastical History*. Hans Eger, "Kaiser und Kirche in der Geschichtstheologie Eusebs von Cäsarea," *Zeitschrift für die neuetestamentliche Wissenschaft und altkirchlichen*

Literatur 38 (1939), Edward Cranz, "Kingdom and Polity in Eusebius of Caesarea," *Harvard Theological Review* 45 (1952), and Friedhelm Winkelmann, "Zur Geschichte des Authentizitätsproblems der *Vita Constantini*," *Klio: Beiträge zur alten Geschichte* 40 (1962) include helpful observations on Eusebius's *Life of Constantine* (cited as *LKK*), as do three fine studies by Salvatore Calderon: *Costantino e il Cattolicesimo* (Florence, 1962); "Teologia politica, successione dinastica, e consecratio in età Constantiniana," in den Boer, *Le culte des souverains*; and "Eusebio e l'ideologia imperiale," in *La trasformazioni della cultura nella tarda antichità: Atti del convegno tennto a Catania*, vol. 1 (Rome, 1985). Nothing, however, is quite as comprehensive as Raffaele Farina, *L'impero e l'imperatore cristiano in Eusebio di Cesarea* (Zurich, 1966). Jean-Marie Sansterre, "Eusèbe de Césarée et la naissance de la théorie césaropapiste," *Byzantion* 42 (1972) contains intriguing speculations about Eusebius's motives. Jean Sirinelli, *Les vues historiques d'Eusèbe de Césarée durant la période prénicéenne* (Dakar, 1961) considers Eusebius's early career. On Lactantius: *Lactance et son temps*, ed. J. Fontaine and M. Perrin (Paris, 1978), and C. Ocker, "*Unius arbitrio mundum regi necesse est*: Lactantius' concern for the Preservation of Roman Society," *Vigiliae Christianae* 40 (1986). Charles Pietri, "Constantin en 324: Propagande et théologie impériales d'après les documents de la *Vita Constantini*," in *Crise et redressement dans les provinces européennes de l'Empire*, ed. Edmond Frézouls (Strasbourg, 1983), expeditiously traverses the distance between rhetoric and reality.

Any investigation of Constantine's piety must start with Eusebius, who is not always to be trusted. Andreas Alföldi, *The Conversion of Constantine and Pagan Rome* (Oxford, 1948) and Hermann Dörries, *Constantine and Religious Liberty* (New Haven, 1960), along with their untranslated essays and those of others collected in *Konstantin der Grosse*, ed. Heinrich Kraft (Darmstadt, 1974), should now be read in conjunction with Barnes's studies of the emperor's personality and administration. There is also much to learn about Constantine's Christianity from Barnes's "Lactantius and Constantine," *Journal of Roman Studies* 63 (1973), from Johannes Straub, "Konstantins christliches Sendungsbewusstein," reprinted in *Regeneratio Imperii: Aufsätze über Roms Kaisertum und Reich im Spiegel der heidnischen und christlichen Publizitik* (Darmstadt, 1972) and from A. H. Drake, "Athanasius's First Exile," *Greek, Roman, and Byzantine Studies* 27 (1986). There are also instructive remarks on this topic in studies that deal with the emperor's ecclesiastical initiatives and legislation L. Voelkl, *Die Kirchenstiftungen des Kaisers Konstantin im Lichte des römischen Sakralrechts* (Cologne, 1964); Clemence Dupont, "Les privilèges des clercs sous Constantin," *Revue d'histoire ecclésiastique* 62 (1967); and Walter Ullmann, "The Constitutional Significance of Constantine the Great's Settlement," *Journal of Ecclesiastical History* 27 (1976). The pagan reaction and senatorial opposition to Constantine in Rome have perhaps been as exaggerated as Constantine's convictions. On that count, David M. Novak, "Constantine and the Senate: An Early Phase of the Christianization of the Roman Aristocracy," *Ancient Society* 10 (1979) provides appropriate remedies.

The fate of Rome and the foundation of Constantinople figure prominently in discussions of the Christianization of the empire. As for Rome, the early chapters of Charles Pietri's splendid history are enlightening—*Roma Christiana: Recherches sur l'église de Rome, son organisation, sa politique, son idéologie de Miltiade à Sixte III (311–440)*, vol. 1 (Paris, 1976). Better still, for Constantine's church foundations in Rome, is Richard Krautheimer, *Three Christian Capitals* (Berkeley, 1983). Krautheimer also has a fine chapter on Constantinople, but that ground is more thoroughly covered in Gilbert Dagron, *Naissance d'une capitale: Constantinople et ses institutions de 330 à 451* (Paris, 1974). J.M.C. Toynbee, "Roma and Constantinopolis in Late-antique Art from 312 to 365," *Journal of Roman Studies* 37 (1947) and J. M. Huskinson, *Concordia Apostolorum: Christian Propaganda at Rome in the Fourth and Fifth Centuries* (Oxford, 1982) study subsequent developments of importance.

CHAPTER TWO
CONSTANTINE'S SHADOW (I)

"Sacrality," Janet Nelson has said, "involves the transmission of other-worldly powers into this world, crosscutting the line between nature and supernature. Sacral rulership therefore transcends the distinction between clerical and secular." Assembled in *Politics and Ritual in Early Medieval Europe* (London, 1986), Nelson's papers concentrate on the Carolingians (the quotation is on p. 72). To appreciate the "crosscutting" in earlier and later medieval history, two volumes are indispensable: Fritz Kern's *Gottesgnadentum und Widerstandsrecht im früheren Mittelalter*, translated by S. B. Chrimes in *Kingship and Law* (New York, 1956), and Ernst Kantorowicz's *The King's Two Bodies* (Princeton, 1957). Less accessible to the general reader yet most influential in my preparation for this undertaking, Percy Ernst Schramm's many essays on *Staatssymbolik* bear directly on the repossession of redeeming politics. Readers interested in medieval iconography and the ideals of kingship may profitably consult the new edition of Schramm's *Die deutschen Kaiser und Könige in Bildern ihrer Zeit, 751–1190* (Munich, 1983), but the first two volumes of his *Kaiser, Könige und Päpste: Beiträge zur allgemeinen Geschichte* (Stuttgart, 1968), cited as *KKP*, relate more closely to matters discussed in this chapter. Wilhelm Kölmel, *Regimen Christianum: Weg und Ergebnisse des*

Gewaltenverhältnisses und des Gewaltenverständnisses (Berlin, 1970) also underscores the importance of themes developed in Constantine's shadow, in this chapter and the next. The range of Kölmel's project excites admiration, as does the impressive collection of ideologies and authoritarian regimes packed into John A. Armstrong's *Nations before Nationalism* (Chapel Hill, 1982), which explores the "constitutive myths" of Western Christendom during the course of its far-reaching study of ethnic and civic identity in European and Middle Eastern history.

On Orosius, Eugenio Corsini's *Introduzione alle Storie di Orosio* (Turin, 1968) still repays study, but Hans-Werner Goetz, *Die Geschichtstheologie des Orosius* (Darmstadt, 1980) offers more ambitious and suggestive interpretations. Slightly different understandings of how, for Orosius, history took on the character of revelation may be teased from the short chapter in Werner Suerbaum's *Vom antiken zum frühmittelalterlichen Staatsbegriff* (Münster, 1977) and Fabrizio Fabbrini's repetitive *Paolo Orosio: Uno Storico* (Rome, 1979). Goetz's treatment, however, is best read with Benoit Lacroix, *Orose et ses idées* (Montreal, 1965), which stresses the influence of personal and public misfortune on Orosius's history and apology. Much less has been made of Salvian's work. A. G. Hamman's "L'actualité de Salvien de Marseilles: Idées sociales et politiques," *Augustinianum* 17 (1977) and Jan Badewien's *Geschichtstheologie und Sozialkritik im Werke Salvians von Marseilles* (Göttingen, 1980) offer judicious assessments. Notwithstanding Theodor Mommsen's fine and provocative paper on Orosius and Augustine, reprinted in *Medieval and Renaissance Studies*, ed. Eugene F. Rice, Jr. (Ithaca, 1959), and the helpful summaries in R.P.C. Hanson, "The Reaction of the Church to the Collapse of the Western Roman Empire in the Fifth Century," *Vigiliae Christianae* 26 (1972), both Orosius and Salvian still await comprehensive exposition and analysis in English. Such neglect is all the more conspicuous now that Walter Goffart has so wonderfully illumined the work of their successors in *The Narrators of Barbarian History: Jordanes, Gregory of Tours, Bede, and Paul the Deacon* (Princeton, 1988).

Of Goffart's narrators, only Gregory of Tours figures in our story, and only his remarks on Clovis in the *Libri historiarum*. By the first decade of the sixth century, Clovis had made the Seine basin the center of a Frankish empire stretching into northern Italy, to the fortresses seized there from the Goths; subsequently Gregory made Clovis an agent of divine vengeance, a sacred king and second Constantine. Ian Woods reports as much and includes interesting speculations about the politics of Clovis's conversion to Christianity in "Gregory of Tours and Clovis," *Revue belge de philologie et d'histoire* 63 (1985). There are informative sections on Gregory, as there are on Orosius and Salvian, in the time-honored work of Pierre Courcelle, *Histoire littéraire des grands invasions germanique*,

3rd ed. (Paris 1964). Also on Gregory and early medieval kingship, Marc Reydellet, *La royauté dans la littérature Latine de Sidoine Apollinaire à Isidore de Séville* (Rome, 1981) displays impressive learning.

The debate about the Germanic origins of sacral kingship is an extension of the controversy over how much of the Middle Ages came from Rome and how much came out of the German forests. Parts of the controversy that touch on redeeming politics are discussed in František Graus, *Volk, Herrscher und Heiliger im Reich der Merowinger* (Prague, 1965) and in the first chapter of J. M. Wallace-Hadrill, *Early Germanic Kingship in England and on the Continent* (Oxford, 1971). The argument is easiest to follow in Robert Folz, "Zur Frage der heiligen Könige," *Deutsches Archiv* 14 (1958), and Folz's translated work has considerable importance for issues raised in this chapter and the next—*The Coronation of Charlemagne* (London, 1974) and *The Concept of Empire in Western Europe from the Fifth to the Fourteenth Century* (London, 1965).

Edward James has published two excellent surveys, *The Origins of France: From Clovis to the Capetians, 500–1000* (New York, 1982) and *The Franks* (Oxford, 1988). The master of Merovingian studies remains Eugen Ewig. Of the many papers in his collection *Spätantikes und fränkisches Gallien*, 2 vols. (Munich, 1976–79), a majority analyzes some aspect of the interpenetration of religious and political life. In volume two, "Das Privileg des Bischofs Berthefrid von Amiens für Corbie von 664 und die Klosterpolitik der Königin Bathild" rehearses the collaboration between royal and episcopal authorities. And "Der Bild Constantins des Grossen in den ersten Jahrhunderten des abendländischen Mittelalters," in volume one, is particularly valuable for the study of *Staatssymbolik* in Constantine's shadow. Studies of the Carolingians in English have been dominated by studies of Charlemagne. Donald A. Bullough, "*Europae Pater*: Charlemagne and His Achievement in the Light of Recent Research," *English Historical Review* 85 (1970), is a helpful historiographical introduction to the field, and Louis Halphen's *Charlemagne et l'empire carolingien* was subsequently translated as *Charlemagne and the Carolingian Empire* (Amsterdam, 1977), unfortunately without annotations. On Charlemagne's government, nothing surpasses F. L. Ganshof, *Frankish Institutions under Charlemagne* (Providence, 1968); on Charlemagne himself, the first two volumes of the commendable collection *Karl der Grosse: Lebenswerk und Nachleben* (Düsseldorf, 1965), edited respectively by Helmut Beumann and Bernhard Bischoff, are packed with promising material for the student of redeeming politics. Attention should especially be directed to Peter Classen's "Karl der Grosse, das Papsttum, und Byzanz" in the first volume. But for Carolingian sociolatry, two papers in Percy Schramm's aforementioned *Beiträge* remain the best points of departure—"Karl der Grosse als König (768–800) im Lichte der Staatssymbolik" and "Karl der Grosse als Kaiser (800–814) im Lichte der Staatssymbolik," both in the first volume.

Pierre Riché, *Les Carolingiens: Une famille qui fit l'Europe* (Paris, 1983), provides useful topical chapters on the church, kingship, and culture. Rosamund McKitterick's *The Frankish Church and the Carolingian Reforms, 789–895* (London, 1977) succeeds reasonably well in clarifying the government's role in ecclesiastical advances, notably those advances in clerical education. But J. M. Wallace-Hadrill's *The Frankish Church* (Oxford, 1983) is now essential; it ranges from the Gallo-Roman period through the ninth century.

For the Carolingians, the ninth century begins with ideological consolidation and ends with dynastic dissolution. Einhard, I believe, was phenomenally important for the consolidation, and for critical assessments of his *Vita Karoli* one may trust Helmut Beumann, *Ideengeschichte Studien zu Einhard und anderen Geschichtsschreibern des früheren Mittelalters* (Darmstadt, 1962), but also consult the relevant chapters of Werner Goez's *Translatio Imperii: Ein Beitrag zur Geschichte des Geschichtsdenkens und der politischen Theorien im Mittelalter und in der frühen Neuzeit* (Tübingen, 1958) and Wolfgang Wehlen, *Geschichtsschreibung und Staatsauffassung im Zeitalter Ludwigs des Frommen* (Lübeck, 1970). The most influential churchman in the ninth century was Hincmar, archbishop of Rheims. Peter McKeon, *Hincmar of Laon and Carolingian Politics* (Urbana, 1978) allows the general reader a glimpse of the ninth-century church as well as an introduction to a lesser-known Hincmar, but Jean Devisse's *Hincmar, archevêque de Reims, 845–882*, 3 vols. (Geneva, 1975–76) is the best study of ecclesiastical influence and ninth-century church life. Walter Ullmann, *The Carolingian Renaissance and the Ideal of Kingship* (London, 1969) stressed, and arguably overstressed, the significance of "religious-ecclesiastical thoughts and actions and institutions" in restricting the development of imperial authority. Ullmann's "Schranken der Königsgewalt im Mittelalter," *Historische Zeitschrift* 91 (1971) advances his argument and should be read in conjunction with Josef Semmler, "Reichsidee und kirchliche Gesetzgebung," *Zeitschrift für Kirchengeschichte* 71 (1960).

Walter Schlesinger, "Die Auflösung des Karlsreich," in the first volume of *Karl der Grosse*, chronicles Carolingian dissolution. Joachim Ehlers, "Karolingische Tradition und frühes Nationalbewusstsein in Frankreich," *Francia* 4 (1976) investigates the contests for power more thoroughly and notes prospects for some "restoration" that are carefully sifted in Ursula Penndorf, *Das Problem der Reichseinheitsidee nach der Teilung von Verdun* (Munich, 1974). For the predominance of regional concerns in the later Carolingian period, review Karl Brunner, *Oppositi-*

onelle Gruppen im Karolingerreich (Vienna, 1979). The best route in English from the Carolingians to the Capetians is Jean Dunbabin, *France in the Making, 843–1180* (Oxford, 1985), which nonetheless understates the importance of Ottonian claims for West Frankish politics. For remarks on the Ottonians, I am indebted to Heinz Löwe, "Kaisertum und Abendland in ottonischer und frühsalischer Zeit," *Historische Zeitschrift* 196 (1963). Helmut Beumann, "Die sakrale Legitimierung des Herrschers in Denken der ottonischer Zeit," in *Königswahl und Thronfolge in ottonisch-frühdeutscher Zeit*, ed. Eduard Hlawitschka (Darmstadt, 1971) more closely examines topics related to our themes. Saxon interventions in Italian church politics shape many of the events discussed in our fifth chapter ("The Imperial Papacy") but earlier Saxon influence is usually overvalued; consult Roland Pauler, *Das Regnum Italiae in ottonischer Zeit: Markgrafen, Grafen, und Bischöfe als politische Kräfte* (Tübingen, 1982).

CHAPTER THREE
CONSTANTINE'S SHADOW (II)

To place the study of medieval political ideology and medieval Christendom's redeeming politics in scholarly context, see John Van Engen's brilliant survey, "The Christian Middle Ages as an Historiographical Problem," *American Historical Review* 91 (1986). And it is especially useful to set remarks on Dante's political ideology alongside studies of the centralization of ecclesiastical power during the twelfth and thirteenth centuries. Readers may wish to start with the fifth chapter of this study to consider the origins of papal imperialism. Canonists' subsequent contributions to the doctrines of papal supremacy, however, must not be forgotten. J. A. Watt, *The Theory of Papal Monarchy* (New York, 1965) introduces important concepts and canonists, but the work of Brian Tierney is of particular and enduring interest—notably his *Origins of Papal Infallibility, 1150–1350* (Leiden, 1972), but also "The Continuity of Papal Political Theory in the Thirteenth Century: Some Methodological Considerations," *Mediaeval Studies* 27 (1965). Kenneth Pennington, *Pope and Bishops: The Papal Monarchy in the Twelfth and Thirteenth Centuries* (Philadelphia, 1984) offers insight into popes' increasing authority over lesser prelates. Of the significant pontificates of the period, Innocent III's has attracted most attention. Readers interested in themes developed in Constantine's shadow and Innocent's clever use of ecclesiological imagery may be referred to Wilhelm Imkamp, *Das Kirchenbild Innocenz' III (1198–1216)* (Stuttgart, 1983). Notwithstanding the literature on the pursuit of papal primacy, Hostiensis and Pope Innocent IV are too often disregarded, but see Michele Maccarrone, "Ubi est papa, ibi est Roma," in *Aus Kirche und Reich: Studien zu Theologie, Politik, und Recht im Mittelalter*, ed. Hubert Mordek (Sigmaringen, 1983) and the chapter on Innocent IV in Kölmel's *Regimen Christianum*.

George Holmes, "Dante and the Popes," in *The World of Dante*, ed. Cecil Grayson (Oxford, 1980) assesses Dante's antagonisms toward Popes Boniface VIII and Clement V. T.S.R. Boase, *Boniface VIII* (London, 1933) is still a valuable introduction to the controversial pontificate that textbooks always associate with the papal hierocratic theory that so distressed Dante. Time has also been kind to Richard Scholz's *Die Publizistik zur Zeit Philipps des Schönen und Bonifaz' VIII* (1903; rpt. Stuttgart, 1962). Comments on Clement's pontificate and the crisis prompting Dante's doubts about papal political authority are scattered in yet another time-honored study, Guillaume Mollat, *Les papes d'Avignon (1305–1378)*, 9th ed. (Paris, 1949). It is also worth noting Carl Stange's speculations about pilgrimage, the papacy, and the composition of the *Divine Comedy*, "Der Jubelablass Bonifaz' VIII in Dantes *Commedia*," *Zeitschrift für Kirchengeschichte* 63 (1950).

William Anderson's *Dante the Maker* (London, 1980) is a good general introduction to Dante's literary career, although Dante's world comes more clearly into focus upon reading John Larner, *Italy in the Age of Dante and Petrarch, 1216–1380* (London, 1980). Larner's treatment of Emperor Frederick II is brief and idiosyncratic, so readers would be wise to consult Thomas Curtis Van Cleve, *The Emperor Frederick II of Hohenstaufen, "Imperator Mundi"* (Oxford, 1972). Charles T. Davis, *Dante's Italy and Other Essays* (Philadelphia, 1984) contains pertinent analysis of theorists and issues, all of which make Dante's dreams of a more perfect order more intelligible, but the spirited and compendious reading of Tuscan civilization and papal politics presented by George Holmes, *Florence, Rome, and the Origins of the Renaissance* (Oxford, 1986) is likely to become the standard gateway to Dante's poetic and political visions.

Joan M. Ferrante, *The Political Vision of the Divine Comedy* (Princeton, 1984) is the best book on Dante's politics, yet Jacques Goudet, *La politique de Dante* (Lyon, 1981) sheds greater light on the arguments of the *De monarchia*. I disagree with Michele Maccarrone's "Il terzo libro della *Monarchia*," *Studi Danteschi* 33 (1955); still, one learns much from its pages and from Giovanni di Giannatale's compatible arguments, "Papa e imperatore in *Monarchia* III, 12," *L'Alighieri* 22 (1981). As Bruno Nardi confirms in *Dal "Convivio" alla "Commedia"* (Rome, 1960), the empire, for Dante, "has its own peculiar spirituality," but that claim is only comprehensible when one appreciates Dante's nostalgia for empire and Dante's "spirituality." To those ends, see Charles T. Davis, *Dante and the Idea of Rome* (Oxford, 1957), Antonio de Angelis, *Il con-*

cetto d'imperium e la comunità soprannazionale in Dante (Milan, 1965), and a much-neglected paper by Edouard Jordan, "le gibelinisme de Dante: La doctrine de la monarchie universelle," in *Mélanges de critique et d'érudition françaises publiés à l'occasion du sixième centenaire de la mort du poète* (Paris, 1921). Kenelm Foster, *The Two Dantes and Other Studies* (Berkeley, 1977) ponders Dante's spirituality and orthodoxy and locates Dante on "the Catholic Left" of his time. From Raoul Manselli, "Dante e gli Spirituali Francescani," *Letture Classensi* 11 (1982), from Manselli's more detailed "Dante e l'*Ecclesia Spiritualis*," in *Dante e Roma* (Florence, 1965), and from Rafaello Morghen, *Dante profeta* (Milan, 1983), I gather that Dante may justifiably be shifted farther to the left, perhaps as far as Ugo Foscolo and other nineteenth-century romantics placed him. Foscolo's *Discorso sul testo della Commedia di Dante*, reprinted in *Studi di Dante*, ed. Giovanni da Pozzo (Florence, 1979) is still worth consulting, and for Dante and radical Dantists, see Aldo Vallone, *Storia della critica dantesca da XIV al XV secolo*, vol. 2 (Padua, 1981).

For background information on early Tudor royalty and rituals, see Peter Iver Kaufman, *The 'Polytyque Churche': Religion and Early Tudor Political Culture, 1485–1516* (Macon, Ga., 1986), but also consult C.S.L. Davis, "Bishop John Morton, the Holy See, and the Accession of Henry VII," *English Historical Review* 102 (1987), Stephen Orgel, *The Illusion of Power: Political Theater in the English Renaissance* (Berkeley, 1975), and John N. King, *Tudor Royal Iconography* (Princeton, 1989).

CHAPTER FOUR
PURITANISM AND CROMWELL'S NEW MODEL ARMY

Persons newly introduced to the study of Puritan sociolatry will be surprised to find that the first and familiar term, *Puritan*, generates greater controversy than the second. Debates about the meanings of the word and the "movement" to which it is applied fill the literature as scholars attempt to distinguish Puritanism either *from* the mainstream or *as* the mainstream of sixteenth- and seventeenth-century English Protestantism. During the 1960s the lines of battle were clearly drawn; Charles H. George and Katherine George, *The Protestant Mind of the English Reformation, 1570–1640* (Princeton, 1961) and J.F.H. New, *Anglican and Puritan: The Basis of Their Opposition, 1558–1640* (Palo Alto, 1964) represented the warring parties. For reviews of the contest, see Paul Christianson, "Reformers and the Church of England under Elizabeth I and the Early Stuarts," *Journal of Ecclesiastical History* 31 (1980) and especially Richard L. Greaves, "The Puritan-Nonconformist Tradition in England, 1560–1700: Historiographical Reflections," *Albion* 17 (1985).

Christopher Hill's grand generalizations about Puritan radicalism, rationalism, and capitalism have always seemed to hover above that conflict
(while causing others, to be sure), and they reward close inspection. His
Society and Puritanism in Pre-revolutionary England (London, 1964), if
only for its suggestive coverage of preaching, prophesying, and "the rats-
bane of lecturing," is a good place to start. His most provocative second
thoughts about the Calvinist creed and social conditions, however, have
been patched into the second volume of his latest collection of papers,
Religion and Politics in Seventeenth-Century England, vol. 2 of *The Collected Essays of Christopher Hill* (Amherst, Mass., 1986). It is no exag-
geration to say that Hill sets the agenda for social theorists, but theologians remain troubled by the problem of definition.

Dewey D. Wallace, *Puritans and Predestination: Grace in English Protestant Theology, 1525–1695* (Chapel Hill, 1982) amply documents that
Puritans and other English Protestants were similarly committed to a
"Reformed theology of grace," and Nicholas Tyacke, *Anti-Calvinists:
The Rise of English Arminianism, 1590–1640* (Oxford, 1987) persuasively argues that the shared commitment dominated university discussions, despite disagreements among reformers over liturgy and church
structure. Read together, Wallace and Tyacke prove that the established
church in late Tudor England was doctrinally as Calvinist as its critics,
ordinarily identified as Puritan nonconformists. Hence, criticism and not
creed made Protestants Puritans. It is tempting to subscribe to that conclusion, and possible to do so intelligently, principally because Patrick
Collinson has provided a veritable Michelin map of religious dissent in
the 1570s and 1580s, *The Elizabethan Puritan Movement* (Berkeley,
1967). Collinson himself, however, has been edging cautiously, yet not
timidly, toward a slightly different view. In *The Religion of Protestants*
(Oxford, 1982) and in some papers collected in his *Godly People* (London, 1983), Collinson acknowledges that religious opposition, "the desire for religious reform," was often consistent with "an intensely conservative world view." He then experiments with a plausible redefinition
whereby severely critical *and* conformist Protestants are distinguishable
as Puritans insofar as they applied generally held doctrines of election and
reprobation to their lives more zealously than other Christians. The argument is unambiguously set forth in the chapter on Puritan "practical
divinity" in Peter Lake's ambitious study of Laurence Chaderton and his
Cambridge friends, *Moderate Puritans and the Elizabethan Church*
(Cambridge, 1982) and, more succinctly, in Lake's "Puritan Identities,"
Journal of Ecclesiastical History 35 (1984). Categories formulated in Jerald C. Brauer's anatomy of practical divinity, "Types of Puritan Piety,"
Church History 56 (1987), constitute a promising step forward along
these lines. Explicitly recognizing the experiential or practical dimensions

of Puritan divinity, some scholars will still insist that differences in creed and kind are more significant than differences in degree when measuring religious dissent and nonconformity. That camp has produced insightful studies, notably John S. Coolidge's *The Pauline Renaissance in England: Puritanism and the Bible* (Oxford, 1970) and Richard L. Greaves's *Society and Religion in Elizabethan England* (Minneapolis, 1981), so the debates continue to be lively.

On both sides of the question, the Puritan sermon is seen as the bridge between doctrine or theory and practice. Edward Dering's complaint that hardly one parish in one hundred could boast an effective preaching ministry is a fine specimen of Tudor overstatement, yet it attests the Puritan obsession with the pulpit and with the established church's alleged indifference. Ivronwy Morgan's nearly forgotten story of *The Godly Preachers of the Elizabethan Church* (London, 1965) is a valuable source for Puritan concerns, as is Paul Seaver's *The Puritan Lectureships: The Politics of Religious Dissent, 1560–1662* (Stanford, 1970). Education of preachers was left to the universities, where the English Reformation and later the Puritan reform of the Reformation incubated. H. C. Porter, *Reformation and Reaction in Tudor Cambridge* (Cambridge, 1958) offers a fine overview, although I think Lake's version of important theological skirmishes during the 1590s is to be preferred to Porter's. In terms of doctrinal and intellectual history, few would dispute that the sixteenth century belongs to Cambridge, but C. M. Dent, *Protestant Reformers in Elizabethan Oxford* (Oxford, 1983) recalls that Oxonian religious activism was by no means negligible. Still, the evidence of Cambridge influence and innovation is impressive: see Stanford E. Lehmberg, *Sir Walter Mildmay and Tudor Government* (Austin, 1964) for the foundation of Emmanuel College, and Winthrop S. Hudson, *The Cambridge Connection and the Elizabethan Settlement of 1559* (Durham, N.C., 1980). As for Puritan attention to schooling, review John Morgan, *Godly Learning: Puritan Attitudes towards Reason, Learning, and Education, 1540–1640* (Cambridge, 1986).

At the universities, would-be preachers learned theology; they read Calvin, Beza, Peter Martyr, and the revered theologians of Heidelberg. R. T. Kendall, *Calvin and English Calvinism to 1649* (Oxford, 1979), Collinson's contribution to *International Calvinism, 1541–1715*, ed. Menna Prestwich (Oxford, 1985), and Dewey Wallace comment on continental influences. Like Christopher Hill, David Zaret favors another approach; *The Heavenly Contract: Ideology and Organization in Prerevolutionary Puritanism* (Chicago, 1985) cogently argues that "organizational pressures" were as decisive as intellectual precedents in the development of Puritan covenantal theology. Zaret refers here to lay initiatives, and interest in the laity's part in Puritan dissent has greatly increased. On one side, scholars contend the English Reformation made only grudging progress through the sixteenth century and they assemble evidence for the vitality of Catholicism among the laity. See the case presented by Christopher Haigh and his allies in *The English Reformation Revised*, ed. Haigh (Cambridge, 1987) and J. J. Scarisbrick, *The Reformation and the English People* (Oxford, 1984). On the other side, Protestantism moves more rapidly and the laity's importance is usually underscored. See, for example, A. G. Dickens, *Lollards and Protestants in the Diocese of York, 1509–1558* (Oxford, 1959); Claire Cross, *Church and People, 1450–1660: The Triumph of the Laity in the English Church* (Atlantic Highlands, N.J., 1976); and John F. Davis, *Heresy and Reformation in the South East of England, 1520–1559* (London, 1983). Final word on the importance and dedication of the Puritan laity may come from studies like Hill's and Zaret's, but it may also come from research on local gentry and local militancy. Visiting Sussex with Anthony Fletcher, *A County Community in Peace and War: Sussex, 1600–1640* (London, 1975), or visiting Essex, "the revolutionary county par excellence," with William Hunt, *The Puritan Movement: The Coming of Revolution in an English County* (Cambridge, Mass., 1983) are good ways to sample that approach, but also see J. T. Cliffe, *The Puritan Gentry: The Great Puritan Families of Early Stuart England* (London, 1984).

The study of "organizational pressures" closer to the center of political power requires colloquy with influential clerics. Patrick Collinson's *Archbishop Grindal, 1519–1583* (Berkeley, 1979) is wonderful. Nothing comparable retrieves Grindal's successor, John Whitgift, but Wallace T. MacCaffery's judicious assessments are commendable, although they are crowded into a small corner of his *Queen Elizabeth and the Making of Policy, 1572–1588* (Princeton, 1981). Thomas Cartwright was never really close to the centers of power, yet he was always at the center of swirls of controversy. A. F. Scott Pearson, *Thomas Cartwright and Elizabethan Puritanism, 1535–1603* (Cambridge, 1925; rpt. Gloucester, Mass., 1966) has no serious rival. And then there is William Laud; the standard biography is still Hugh Trevor-Roper's *Archbishop Laud, 1573–1645*, 2nd ed. (London, 1962).

For Laud's administration and the origins of the English Civil War, consult John S. Morrill's bibliography, *Seventeenth-Century Britain* (Hamden, Conn., 1980). Morrill himself shrewdly reconstructs "The Religious Context of the English Civil War," *Transactions of the Royal Historical Society*, 5th ser., 34 (1984) and assembles essays that enrich our understanding of Puritanism as a factor in the war's escalation, *Reaction to the English Civil War, 1642–1649* (London, 1982). J. P. Sommerville, *Politics and Ideology in England, 1603–1640* (London, 1986), however, shows it is still possible to ponder the conflict without Puritanism. Certainly once the country was in arms, local political interests were likely to determine loyalties. Contemplating the critical debates between 1640 and 1642, one is nonetheless struck by the force of Anthony Fletcher's claims that religiously inspired suspicions about popish conspiracies were crucial, if not causal—*The Outbreak of the English Civil War* (London, 1981). And whether or not one agrees that Puritanism was inherently politically subversive, Michael Walzer's arguments to that effect demand careful consideration, *The Revolution of the Saints: A Study in the Origins of Radical Politics* (Cambridge, Mass., 1965).

John F. Wilson's work on *The Pulpit in Parliament: Puritanism during the English Civil Wars, 1640–1648* (Princeton, 1969) documents the revolutionary impulse in later Puritanism's redeeming politics; Christopher Hill, *God's Englishman: Oliver Cromwell and the English Revolution* (New York, 1970) introduces the leading revolutionary. As entertaining and plausible as Hill's observations are, his position on the early radicalization of Cromwell's army will not survive Mark Kishlansky's analysis of the soldiers' special interests and political consciousness, *The Rise of The New Model Army* (Cambridge, 1979), for which also see Clive Holmes, *The Eastern Association in the English Civil War* (Cambridge, 1974). Both Kishlansky and Austin Woolrych, *Soldiers and Statesmen: The General Council of the Army and Its Debates, 1647–1648* (Oxford, 1987) volunteer fresh readings of the army's march to Putney, but A.S.P. Woodhouse's introduction to the collection of relevant texts, *Puritanism and Liberty* (London, 1938), is still fascinating.

If the Puritan preachers' influence among the soldiers was as great as Leo Solt implies, the New Model's religious consciousness was rather suddenly raised and radicalized. But it is wise to remain prudently sceptical about such influence. Solt's *Saints in Arms* (Stanford, 1959) is nonetheless a useful review of the preachers' assurances of the army's righteousness, as is Tai Liu, *Discord in Zion: The Puritan Divines and the Puritan Revolution* (The Hague, 1973). A number of studies permit readers to place the preachers' assurances in the context of Puritan spiritualism and millenarianism: Geoffrey F. Nuttall, *The Holy Spirit in Puritan Faith and Experience* (Oxford, 1946); William M. Lamont, *Godly Rule: Politics and Religion, 1603–1660* (London, 1969); Paul Christianson, *Reformers and Babylon: Apocalyptic Visions from the Reformation to the Eve of the Civil War* (Toronto, 1978); and Katharine R. Firth, *The Apocalyptic Tradition in Reformation Britain, 1530–1645* (Oxford, 1979). Eric C. Walker, *William Dell, Master Puritan* (Cambridge, 1970) avoids some troubling issues, but much can be mined from an unexpected source, Theodor Sippell's provocative monograph, "William Dells Programm einer 'lutherischen' Gemeinschaftsbewegung," *Zeitschrift für Theologie und Kirche*, Ergänzungsheft 3 (1911).

CHAPTER FIVE
THE IMPERIAL PAPACY

The earliest churches' concepts of clerical authority, to which this chapter alludes, are part of the imperial papacy's history. Luigi I. Scipioni, *Vescovo e populo: L'esercizio dell'autorità nella chiesa primitiva* (Milan, 1977) gives a good account of the "monarchialization" of the episcopacy, that is, the concentration of power and the development of Christianity's first ministries. Michele Maccarrone, *Apostolicità, episcopato e primato di Pietro* (Rome, 1979) discusses later efforts to concentrate ecclesiastical power in Rome. Those efforts during the early Middle Ages should only be considered alongside accounts of Byzantine and Lombard regimes in Italy, for which general readers are fortunate to have Jeffrey Richards, *The Popes and the Papacy in the Early Middle Ages, 476–752* (London, 1979). For papal proprietary interests in Italy, however, Thomas F. X. Noble, *The Republic of St. Peter: The Birth of the Papal State, 680–825* (Philadelphia, 1984) is essential, and Peter Partner, *The Lands of St. Peter: The Papal State in the Middle Ages and the Early Renaissance* (London, 1972) permits readers to track papal government through the pontificate of Gregory VII and beyond. Still, it is hardly possible to relate the church's territorial administrations to issues that bear more directly on papal redeeming politics—to the formulation of papal ideology, the direction of papal diplomacy—without a sound, pontificate-by-pontificate report. For the period in question, I prefer Erich Caspar's judicious *Geschichte des Papsttums von den Anfängen zur Höhe der Weltherrschaft*, 2 vols. (Tübingen, 1930–33). Bernhard Schimmelpfennig, *Das Papsttum: Grundzüge seiner Geschichte von der Antike bis zur Renaissance* (Darmstadt, 1984) knows no close contender among more recent surveys and certainly warrants translation.

The study of medieval papal ideology during the last quarter century would have been much less lively were it not for the controversial interpretations of Karl Morrison and Walter Ullmann. Morrison's *Tradition and Authority in the Western Church, 300–1140* (Princeton, 1969) is a marvelous book. It measures the relative importance of precedent and discretion in pontiffs' ecclesiological and political pronouncements. Accounts of popes and leading prelates of the Frankish and early Ottonian periods are especially compelling. Gregory VII, however, seems slightly out of focus; although Morrison correctly identifies Gregory's emphasis on discretion (whereby whatever the pontiff wills is canonical), *Tradition*'s insistence on Gregory's contempt for antiquity requires qualification. Walter Ullmann finds imperial pretensions everywhere in papal history. What distinguishes Gregory VII from his predecessors, therefore, is not ideology but the determination to realize the claims of hierocratic theorists who specified that the church should rule the world or, at least in critical matters, rule the rulers of the world. Despite some telling criticisms in Friedrich Kempf's "Die päpstliche Gewalt in der mittelalterlichen Welt," *Miscellanea historiae pontificae* 21 (1959), Ullmann's *The Growth of Papal Government in the Middle Ages: A Study in the Ideological Relations of Clerical to Lay Power*, 2nd ed. (London, 1962) is still justifiably known as *the* textbook on papal monarchy, and Ullmann's contributions to our understanding of the busy and influential fifth century are immense, less striking in *Growth*, perhaps, than in his last volume, *Gelasius I (492–496): Das Papsttum an der Wende der Spätantike zum Mittelalter* (Stuttgart, 1981). To elucidate Boniface I's pontificate, I have used both Ullmann and Charles Pietri's *Roma Christiana*. Percy Schramm, of course, has also imposed his stamp on the study of the papal *imitatio imperii*. The fourth volume of his *Beiträge* (Pt. 1, Stuttgart, 1970) includes his grand chronicle of "*Sacerdotium* und *Regnum* im Austausch ihrer Vorrechte" as well as several probing papers on the reform papacy of the eleventh and twelfth centuries.

The urge to think of that *Reformpapsttum* as something Gregory VII created, as a reflection of his personality, is nearly irrepressible. He is said to have been the power behind the scenes long before his election, and he knew virtually every progressive at the courts of his predecessors, several of whom were themselves notable reformers; see Enzo Petrucci, *Ecclesiologia e politica di Leone IX* (Rome, 1977) and Tilmann Schmidt, *Alexander II und die römische Reformgruppe seiner Zeit* (Stuttgart, 1977). As impertinent as Gregory VII may occasionally seem, much that he tried obliged current expectations. His strides against simony were part of a long march. With the publication of Johannes Laudage's *Priesterbild und Reformpapsttum im 11. Jahrhundert* (Cologne, 1984), it is clear that even his most extreme statements against lay investiture must be considered in the context of previous and prevailing discontent with lay interference in church affairs. And lay interference sometimes encouraged reformers and reform; scc John Howe, "The Nobility's Reform of the Medieval Church," *American Historical Review* 93 (1988). To what extent, then, was Pope Gregory VII in step? out of step? out of bounds? That such questions—more elegantly expressed, to be sure—should generate a vast literature is quite predictable. I. S. Robinson has admirable command of it, and his magnificent bibliography, "Pope Gregory VII (1073–1085)," 36 *Journal of Ecclesiastical History* (1985) is a windfall for specialists and nonspecialists alike.

Of the books that bring nonspecialists closer to Gregory VII, his times, and his troubles, Uta-Renate Blumenthal's *The Investiture Controversy: Church and Monarchy from the Ninth to the Twelfth Century* (Philadelphia, 1988) is especially commendable, as is Gerd Tellenbach's *Church,*

State, and Christian Society at the Time of the Investiture Contest, translated by R. F. Bennett (Oxford, 1948). Tellenbach stresses the pope's dedication to ecclesiastical liberties and the politicization of the theological concept *libertas ecclesiae*. To explain Gregory's commitments to liberty and reform, it is best to investigate his commerce with Cluny, as did H.E.J. Cowdrey, *The Cluniacs and the Gregorian Reform* (Oxford, 1970). Also pertinent is Marcel Pacaut, "Ordre et liberté dans l'église: L'influence de Cluny aux XIe et XIIe siècles," in *The End of Strife*, ed. David Loades (Edinburgh, 1984). Equally revealing, Gregory's work in concert with jurists is reviewed by Horst Fuhrmann in "Das Reformpapsttum und die Rechtswissenschaft," in *Investiturstreit und Reichsverfassung*, ed. Josef Fleckenstein (Sigmaringen, 1973), and his debts to the pope he respected most are analyzed by Gerhart Ladner, "Gregory the Great and Gregory VII: A Comparison of Their Concepts of Renewal," reprinted in his *Images and Ideas in the Middle Ages*, vol. 2 (Rome, 1983). All agree that comprehensive and significant results are obtained only when Gregory VII's commitments and concepts are collated with interpretations of his monumental struggle against Emperor Henry IV, culminating perhaps at Canossa in 1077 but ending years later with Gregory's death in exile.

Harald Zimmermann has published the most intriguing reconstruction concerned with Canossa as both historical confrontation and metaphor, *Der Canossagang von 1077: Wirkungen und Wirklichkeit* (Mainz, 1975). Christian Schneider dispels some misleading conjectures about preliminaries, *Prophetisches Sacerdotium und heilsgeschichtliches Regnum im Dialog, 1073–1077: Zur Geschichte Gregors VII und Heinrichs IV* (Munich, 1972). Jürgen Vogel, *Gregor VII und Heinrich IV nach Canossa: Zeugnisse ihres Selbstverständnisses* (Berlin, 1983) takes the tale to Gregory's death, blaming the tragedy on the pope's inflexibility. To read the essays by Gerd Tellenbach, Carl Erdmann, Henri Xavier Arquillière, and Albert Brackmann, assembled with others in *Canossa als Wende*, ed. Hellmut Kämpf (Darmstadt, 1963), however, is to be reassured that distributions of blame and *Bedeutung* rarely stand uncontested for long. The pope and his apologists, of course, presented the confrontation at Canossa, events and exchanges preceding it, and the wreck of the apparent reconciliation in order to ennoble their case for papal supremacy. Their offensives in the war of words are the very stuff from which the imperial papacy can be recomposed as a chapter in the history of Christian sociolatry.

I. S. Robinson, *Authority and Resistance in the Investiture Contest: The Polemical Literature of the Late Eleventh Century* (Manchester, U.K., 1978) describes the warfare economically, identifying the central preoccupations of both parties. Nothing comparable to Robinson's *Au-*

thority has been written on the rhetoric of the Gregorian reform, for which Gregory VII's register is naturally an indispensable source. Thanks to Ephraim Emerton, who selected and translated strategic documents in *The Correspondence of Pope Gregory VII* (New York, 1932), general readers may judge for themselves the tone and substance of papally authorized polemics. Erich Caspar's shrewd judgments, however, will be hard to dismiss. His "Gregor VII in seinen Briefen," *Historische Zeitschrift* 130 (1924) picked holes in the letters' logic yet admired their personal appeal. Of the doctrinal letters, the second justification Gregory sent to Hermann of Metz is probably the most informative and had the most significant afterlife, for which see John Gilchrist, "The Reception of Pope Gregory VII into Canon Law," *Zeitschrift der Savigny-Stiftung für Rechtsgeschichte, kanonistische Abteilung* 59 (1973). Other notable essays on the correspondence include Alexander Murray, "Pope Gregory VII and His Letters," *Traditio* 22 (1966) and I. S. Robinson, "The Dissemination of the Letters of Pope Gregory VII during the Investiture Controversy," *Journal of Ecclesiastical History* 34 (1983).

Compressed appraisals of Gregory VII and the sacerdotalism and imperialism associated with his reform and rule of the church are common fare. Few recent wrap-ups, however, are as good as Rudolf Schieffer's "Gregor VII—Ein Versuch über die historische Grösse," *Historisches Jahrbuch* 97–98 (1978), Werner Goez's "Zur Persönlichkeit Gregors VII," *Römische Quartalschrift für christliche Altertumskunde und Kirchengeschichte* 73 (1978), and Karl Morrison's "The Gregorian Reform," in *Christian Spirituality: Origins to the Twelfth Century*, ed. Bernard McGinn and John Meyendorff (New York, 1985).

Predictably, Robinson's aforementioned bibliography shows the limits of summary assessments. One learns quickly that Gregory VII's diplomacy inspires a wide range of opinions about the occasions and aims of his interventions. One also learns of the extraordinary range of John Cowdrey's interests in Gregorian initiatives and in their local effects. Cowdrey's studies of England, Spain, and southern Italy are unfailingly intelligent and suggestive. Of particular value is the story of how Gregory and his successor Desiderius (as Victor III) made common cause against the emperor, in H.E.J. Cowdrey, *The Age of Abbot Desiderius: Montecassino, the Papacy, and the Normans in the Eleventh and Early Twelfth Centuries* (Oxford, 1983).

There are several routes from the death of Gregory VII, through the achievements of his immediate successors, to the pontificates of Innocent II and Anacletus II, where this chapter concludes. From studies of local impact like those of Cowdrey and his student, G. A. Loud, *Church and Society in the Norman Principality of Capua, 1058–1197* (Oxford, 1985), one gets the impression of fundamental continuity. When the pol-

itics of Pope Paschal II (1099–1119) is featured, as in Glauco Maria Can-
tarella's *Ecclesiologia e politica nel papato di Pasquale II: Linee di una
interpretazione* (Rome, 1982), one must take discontinuities and compromises very seriously.

Still another route has been tried by scholars interested in curial politics. Hans-Walter Klewitz, *Reformpapsttum und Kardinalkolleg* (Darmstadt, 1957), specifically his paper on "Das Ende des Reformpapsttum,"
published in 1939, tracks developments that led to the double election of
1130. Rudolf Hüls, *Kardinäle, Klerus, und Kirchen Roms, 1049–1130*
(Tübingen, 1977) takes a similar approach in its final chapter on party
politics (*die Machtverteilung*) in Rome. This is important because Franz-
Josef Schmale, *Studien zum Schisma des Jahres 1130* (Cologne, 1961)
claims that contests between conservative and reformist cardinals preceded the disputed election, that those contests reflected divisions among
churchmen throughout Europe, and that conservatives capitalized on the
ambitions of Anacletus and the Pierleone family while reformers gravi-
tated toward Innocent and his seasoned, resourceful chancellor, Haimeric. Werner Malaczek, "Das Kardinalskollegium unter Innocenz II und
Anaklet II," *Archivum Historiae Pontificae* 19 (1981) insists Innocent
and Haimeric built rather than borrowed the consensus for reform.
Moreover, reform and ideology, according to Malaczek, were not principal concerns of the Innocentians, who experimented with alliances and
innovations chiefly to unseat their rivals. Pier Fausto Palumbo, *Lo scisma
del MCXXX* (Rome, 1942) speaks up for Anacletus and is still valuable;
his "Nuovi studi (1942–1962) sullo scisma di Anacleto II," *Bulletino
dell'istituto storico italiano per il medio evo* 75 (1963) is largely a response to Schmale. For the rhetoric of redeeming politics and the smear
campaigns against Anacletus, see Palumbo's *Lo scisma*, Mario da Bergamo (Luigi Pellegrini), "Osservazioni sulle fonti per la duplice elezione
papale del 1130," *Aevum* 39 (1965), and Aryeh Graboïs, "Le schisme de
1130 et la France," 76 *Revue d'histoire ecclesiastique (1981)*. Agreeing
with Malaczek and Palumbo, Mary Stroll, *The Jewish Pope: Ideology
and Politics in the Papal Schism of 1130* (Leiden, 1987) doubts the importance of ideology and declares Anacletus "eminently *papabile.*"

CHAPTER SIX

JOHN CALVIN'S GENEVA

Heading to Calvin's Geneva now means traveling through a relatively
new field of study and a robust crop of books and papers on the nontheo-
logical conditions for religious reform in sixteenth-century urban centers.
Bernd Moeller's seminal *Reichsstadt und Reformation* (Gütersloh, 1962),
available in English in *Imperial Cities and the Reformation: Three Essays*

(Philadelphia, 1972), reawakened interest in the sacralization of civic order. Subsequently scholars have probed for elites, interest groups, social conflicts, and political power struggles that hastened or retarded religious reform. Readers may sample results in Robert W. Scribner's concise account of "Civic Unity and the Reformation in Erfurt," *Past and Present* 66 (1975), in papers collected in *Stadtbürgertum und Adel in der Reformation / The Urban Classes, the Nobility, and the Reformation*, ed. Wolfgang J. Mommsen (Stuttgart, 1979) and in *The German People and the Reformation*, ed. R. Po-Chia Hsia (Ithaca, 1988). Hsia has also published a valuable study of the urban context of the Courter-Reformation, *Society and Religion in Münster, 1535–1618* (New Haven, 1984). Susan C. Karant-Nunn's *Zwickau in Transition, 1500–1547: The Reformation as an Agent of Change* (Columbus, Ohio, 1987) is interesting for its nearly exclusive concentration on Protestantism's deleterious effects. Among the challenges to Moeller's propositions, however, Steven Ozment's *The Reformation in the Cities* (New Haven, 1975) is still the most direct, while the final word so far on corporate policies and new pieties during the Reformation's first and critical decade is Heinrich Richard Schmidt, *Reichsstädte, Reich, und Reformation: Korporative Religionspolitik, 1521–1529/30* (Wiesbaden, 1986).

Although it extends into territories covered by Schmidt, Thomas A. Brady's *Turning Swiss: Cities and Empire, 1450–1550* (Cambridge, 1985) should be widely consulted on the influence of urban oligarchies and religious reform on the deterioration of Habsburg hegemony. Its bibliography is blue-chip. Brady is also known as one of the perceptive Strasbourg-watchers whose observations illustrate and advance the social history of the Reformation. (Strasbourg, of course, was Calvin's refuge for several years.) Brady's *Ruling Class, Regime, and Reformation in Strasbourg, 1520–1555* (Leiden, 1978) heads a long list of more or less "Moellerian" volumes that should include Erdmann Weyrauch, *Konfessionelle Krise und soziale Stabilität: Das Interim in Strassburg (1548–1562)* (Stuttgart, 1978), René Bornert, *La réforme protestante du culte à Strasbourg au XVIᵉ siècle (1523–1598): Approche sociologique et interprétation théologique* (Leiden, 1981), Miriam Usher Chrisman, *Lay Culture, Learned Culture: Books and Social Change in Strasbourg* (New Haven, 1982), and Lorna Jane Abray, *The People's Reformation: Magistrates, Clergy, and Commons in Strasbourg, 1500–1598* (Ithaca, 1985). Franziska Conrad's *Reformation in der bäuerlichen Gesellschaft: Zur Rezeption reformatorischer Theologie im Elsass* (Wiesbaden, 1984) stays in the neighborhood of Strasbourg but studies the sacralization of rural society. That volume and Marijn de Kroon's *Studien zu Martin Bucers Obrigkeitsverständnis: Evangelisches Ethos und politisches Engagement* (Gütersloh, 1984) are equally relevant here and among contextual studies of the development of sectarian Protestantism, to which our eighth chapter refers.

There are good books on Geneva as well. E. William Monter, *Calvin's Geneva* (New York, 1967) is a splendid introduction. His *Studies in Genevan Government (1536–1605)* (Geneva, 1964) is stocked with more technical information, and his papers on "Virtue and Money in Calvinist Geneva," in his *Enforcing Morality in Early Modern Europe* (London, 1987) intelligently report on commerce and the consistory. For the consistory, the second volume of Walther Köhler's *Zürcher Ehegericht und Genfer Konsistorium* (Leipzig, 1942) is absolutely essential, but also see Robert M. Kingdon's fine essays on crime, punishment, morality, and the Reformed Church in Calvin's Geneva, *Church and Society in Reformation Europe* (London, 1985). Kingdon's *Geneva and the Coming of the Wars of Religion in France, 1555–1563* (Geneva, 1956) and *Geneva and the Consolidation of the French Protestant Movement, 1564–1572* (Geneva, 1967) discuss city life and remind us that Calvin sometimes saw Geneva as a staging area for the French Reformation.

But influential Frenchmen were unimpressed by Calvin's successes in Geneva. Currently, few scholars question Calvin's achievement; the question is how radically his reformation broke with its past. In Carlos Eire's *War against the Idols: The Reform of Worship from Erasmus to Calvin* (Cambridge, 1986), the title of one chapter, "From Iconoclasm to Revolution," suggests an answer, yet it does not signal how cleverly the answer is argued. For Calvin and late medieval exegesis and theology, see E. P. Meijering, *Calvin wider die Neugierde* (Nieukoop, 1980), Alister E. McGrath, "John Calvin and Late Medieval Thought," *Archiv für Reformationsgeschichte* 77 (1986), and Thomas F. Torrance, *The Hermeneutics of John Calvin* (Edinburgh, 1988).

Calvin's break with his past, his alleged abandonment of humanistic interests, was once thought complete. But William J. Bouwsma's *John Calvin: A Sixteenth-Century Portrait* (Oxford, 1988) analyzes anxieties, contradictions, and enduring cultural influences, maintaining persuasively that "Calvin was still wrestling as inconclusively with the same inner demons at the end of his life as when he first arrived in Geneva" (p. 4). Alexandre Ganoczy, *Le jeune Calvin: Genèse et évolution de sa vocation réformatrice* (Wiesbaden, 1966)—translated as *The Young Calvin* (Philadelphia, 1987)—chases down "the origin and evolution of Calvin's calling as a reformer." Together, Bouwsma and Ganoczy should appease the most insatiable appetite for elegantly argued yet confessionally indifferent biographical literature.

It is an article of faith that proceedings from interdisciplinary congresses and other *miscellanea* dispel more confusion than they create. Three recent collections on Calvin and Calvinism tend to corroborate:

Calvinus Ecclesiae Genevensis Custos, ed. Wilhelm Neuser (Frankfurt, 1984); *International Calvinism, 1541-1715*, ed. Menna Prestwich (Oxford, 1985); and *Calviniana: Ideas and Influence of Jean Calvin*, ed. Robert Schnucker (Kirksville, Mo.; 1988). Nonetheless, the "clusters of intellectual problems ... worthy of further study," identified by David Steinmetz, are still worthy of further study: see his "The Theology of Calvin and Calvinism," in *Reformation Europe: A Guide to Research*, ed. Steven Ozment (St. Louis, 1982). Wilhelm Niesel, *The Theology of Calvin* (Philadelphia, 1956) tempts us, as general presentations often do, to conclude that most problems have been resolved, but it remains a useful introduction. On Calvin's theology, however, also see Edward A. Dowey, *The Knowledge of God in Calvin's Theology*, 2nd ed. (New York, 1965), T.H.L. Parker, *Calvin's Doctrine of the Knowledge of God*, rev. ed. (Edinburgh, 1969), Charles Boyer, *Calvin et Luther: Accords et différences* (Rome, 1973), and Charles Partee, "Calvin's Central Dogma Again," *Sixteenth Century Journal* 18 (1987). We may well doubt the ultimate outcome, yet Richard Stauffer's *L'Humanité de Calvin* (Neuchâtel, 1964), "Un Calvin reconnu: Le prédicateur de Genève," *Bulletin: Société de l'histoire de Protestantisme française* 123 (1977), *Dieu, la création, et la providence dans la prédication de Calvin* (Bern, 1978), and "Calvin et la catholicité évangélique," *Revue de théologie et de philosophie* 115 (1983) are fascinating efforts to tease from his theology and preaching a kinder, gentler Calvin.

André Bieler, *La pensée économique et sociale de Calvin* (Geneva, 1959) holds fast to a gentler Geneva than the one reconstituted in histories of the Reformation that tended to make Calvin's city a police state. Bieler writes of policy, regulation, and biblical theology that was solicitous of creditors, debtors, and derelicts. For related comments, see Ronald S. Wallace, *Calvin's Doctrine of the Christian Life* (Edinburgh, 1959) and W. Fred Graham, *The Constructive Revolutionary: John Calvin and His Socio-Economic Impact* (Richmond, Va., 1971). The better snapshots and summaries of Calvin's political vision still consider whether the apparently authoritarian and undemocratic reformer could have fathered modern democracy and capitalism: Hans Baron, "Calvinist Republicanism and Its Historical Roots," *Church History* 8 (1939); Erik Wolf, "Theologie und Sozialordnung bei Calvin," 42 *Archiv für Reformationsgeschichte* (1951); J. W. Allen, *A History of Political Thought in the Sixteenth Century*, rev. ed. (London, 1957); Sheldon S. Wolin, *Politics and Vision: Continuity and Innovation in Western Political Thought* (London, 1961); and David Little, *Religion, Order, and Law: A Study in Pre-revolutionary England* (Oxford, 1970). It is surprising how little some surveys have to say about Calvin and Geneva; for instance, Thomas G. Sanders, *Protestant Concepts of Church and State* (New York, 1964) and Quentin Skinner, *The Foundations of Modern Political Thought*, vol. 2 (Cambridge, 1978). Hans Scholl, *Reformation und Politik: Politische Ethik bei Luther, Calvin, und den Frühhugenotten* (Stuttgart, 1976) is useful for purposes of comparison and for its emphasis on sermon literature.

On the question of Calvin's modernity, I think the weight of the evidence favors Hermann Vahle's conclusion that Calvin cannot be credited for later appeals to popular sovereignty, although his ideals and ecclesiology had politically liberalizing effects—"Calvinismus und Demokratie im Spiegel der Forschung," *Archiv für Reformationsgeschichte* 66 (1975). One could argue, then, as does Ralph C. Hancock, *Calvin and the Foundations of Modern Politics* (Ithaca, 1989), that the theology of the *Institutes*, which "explodes the simple dichotomy between secular and religious concerns," and progressive political ideology are not irreconcilable. The question that more directly relates to this chapter, however, is whether (or to what extent) Calvin's ideals evolved with or ahead of the redeeming politics of the Genevan magistracy. The best book by far on that issue is Harro Höpfl's *The Christian Polity of John Calvin* (Cambridge, 1982), but Höpfl seems to me to underestimate Calvin's sense of the corporate character of redemption and sanctification, which Bieler's *Pensée économique* and particularly Josef Bohatec's *Calvins Lehre von Staat und Kirche mit besonderer Berücksichtigung des Organismusgedankens* (Breslau, 1937) place in the foreground. I am indebted to Bohatec, Bieler, and Höpfl, but also to Marc Chenevière, *La pensée politique de Calvin*, (1937; rpt. Geneva, 1970) and Jürgen Baur, *Gott, Recht, und weltliches Regiment im Werke Calvins* (Bonn, 1965). Roger Stauffenegger, *Eglise et société: Genève au XVIIᵉ siècle*, 2 vols. (Geneva, 1983) studies Calvin's legacy and the next century in Geneva, "la cité de Dieu" and "la cité terrestre."

CHAPTER SEVEN
AUGUSTINE'S CITIES OF GOD

Stauffenegger borrowed his cities from Augustine or from the army of theorists who took their metaphors, phrases, and ideas from *The City of God*, which Augustine composed during the last twenty years of his career. For background and biography, of course, readers will find the first twenty as important. George Lawless, *Augustine of Hippo and His Monastic Rule* (Oxford, 1987) contains a discerning study of Augustine's "mind and milieu" during the decade after his conversion (386–396). The sixteenth centenary of that conversion occasioned bushels of work but nothing, I suspect, keener than Paula Fredriksen's "Paul and Augustine: Conversion Narratives, Orthodox Traditions, and the Retrospective

Self," *Journal of Theological Studies* 37 (1986). Excellent summaries of Augustine's quarrels with Manicheans, Donatists, and Pelagians distinguish Gerald Bonner's *Augustine, Life and Controversies* (London, 1963). Peter Brown, *Augustine of Hippo* (London, 1967) brings admirable order to his subject's life and thought; Brown's is *the* biography of Augustine, and to explore supplementary considerations with the same thoughtful and entertaining guide, see Brown's *Religion and Society in the Age of Augustine* (London, 1972). Notable accounts in other languages include Henri Marrou, *Saint Augustin et la fin de culture antique* (Paris, 1938), André Mandouze, *Saint Augustin: L'aventure de la raison et de la grâce* (Paris, 1968), and Alberto Pincherle, *Vita di Sant'Agostino* (Rome, 1980). Isabelle Bochet, *Saint Augustin et le désir de Dieu* (Paris, 1982) helpfully reevaluates Augustine's apparent dualism to correct misleading inferences commonly drawn from his reflections on his own, others', and original sin. For his philosophical sources, see Jean Pepin, *"Ex Platonicorum persona": Etudes sur les lectures philosophiques de saint Augustin* (Amsterdam, 1977), Marcia L. Colish, *The Stoic Tradition from Antiquity to the Middle Ages*, vol. 2 (Leiden, 1985), and Gerard O'Daly, *Augustine's Philosophy of Mind* (Berkeley, 1987). Among general surveys of Augustine's thinking, Henry Chadwick, *Augustine* (Oxford, 1986) and Jaroslav Pelikan, *The Mystery of Continuity: Time and History, Memory and Eternity in the Thought of Saint Augustine* (Charlottesville, Va., 1986) provide fine day-trip introductions. Etienne Gilson, *The Christian Philosophy of Saint Augustine* (New York, 1967) and Eugene TeSelle, *Augustine, the Theologian* (New York, 1970) demand somewhat lengthier stays.

The starting point for any study of Augustine's *De civitate Dei* remains Gustave Bardy's introduction in *Bibliothèque augustinienne*, 5th ser., 33 (1959). Bardy's notes for that edition enlighten ceaselessly. On Christians' responses to the fall of Rome, of which the *De civitate* is certainly the most unforgettable, see Otto Zwierlein, "Der Fall Roms im Spiegel der Kirchenväter," *Zeitschrift für Papyrologie und Epigraphik* 32 (1978) and Jaroslav Pelikan, *The Excellent Empire: The Fall of Rome and the Triumph of the Church* (San Francisco, 1987). Paolo Brezzi, "Riflessioni sulla genesi del *De Civitate Dei* di Sant'Agostino," *Perennitas: Studi in onore di Angelo Brelich*, ed. Giulia Piccaluga (Rome, 1980) looks beyond Rome's humiliation for other provocations for Augustine's work. Also see Brezzi's *Analisi ed interpretazione del "De Civitate Dei" di Sant'Agostino* (Tolentino, 1960) and Jean-Claude Guy, *Unité et structure logique de la "Cité de Dieu" de saint Augustin* (Paris, 1961). Undeniably, and whatever other justifications for the *City* may be contemplated, Augustine's *opus arduum* deliberately rewrites Rome's history in light of Rome's recent tragedy, so consult Klaus Thraede, "Das antike Rom in

Augustins *De civitate Dei*," *Jahrbuch für Antike und Christentum* 20 (1977) and Salvatore d'Elia, *Studi sulla civiltà del Basso Impero* (Naples, 1981).

The histories of Rome and empire throw into greater relief what Augustine has to say about the fortunes and destiny of the city of God. But investigations have not made incontestably clear to what that city refers. The church, a likely candidate at first glance, becomes less likely as studies of Augustine's ecclesiology reveal its complexity. See Joseph Ratzinger, *Volk und Haus Gottes in Augustins Lehre von der Kirche* (Munich, 1954), Yves Congar, "*Civitas Dei* et *Ecclesia* chez saint Augustin," *Revue des études augustiniennes* 3 (1957), Rémi Crespin, *Ministère et sainteté: Pastorale du clergé et solution de la crise Donatiste dans la vie et la doctrine de saint Augustin* (Paris, 1965), Emilien Lamirande, *Etudes sur l'ecclésiologie de saint Augustin* (Ottawa, 1969), and Ulrich Duchrow, *Christenheit und Weltverantwortung: Traditionsgeschichte und systematische Struktur Zweireichelehre* (Stuttgart, 1970). To speculate about the earthly presence of the city of God in the context of this chapter's understanding of Augustine's "personalist platform," I have drawn from several scholars: Wilhelm Kamlah, *Christentum und Geschichtlichkeit*, 2nd ed. (Stuttgart, 1959); Paolo Brezzi, "Una *civitas terrena spiritualis* come ideale storico-politico di Sant'Agostino," *Augustinus Magister* 2 (1954); Gerhart Ladner, *The Idea of Reform* (New York, 1967); and Berndt Hamm, "Unmittelbarkeit des göttlichen Gnadenwirkens und kirchliche Heilsvermittlung bei Augustin," *Zeitschrift für Theologie und Kirche* 78 (1981).

The ultimate objective of Augustine's personalist platform was the redemption of human will. Much of the literature on that prospect reminds us how difficult it is to reconcile choice in such a critical matter with Augustine's uncompromising insistence on God's sovereignty. Gotthard Nygren, *Das Praedestinationsproblem in der Theologie Augustins* (Göttingen, 1956) knows the problem; John Rist, "Augustine on Free Will and Predestination," *Journal of Theological Studies* 20 (1969) volunteers one creditable solution, but J. Patout Burns, *The Development of Augustine's Doctrine of Operative Grace* (Paris, 1980) and the papers collected in Gerald Bonner, *God's Decree and Man's Destiny: Studies on the Thought of Augustine of Hippo* (London, 1987) should not be overlooked. In some places, I believe, Augustine himself worked deliberately toward a reconciliation. See Peter Iver Kaufman, *Augustinian Piety and Catholic Reform: Augustine, Colet, and Erasmus* (Macon, Ga., 1982) for the *Confessions* and the *De gratia et libero arbitrio* and Domenico Marfioti's *L'uomo tra legge e grazia* (Brescia, 1983) for the *De spiritu et littera*.

This chapter shows Augustine altered rather than abandoned the themes of Christian sociolatry, while he renegotiated the relationship between personal and political redemption. For the renegotiation, we concentrate on the *De civitate Dei*. Unsupported by evidence from Augustine's appeals during the Donatist controversy, however, our claims would be weaker, so the controversy is nearly as important as the crisis that compelled Augustine to compose his *City*. Details of the Donatists' schism early in the fourth century can be retrieved from Bernhard Kriegbaum's *Kirche der Traditoren oder Kirche der Märtyrer: Die Vorgeschichte des Donatismus* (Innsbruck, 1986). Jean-Paul Brisson, *Autonisme et christianisme dans l'Afrique romaine* (Paris, 1958) and W.H.C. Frend, *The Donatist Church*, 3rd ed. (Oxford, 1985) search for precedents and preconditions deeper in the history of North African Christianity. Frend was among the first to challenge explanations of the Donatists' numerical superiority in Numidia that emphasized theology or religious fanaticism. He and Emin Tengstrom, *Donatisten und Katholiken: Soziale, wirtschaftliche, und politische Aspekte einer nordafrikanischen Kirchenspaltung* (Göteborg, 1964) prefer explanations that turn on material conditions. On the literary remains of the controversy and its prehistory, Paul Monceaux's *Histoire littéraire de l'Afrique chrétienne*, 7 vols. (Paris, 1901–23) is still valuable. Robert Joly, "Saint Augustin et l'intolérance religieuse," *Revue belge de philologie et d'histoire* 33 (1955) and Ernst Ludwig Grasmück, *Coercitio: Staat und Kirche im Donatistenstreit* (Bonn, 1964) discuss Augustine's appeals for government intervention; *Actes de la conférence de Carthage en 411*, ed. Serge Lancel, vol. 1 (Paris, 1972) covers Augustine's conduct during the government's hearings.

J. Patout Burns, "Augustine's Role in the Imperial Action against Pelagius," *Journal of Theological Studies* 30 (1987) suggests that Augustine's approval of government intervention was based more on conviction than on circumstance and convenience. Efforts to reconstruct that conviction and to incorporate it in the study of Christian sociolatry would be resisted by Robert Markus, who argues formidably that the *City of God* is an attack on "the arrogance of Roman imperial jingoism" and leaves no room for redeeming politics. The latest edition of Markus's *Saeculum: History and Society in the Age of Saint Augustine*, 2nd ed. (Cambridge, 1988) contains a new and valuable introduction. Others similarly stress Augustine's pessimism regarding the perfectibility of political institutions: Ernest L. Fortin, "Augustine's *City of God* and the Modern Historical Consciousness," *Review of Politics* 41 (1979); Franz Weissengruber, "Zu Augustins Definition des Staates," *Römisches historische Mitteilungen* 22 (1980); and Charles Norris Cochrane, *Christianity and Classical Culture*, (1940; rpt. Oxford, 1980). Nonetheless, acknowledging imperfectibility, one can still write expansively of the empire's redemptive roles, for which, see Johannes Straub, "Augustins Sorge um die *regeneratio imperii*: Das *Imperium Romanum* als *civitas terrena*," *Histo-*

risches Jahrbuch (1954), reprinted in Straub's *Regeneratio Imperii: Auf-sätze über Roms Kaisertum und Reich im Spiegel der heidenischen und christlichen Publizistik* (Darmstadt, 1972), Michael Wilks, "Roman Empire and Christian State," *Augustinus* 12 (1967), and Hubert Cancik, "Augustin als constantinischer Theologe," in *Der Fürst dieser Welt*, ed. Jacob Taubes (Munich, 1983).

CHAPTER EIGHT
SECTARIAN DUALISM AND SOCIOLATRY

Two fine bibliographical and historiographical essays are available to general readers: Werner O. Packull, "Some Reflections on the State of Anabaptist History: The Demise of a Normative Vision," *Science religieuses / Studies in Religion* 8 (1979) and James M. Stayer, "The Anabaptists," in Ozment, *Reformation Europe*. Packull, Stayer, and Klaus Deppermann collaborated to sketch the difficulties involved in one critical historiographical issue in "From Monogenesis to Polygenesis: The Historical Discussion of Anabaptist Origins," *Mennonite Quarterly Review* 49 (1975).

The polygenesis (or multiple causes and conditions) of radical reform in the sixteenth century appears to be the topic of choice in the 1980s, although, for background information, nothing has replaced George Huntston Williams's awesome survey, *The Radical Reformation* (Philadelphia, 1962). Nonetheless, the insistence that the sectarian Protestants' protests did not originate from a single "theological root" or in a single setting has transformed the study of the Reformation's radicals. Hans-Jürgen Goertz wholly subscribes to polygenesis, and his *Die Täufer: Geschichte und Deutung* (Munich, 1980) is filled with fresh insights on Anabaptism and sixteenth-century anticlericalism. But a later essay suggests that Goertz, and perhaps his accomplices, though pleased to jettison the content of the "normative vision" of Anabaptist history, are willing to retain its trajectories. Compare Goertz's "Das Täufertum—ein Weg in die Moderne?" in *Zwingli und Europa*, ed. Peter Blickle, Andreas Lindt, and Alfred Schindler (Zurich, 1985) with *The Recovery of the Anabaptist Vision*, ed. Guy E. Hershberger (Scottdale, Pa., 1957).

On Zwingli and Zurich, Gottfried W. Locher's work exhibits exceptional erudition; *Die zwinglische Reformation im Rahmen der europäischen Kirchengeschichte* (Göttingen, 1979) is tremendously useful. Still, careful readers of even his translated essays, in *Zwingli's Thought: New Perspectives* (Leiden, 1981), will sense that Locher is sometimes more disposed to praise than probe his subject's ideas and that he largely ignores the effects on Zwingli of the intensification of hostilities in Zurich. Also relevant to our topic is Locher's *Die evangelische Stellung der*

Reformatoren zum öffentlichen Leben (Zurich, 1950). Heinrich Schmid's *Zwinglis Lehre von der göttlichen und menschlichen Gerechtigkeit* (Zurich, 1959) reminds us that theological considerations were important in Zwingli's evaluation of civic order, as does Joachim Rogge's "Zwingli the Statesman," in *Huldrych Zwingli, 1484–1531: A Legacy of Radical Reform*, ed. E. J. Furcha (Montreal, 1985). Any work on righteousness and redeeming politics in Zurich, however, invites comparison with analyses of Luther's doctrine of justification and appraisal of worldly justice, for which comparison Berndt Hamm, *Zwinglis Reformation der Freiheit* (Neukirchen-Vluyn, 1988) is a trustworthy introduction. Like Locher, W. P. Stephens is inclined to emphasize Zwingli's independence from Luther. Stephens's comprehensive review of *The Theology of Huldrych Zwingli* (Oxford, 1986) also argues for development rather than discontinuity in Zwingli's thinking, an argument that somewhat minimizes the radicals' influence on their paladin and then chief opponent in Zurich. For general readers, however, Stephens is the best guide to Zwingli's theology. Zwingli's career and a more encompassing appreciation of "the radical challenge" during the 1520s are lodged accessibly in G. R. Potter's capacious *Zwingli* (Cambridge, 1976).

Potter referred to Harold Bender's biography, *Conrad Grebel, 1498–1526* (Goshen, Ind., 1950), as "a favorable, almost enthusiastic account" and called for some correction. The assessment is fair, yet Bender's *Grebel* is a valuable mine of information as well as a monument to the now supplanted "normative vision" of Anabaptist history. Heinold Fast's more recent biographical sketch is a blend of bedrock reality and soaring speculation. Originally composed for Hans-Jürgen Goertz's anthology, *Radikale Reformation* (Munich, 1978), it is available in translation in *Profiles of Radical Reformers* (Scottdale, Pa., 1982). Specimens from the Zurich controversies have been collected and translated in *The Sources of Swiss Anabaptism: The Grebel Letters and Related Documents*, ed. Leland Harder (Scottdale, Pa., 1985), enough evidence for general readers to make their own assessments of the biographers' enthusiasms.

One of the first challenges to the normative vision, Hans J. Hillerbrand's "The Origin of Sixteenth-Century Anabaptism: Another Look," *Archiv für Reformationsgeschichte* 53 (1962), appeals against Bender's presumption of "monogenesis." Insofar as Hillerbrand relates Grebel's ideas to those of Thomas Müntzer, he makes Hans-Jürgen Goertz's early work, *Innere und äussere Ordnung in der Theologie Thomas Müntzers* (Leiden, 1967), and Klaus Ebert, *Thomas Müntzer: Von Eigensinn und Widerspruch* (Frankfurt, 1987) particularly relevant to the presentation of Grebel's radicalism. On the issue of Grebel's intellectual indebtedness and originality, also see Martin Brecht, "Herkunft und Eigenart der Taufanschauung der züricher Täufer," *Archiv für Reformationsgeschichte*

64 (1973) and the chapter on Swiss "appropriations" in Calvin Augustine Pater, *Karlstadt as the Father of the Baptist Movements: The Emergence of Lay Protestantism* (Toronto, 1984) as well as remarks scattered in Clarence Bauman, *Gewaltlosigkeit im Täufertum* (Leiden, 1968) and Kenneth Ronald Davis, *Anabaptism and Asceticism: A Study in Intellectual Origins* (Scottdale, Pa., 1974).

Explaining Zwingli's reformation and Grebel's radicalism is difficult unless the stage in Zurich is adequately set, so consult Hans Morf, "Obrigkeit und Kirche in Zürich bis zu Beginn der Reformation," *Zwingliana* 13 (1970) for magistrates' attitudes toward the bishop of Constance and Zurich's Catholic "establishment," Heinold Fast, "Reformation durch Provokation: Predigtstörungen in den ersten Jahren der Reformation in der Schweiz," in *Umstrittenes Täufertum, 1525–1975*, ed. Hans-Jürgen Goertz (Göttingen, 1975), and J. F. Gerhard Goeters, "Die Vorgeschichte des Täufertums in Zürich," in *Studien zur Geschichte und Theologie der Reformation*, ed. Luise Abramowski and Goeters (Neukirchen, 1969) for the radicals' early interests and alliances. James M. Stayer and Martin Haas resourcefully developed Goeters's position into a "contextual" solution to the problems concerning the character of separatist sentiments. Stayer's "Die Anfänge des schweizerischen Täufertums im reformierten Kongregationalismus" and Haas's "Der Weg der Täufer in die Absonderung" appeared in *Umstrittenes Täufertum*, but also consider Stayer's "The Revolutionary Beginnings of Swiss Anabaptism," in *The Origins and Characteristics of Anabaptism*, ed. Marc Lienhard (The Hague, 1977); "The Swiss Brethren: An Exercise in Historical Definition," *Church History* 47 (1978); and Haas's "Täufertum und Volkskirche— Faktoren der Trennung," *Zwingliana* 13 (1970–72). I am less inclined than Stayer, Haas, and Goertz to understate the importance of Grebel's conflicts with Zwingli; see Kaufman, "Social History, Psychohistory, and the Prehistory of Swiss Anabaptism," *Journal of Religion* 68 (1988). And although many materialist or contextualist explanations of separatism exhibit incontrovertible good sense, note Charles Nienkirchen's criticisms, "Reviewing the Case for a Non-Separatist Ecclesiology in Early Swiss Anabaptism," *Mennonite Quarterly Review* 56 (1982). For more on the controversy between Grebel and Zwingli, see John Howard Yoder, *Täufertum und Reformation in der Schweiz* (Karlsruhe, 1962), which persuasively maintains that the crisis compelled Zwingli to reevaluate his reform and, in some respects, to turn reactionary. Robert Walton, *Zwingli's Theocracy* (Toronto, 1967) sorts things out differently; Zwingli, he claims, was consistent—an opinion quite compatible with those of Locher and Stephens. Grebel, however, turned unreasonable and too radical to realize goals that had formerly united all Zurich reformers, or at least seemed to unite them. Wilhelm H. Neuser, *Die reformatorische*

Wende bei Zwingli (Neukirchen-Vluyn, 1977) inexplicably dodges the issue altogether, so for Zwingli's trials, triumphs, and redeeming politics, see Bernd Moeller, "Zwinglis Disputationen: Studien zu den Anfängen der Kirchenbildung und des Synodalwesens im Protestantismus," *Zeitschrift der Savigny-Stiftung für Rechtsgeschichte, kanonistische Abteilung 56* (1970) and 60 (1974).

Zwingli's disputations and Grebel's disappointments and death roughly coincide with the emergence of radical religious responses to reform in Strasbourg, which the following ponder quite helpfully: Klaus Deppermann, "Die strassburger Reformatoren und die Krise der deutschen Täufertums in Jahre 1527," *Mennonitische Geschichtsblätter* 30 (1973); and Hans-Werner Musing, "Karlstadt und die Entstehung der strassburger Täufergemeinde" and Marc Lienhard, "Les autorités civiles et les Anabaptistes: Attitudes du magistrat de Strasbourg, 1526–1532," in the latter's *Origins and Characteristics of Anabaptism*. R. Emmet McLaughlin, *Caspar Schwenckfeld, Reluctant Radical* (New Haven, 1986) has important things to say about "the drift of events in Strassburg." Klaus Deppermann's *Melchior Hoffman: Soziale Unruhen und apokalyptische Visionen im Zeitalter der Reformation* (Göttingen, 1979; trans., Edinburgh, 1987) contains several chapters that contribute significantly to the literature on piety and polity in Strasbourg. Deppermann's *Hoffman* also discusses the development of Anabaptist authoritarianism, on which the final word, however, is likely to come from studies of Melchiorite influence in Münster.

Münster's eclectic reformer Bernard Rothmann figured prominently in James M. Stayer's revision of conventional wisdom about the political ethics of sectarians, *Anabaptists and the Sword* (Lawrence, Kans., 1972), but also consult Martin Brecht, "Die Theologie Rothmanns," in *Anabaptistes et dissidents au XVIᵉ siècle*, ed. Jean-Georges Rott and Simon Verheus (Baden-Baden, 1987). Stayer's superb summary, "Christianity in One City: Anabaptist Münster, 1534-1535," in *Radical Tendencies in the Reformation: Divergent Perspectives*, ed. Hans J. Hillerbrand (St. Louis, 1988) again introduces Rothmann yet reflects on Melchiorite principles and demographic factors as well. Otthein Rammstedt, *Sekte und soziale Bewegung: Soziologische Analyse der Täufer in Münster (1534/35)* (Cologne, 1966) stirs up evidence of sectarian sociolatry. More evidence might be expected from Waldshut, but for now, see Torsten Bergsten, *Balthasar Hubmaier: Seine Stellung zu Reformation und Täufertum* (Kassel, 1961). A number of other works dealing with the popularity and eccentricity of sectarian Protestantism are accessible to general readers, among which, see Cornelius Krahn, *Dutch Anabaptism: Origin, Spread, Life, and Thought, 1450–1600* (The Hague, 1964), William Klassen, *Covenant and Community* (Grand Rapids, 1968), Claus-Peter Clasen,

Anabaptism: A Social History, 1525–1618 (Ithaca, 1972), and Werner O. Packull, *Mysticism and the Early South German-Austrian Anabaptist Movement, 1521–1531* (Scottdale, Pa., 1977). For Sattler and Schleitheim, rely on Arnold Snyder, *The Life and Thought of Michael Sattler* (Scottdale, Pa., 1984), which further illumines sectarian separatism in Strasbourg, but consider the objections of Dennis D. Martin, "Monks, Mendicants, and Anabaptists: Michael Sattler and the Benedictines Reconsidered," *Mennonite Quarterly Review* 60 (1986) and the Schleitheim of Hans-Jürgen Goertz, "Zwischen Zweitracht und Eintracht: Zur Zweideutigkeit täuferischer und mennonitischer Bekentnisse," *Mennonitische Geschichtsblätter* 43/44 (1986/1987).

INDEX

Abbot, George (archbishop of Canterbury), 67

absolutism, 3, 46, 51

Admonition generalis, 37

Aeneas, 137

Agobard (bishop of Lyon), 39n

Alcuin (abbot of St. Martin's, Tours), 36, 38–39

Alexander II (pope), 82, 189

Ambrose (bishop of Milan), 32, 94, 96, 116–17

Anacletus II (pope), 99–102, 191–92

Anastasius (bishop of Thessalonica), 92

Anselm (bishop of Lucca), 88

antinomianism, 73–74

Antioch, church and patriarchs of, 25–26, 80, 101–3

Arcadius (emperor), 96

Arles, sepulchral reliefs, 17

Arnulf of Lisieux, 99–100

Athanasius (bishop of Alexandria), 25

Augustine (bishop of Hippo), 27, 128, 196–99; on Christian empire, 144–49; *City of God*, 8, 27, 130–37, 142–48; against Donatists, 138–47, 199; and Eusebean sociolatry, 129–32, 137, 199–200; as historian, 47, 132–35; and Orosius, 29, 144–45, 178; on personal redemption, 146–48, 198; on political crisis, 143, 150

Augustus (emperor), 31–32, 45–47, 145

Avignon, 41–43, 47–48, 151

Barnes, Robert, 64

Bauman, Clarence, 157, 202

Baxter, Richard, 61–62

Benedict XI (pope), 41

Bern, 107–8, 119–21

Bernard of Clairvaux, 100–101, 110

Berthelier, Philibert, 119, 121

Beza, Theodore, 185

Bieler, André, 105–6, 195–96

Bilney, Thomas, 64

Bockelszoon, Jan (Jan of Leiden), 166–68

Boniface I (pope), 89, 91–92, 189

Boniface VIII (pope), 41, 182

Bonizo (bishop of Sutri), 85n, 88

Bradstreet, Simon, 64

Brescia, siege of, 43

Brezzi, Paolo, 147n, 197–98

Brixen, synod of, 85

Bruno (bishop of Segni), 88

Bucer, Martin, 108, 150–51, 161–65, 193

Bullinger, Heinrich, 119, 122, 168

Burgundians, 31, 34, 39

Byzantium, 9, 35–36, 82, 86–87. *See also* Constantinople

Caecilian (bishop of Carthage), 139, 141, 143

Caius College, Cambridge, 70

Calderon, Salvatore, 176

Calvin, John, 7, 105–6, 129, 166, 168, 192–96; and the Genevan consistory, 117–25; on election, 110–15, 124; and English Protestants, 65–66, 184–85; on the magistracy, 113–17, 122, 124; on the ministry, 108–11, 115–16, 118, 124; and sectarian Protestants, 111, 113–14

Canossa, 84–85, 94, 190

Capito, Wolfgang, 161–63

Carthage, 80, 137; council of (411), 143–44

Cartwright, Thomas, 65–66, 186

Caspar, Erich, 104, 188, 191

Catherine of Aragon, 58

Chaderton, Laurence, 63–64, 184

charisma, 3–4, 22–23, 56–57. *See also* Rome: selection consecration of emperors by; sociolatry, and divine kingship

Charles I (king of England), 60–61, 74–75

Charles V (emperor), 59

Christ's College, Cambridge, 63, 66

Cino da Pistoia, 42

Circumcellions, 139n, 140

Clement III (pope), 98. *See also* Wibert

Clement V (pope), 41–42, 50, 182

Clovis (king of the Franks), 34–35, 56n, 178

Cluny, 190